Th

DATE DUE

The Surplus American

How the 1% Is Making Us Redundant

BY

Charles Derber

AND

Yale Magrass

Paradigm Publishers
Boulder • London

Copyright © 2012 Paradigm Publishers

Published in the United States by Paradigm Publishers, 5589 Arapahoe Avenue, Boulder, CO 80303 USA.

Paradigm Publishers is the trade name of Birkenkamp & Company, LLC, Dean Birkenkamp, President and Publisher.

Library of Congress Cataloging-in-Publication Data

Derber, Charles.
  The surplus American : how the 1% is making us redundant / by Charles Derber and Yale Magrass.
     p. cm.
  Includes bibliographical references and index.
  ISBN 978-1-61205-249-6 (hardcover : alk. paper)—ISBN 978-1-61205-250-2 (pbk. : alk. paper)
  1. Underemployment—United States. 2. Unemployment—United States. 3. Unemployed—United States. I. Magrass, Yale R. II. Title.
  HD5709.2.U6D47 2012
  331.13'7973—dc23

                                                    2012017750

Printed and bound in the United States of America on acid-free paper that meets the standards of the American National Standard for Permanence of Paper for Printed Library Materials.

Designed and Typeset by Straight Creek Bookmakers.

16 15 14 13 12   1 2 3 4 5

From: Charles Derber
To: The Occupy Generation

From: Yale Magrass
To: José, Miguel, and David

Contents

Part I

You're Fired

I

Americans as a Surplus People

An economic neutron bomb is exploding in the nation. The neutron bomb is an explosive developed by the United States that has the peculiar characteristic of killing people while preserving property.[1] What a convenient truth: with this economic weapon, money can be made without the workers.

We dub this emergent United States a society of "surplus people." The economic neutron bomb does not necessarily kill all the people, but it makes most of them redundant. They are not needed in the current system, as designed by those in power. The economy functions profitably without them. The great majority constitutes a mass surplus population.

This does not mean that there is not much important work to be done in America. In a different economic system, it would be entirely rational to hire these workers in useful—indeed essential—new jobs. The United States could and should put millions of people to work in creating a new social, economic, and environmental infrastructure. Creating this infrastructure is crucial to the well-being of the nation. Unemployment and surplus people could be reduced drastically in a rational course to save the nation itself. But the current American political economy has committed itself to a different path—and it would take something approaching a revolution to change it.

Surplus people, then, are "surplus" only within a system that has made them so. A more rational and sustainable economy, organized on the basis of human need and social rationality, could employ all Americans. But in this book, we show that Americans are becoming surplus by design, a form of contrived or artificial surplus, a casualty of short-sighted

3

greed. We need to emphasize at the beginning that there are entirely rational, indeed vital alternatives and solutions that could employ all Americans who want work in useful and necessary jobs, and could even bring profit to elites in the long term. Americans would not be surplus and the nation would prosper, but the current American political economy does not permit this utterly rational and essential change to happen.

In a sense, then, the term *surplus people* could be misleading. It might suggest that there is something wrong with the people or that there is no way to employ them usefully. Since exactly the opposite is true, and we can and need to employ them for the very survival of our country, they are not existentially "surplus." Rather, we call them *surplus* in this book because the deeply irrational system we live in has condemned them to a surplus position and refuses, against all reason, to offer them essential work. Surplus people, then, is a label appropriate only to highlight the irrationality of the current order, and to spotlight the human tragedy of rendering surplus a population that desperately needs to be employed if the country and, in fact, the planet, is to survive.

At the heart of this problem is the calculation by elites that they can make more profit by radically reducing reliance on US workers and US infrastructure, using instead foreign workers or replacing workers with robots or other new technology, while relying on infrastructures in other nations. Turning Americans into surplus workers is utterly irrational when so much useful work must be done immediately in America—for example, to create an entirely new and clean environmental and social infrastructure at home. But the current system and its leadership do not permit this rational course to be pursued.

In the end, this reflects something deeply irrational but central to US capitalism. The core concern of corporate elites is profit, not jobs. And if more profits can be made by shifting production abroad, elites will take that path. Doing so brings massive short-term profits at the cost of jobs and domestic infrastructure, but it is profoundly irrational, even for elites in the long term, because it will produce massive domestic deterioration and revolt. Nonetheless, it is the decision—one of short-term profit-seeking over long-term social health and full employment—that US employers have made.

The irrationality of the current "surplus system" cannot be overstated. But such irrationality is manifest throughout our public life. For example, the suicidal disregard of climate change is the most irrational set of decisions that any society could make. Yet, the United States continues in denial and rejects the climate change decisions that could actually make money, employ workers, and save the planet.[2] The irrationality of making a surplus population under current circumstances is thus just one expression of a political economy that is irrational to its core.

Another name for the political economy of the United States is, of course, corporate capitalism. We shall show here that American capitalism has repeatedly created deep crises of mass surplus people, a crisis that gets worse and worse as the system globalizes, militarizes, matures, and declines. The irrationality of creating a mass surplus population cannot be disentangled from the irrationality of the larger economic system, nor can it be solved until that larger systemic irrationality is fixed.

The analysis of surplus is thus a window into the history and crises of the US economic and political order. There is a long tradition of political economy, a field devoted to critical analysis of Western corporate capitalism that has gone largely silent in the United States. But the severe economic problems of the US Great Recession, and especially the new surplus people crisis it has produced—along with the crises of the Eurozone and the larger global economy—require an intellectual revolution and revival. We have found there is no way to understand the surplus crisis without delving once again deeply into the irrationalities of a now globalized US capitalism that brings deep inequalities between a super-affluent 1 percent and a 99 percent increasingly destined for surplus.

Let us be clear: the problem of surplus is the most glaring example of a systemic irrationality that is catastrophic in its consequences. Capitalist political economy creates not only a surplus crisis but also crises of inequality, militarism, and climate change that threaten the abilities of most people not just to find work but to survive with a civilized lifestyle on a habitable planet. We focus throughout this book, then, not just on surplus people and the elites who control their fates, but on corporate political economy. We pay special attention to the elites who have made surplus an integral part of an un-sustainable economic and social future for people everywhere, including eventually for the 1 percent themselves, for the path they have chosen puts them unwittingly on a suicide mission.

Since the systemic roots and causes of the surplus crisis remain largely invisible, political leaders are unable to truly grasp the dimensions of the problem, failing to recognize that capitalist irrationality prevents reintegrating surplus people back into the economy with a meaningful life. It is also likely that many leaders do not want to see the depth of the problem because acknowledging it could undermine their legitimacy, wealth, and power. In February 2011, President Barack Obama met with Steve Jobs shortly before Jobs died. He asked Jobs why virtually all the 70 million iPhones, 30 million iPods, and 59 million other Apple products are made outside the United States. Couldn't some of Apple's remarkable digital-age miracles be made at home? Jobs, whose software and hard-ware infrastructure is entirely globalized, told the President, "Those jobs aren't coming back," a sentiment also expressed unequivocally by Michael Dell, the founder of Dell, Inc., and representing the global mindset of the entire corporate elite.[3]

This reflects the way globalized corporate capitalism works today and shows that the very problems it creates cannot be fixed within capitalist boundaries. The consequences are dire. Surplus people are not a happy lot. People, after all, need to be needed. Without a role in society, they lack meaning and the means of survival. As long as politicians are committed to serving corporate interests, they are incapable of solving the problem because they must blind themselves to the crises' underlining roots and cannot propose solutions that ultimately threaten the 1 percent. The result is inevitably mass social discontent as the crisis grows worse. In our imagined dystopia of 2020 (an important part of this book), millions of people are in open revolt, converging on Wall Street to express their outrage and despair.

We wrote our first draft just months before the Occupy Movement exploded in the United States in 2011. As experi-enced writers, we were accustomed to analyzing history. But we were not in the habit of predicting the future. Here, we had written a book scripted around a conflict between elites and protesters on Wall Street before it had actually occurred.

The Occupy Movement reinforced certain underlying truths. One is that the problem stems from an innate irrationality, which can only be addressed through deep changes in the entire economic and political system. A second is that the seeds of the future lie in the present. The year 2020, as we initially conceived it, was an eerie extrapolation of what was about to happen today in the United States. That helps explain why our analysis proved prophetic. But our present circumstances—in which the reality of surplus populations was becoming too great and painful to ignore—were an extrapolation of forces unfolding over hundreds of years, at least since the end of the Middle Ages. Our dystopia was actually a history and an account of today's events, as well as a prognosis of things to come.

Buckle your seat belt. The story of surplus people—and of the deeply irrational system that has scripted it—is more stomach churning than a roller-coaster. But, as in the carnival, the experience should be exciting and enlightening.

·⌁·

2

Who Are the Surplus People?

They Are the Unemployed but They Include Many Other Unfortunate Souls

How to define surplus people? Doing so is not as easy as it might seem, nor is there a theoretical tradition in social sciences that has made the idea precise, familiar, or even plausible. After all, a society that has determined that it doesn't need its people is hard to grasp. Society is its people, is it not? For most readers, an economic neutron bomb that eliminated the people would no longer be a society. It would be the absence of society.

This may make a "surplus people" seem nonsensical, but consider this: while it is hard to imagine a society without people, it is much less difficult to imagine a society with a vast unemployed population. We suspect that many readers might already have identified "surplus people" as those who can't find a job, and millions of American workers already suspect that US elites have embraced an economic strategy destined to increase mass unemployment.

A focus on unemployment understates the catastrophic magnitude of the surplus people crisis. True, the unemployed are a core group in the surplus population, the one that is nakedly surplus. They have no economic role in the current social order and appear to be an unwanted burden on society. They are growing rapidly in the United States, with striking, tragic growth in the long-term or permanent unemployed, a group that has grown bigger after each business cycle and has become almost 50 percent of the total official unemployed after the 2008 meltdown.[1] Even though there is much useful work to be done, as emphasized above, US elites have determined that it is better to utilize workers abroad and use new technology to maximize short-term profit, even though the cost of sustaining and controlling a "surplus people" nation is high, especially in the long run.

The unemployed are not just those officially counted as such. Those too discouraged to look for work are not counted, but they are part of the unemployed surplus. Discouraged workers are one segment of a larger number of workers defined as "marginally attached"—those who want a job and have looked for work during part of the previous year but are not counted as unemployed because they haven't looked in the previous month—who also are surplus. So, too, are the underemployed—those working less than they want or need to get by. These include mushrooming numbers of involuntary part-timers. We will call the unemployed, underemployed, and marginally attached workers the "Category 1" surplus population, much larger than registered in the official unemployment rate.[2] And, among minorities, young people, those not college educated, and those from low-income backgrounds, the unemployment and larger Category 1 rate is dramatically higher than the official national rate—approaching 50 percent in the case of young male African Americans.[3]

The unemployed are the radioactive core of the surplus population but just one of six surplus groups. We will use "Category 2" to refer to those who have been forced or induced to leave the labor force. This includes prisoners and mental hospital inmates, and also many soldiers, college students, and elementary and high school students who were legally required to stay in school as part of an effort to end child labor. Also within this category are women who were seduced into becoming housewives so they would not compete with male workers, as well as retired workers, who would otherwise be competing with younger workers for scarce jobs.

Not all students, housewives, or retirees count as surplus people. If members of any of these groups do not want to work and choose voluntarily to stay permanently out of the labor force, they are not surplus. The surplus are those who *want* to work but because of shrinkage in the labor market—due to decisions made by US economic elites—are not able to get jobs. Students who have chosen education because it is a reliable way into the labor force should not necessarily be seen as surplus in the long term. In Germany, students, even while in school, are integrated into paid apprentice work and thus cannot be considered surplus.[4] Because US employers offer far less on-the-job training, and outsource training to schools, they are able to keep students out of the labor market for a temporary period. For many students, this increasingly leads to long-term unemployment. If the economy were organized on a different and more rational foundation, focused on social development rather than short-term profits, all these students could be put to work.

Similar considerations apply to retirees, the largest number of people in this second surplus category. Before 1986, most US workers were required to quit by age 65, thus forced into surplus status and preventing even greater competition for scarce jobs between younger and older workers. There would be plenty of useful work for all if elites put the US economy on a different foundation. But by pursuing the current economic strategy of short-term profit, based on foreign labor and new technology, large percentages of older people must be lured out of the labor force. Many may have wanted to retire and might thus not be considered as surplus. But what about those who want to continue to work? Their exclusion from the labor force allows employers to fire them and hire cheaper younger workers who would otherwise be surplus and more disruptive, thus saving money by creating a pool of senior surplus workers.

Many members of Category 2 are invisible or masked surplus people who have been sucked into what we call "surplus-absorption" institutions: the military, the police, prisons, the schools, old-age homes, and mental institutions. For many housewives, the family itself is a major "surplus-absorption" institution, something that the feminist movement and writers such as Betty Friedan implicitly realized when they described the housewife role as the "problem with no name."[5]

Surplus-absorption institutions are overwhelmingly important in a society with a mass surplus population, such as the United States. As the surplus population grows, the police and prisons, the military, and the schools siphon off mass discontent and revolt. They offer people the illusion of purpose and hope, and pluck them out of the wasteland of naked unemployment into a fantasy world of purpose and possibility.

The third major surplus group are those involved in "make-work." They are all those employed primarily for the sake of having them working rather than because their labor is needed to yield profit or social value. This is a very large and diverse group, including many people hired by government simply to create jobs, even though the jobs create no profit or value. It also includes government bureaucrats working largely to build and feather their own nest or enforce meaningless rules. And it includes managers and administrators in the private sector who are carrying out entirely unprofitable or unnecessary labor.

To be specific, members of Category 3 include some employed in Keynesian[6] public works; conductors on completely automated elevators, buses, planes, and trains; cashiers continuing to be employed when their activity is completely automated by scanners; and some artists, teachers, social workers, government bureaucrats, and record keepers. For these individuals, to be unemployed would be destabilizing, so it is better to give them something to do and make them think they have a purpose. This is problematic, however, because it is expensive. You must pay them more than you would if they were idle.

A fourth surplus group is people who are hired to control the unemployed and manage the surplus-absorption institutions. They work simply to keep the other groups of surplus people in line, functioning as a "worthy" surplus population employed to control the "unworthy." They include police, military officers, prison guards, many teachers, many therapists or managers in mental hospitals, and managers of government make-work projects. Yet they all fit into the large pool of surplus people and are a way of dividing and conquering, managing one sector of the surplus population by the other and thus killing two surplus birds with one stone.

The fifth category of surplus people is more controversial. Category 5 contains people hired by corporations or smaller businesses who carry out profitable labor that is either socially unnecessary or harmful. From a capitalist perspective these people are not surplus, because they contribute to profitable enterprise. But from a larger societal perspective, they are indeed surplus since they are doing a form of make-work, intended to enrich small elites but not contributing to real social needs or the sustaining of society itself—and very often contributing to its decline.

This fifth category is an enormous group, since so much of the American economy is devoted to socially destructive or unnecessary labor. It includes people in food services who create or serve dangerous or unhealthy food substances such as trans-fats; cigarette company executives, employers, and tobacco growers; owners, managers, and employers in dirty coal plants; engineers devising fracking oil technologies; and endless others.

A key subset of Category 5 is jobs created by the financial sector. The 2008 financial meltdown made clear that while the current financial system generated huge wealth and employment before the Great Recession, it was unsustainable and both socially and economically destructive. It generated many jobs both on and off Wall Street through leverage and bubbles, but, as we discuss later, these can be viewed as surplus "bubble jobs," absorbing surplus people but only for a short period until the bubble pops. Bubble jobs are staffed by a crucial and large group of disguised surplus workers, whose jobs create an impression of increasing employment in periods before a bust, and also the impression that employment is going up when it is really declining, as we show in our historical discussion.

There is a sixth group who might be considered surplus, although their status is ambiguous. This group includes everyone whose jobs are created or whose pay is artificially inflated to boost consumption and thus stimulate the economy and boost profits, or to control discontent and stabilize the economic regime.

This Category 6 surplus is a disguised surplus group, with many jobs that are unnecessary from a capitalist perspective and many workers who are paid more than their labor is worth to their employers. Their jobs exist primarily to give them a sense that they are not surplus but have a social role, through which they can live well enough to consume. Of course, we are talking here about the lucky among the surplus population. There are others who are locked up or live near destitution.

Considering these six categories, we can define *surplus people* as including all the following: (1) those who lack work entirely or lack sufficient work to eat and live; (2) those forced or pressured to leave the workforce and are warehoused in custodial or surplus-absorbing institutions; (3) those who work only to control those who lack work; (4) those who do "make-work," that is, jobs that have no real economic or social value; (5) those who engage in profitable work with market value but with jobs that are socially unsustainable and destructive; and (6) those whose jobs are unnecessary, often with inflated pay, and are a disguised surplus population. This already encompasses the majority of Americans. Our dystopia of 2020 America—a nation of surplus people—has arrived.

·⤜·

3

How to Make Money from the Creation of Surplus People

The 1 Percent's Strategy to Maximize Profits by Minimizing US Employment

Why has the surplus people crisis erupted? What is it that creates an America made up of millions of surplus people? And why have the numbers of such people mushroomed so radically in our recent history?

The answer is that the American capitalist economy is, by its nature, inherently surplus-producing. Its main product is twofold; first is very high short-term profits based increasingly on global production, and second (and related to the first) is the rising mass of US surplus people themselves.

The production of surplus people is not new. It has existed for centuries, taking its modern form with the rise of Western capitalism itself. In later sections we will trace the history of the American economy, to show the key forms and phases that surplus people production has taken.

But let's now focus on the grim realities of today—explaining why America faces a super-crisis of surplus populations. Mass surplus people production is a mark of mature capitalist systems: as economies "age" they produce more and more surplus people. This is connected to long-term tendencies in capitalist economies toward protracted crises and decline as well as short-term profit-seeking strategies taken by current US elites. It is also connected to contemporary shifts in the global economy, and to the decline of the United States relative to other rising economic powers.

The contemporary crisis represents a novel phase. The US elites have embraced a comprehensive business strategy that transforms the nation itself into a surplus people. Profit today has become inseparable from the manufacture of American surplus populations, already representing a majority of the American people. This is not a rational long-term strategy for the country, nor even in all likelihood for US elites. But corporate leaders have committed to it and government allies have made it stick, despite the enormous short-term and long-term costs.

Why would government leaders embrace such an irrational and destructive course? Corporate leaders can do so for obvious reasons: they can make immense short-term profits and do not have to incur the short-term or longer-term social costs. All these costs—whether of high unemployment or prisons or poor health—are borne by the government and the population itself.

Why would the government embrace this decision when it has to confront the enormous costs to the society and the population? This question is a major theme of our work, and it relates to the power of money in politics. Government has become, to a frightening degree, a wholly owned subsidiary of the corporate elite. Politicians follow policies benefiting corporate elites even when they harm US voters and people. This is not new in capitalism, but the control of money over politics has deepened and led to far more lethal consequences for the nation and US workers in a globalized age.

US corporations now seek profits and become profitable largely through mechanisms that increase all six of the surplus groups delineated in the previous chapter. This represents a potentially terminal social as well as economic phase. If it is not reversed through major social movements of the surplus people, such as the Occupy Movement, it will lead inevitably to rapid and permanent decline of the United States itself.

We will show that this strategy is institutionalized and extremely difficult to reverse. Corporations, political leaders, and the media are all complicit. And it is part of a worldwide economic transformation that has developed its own inexorable momentum.

Before we describe the nature and roots of this "surplus" corporate strategy, we need to say something about corporate and other elite motives. The key motive is nothing new; it is making money, always the driving engine of the US economy and always creating surplus people.

Nonetheless, the current phase involves a shift toward mass surplus people production tied to a new globally systemic profit strategy. It carries more lethal consequences, namely the creation of a "surplus nation" in which, in the language of the Occupy Movement, the 1 percent render the 99 percent of America "surplus."

In describing this "surplus strategy," we need to offer three caveats. First, 99 percent are unlikely to become surplus; the number will be a large majority of the population if current trends continue, but it won't include everyone. Certain productive jobs will remain in the American "surplus nation."

Business elites and many mainstream economists, it should be noted, will applaud the redistribution of jobs from the United States to poor nations as both efficient and socially just. American companies will continue to employ some American workers while raising their own efficiency by reducing labor and regulatory costs and outsourcing the majority of jobs to global workers who desperately need and deserve them. Outsourcing creates pain in the United States but a whole world of new opportunity to escape poverty in the impoverished nations of Africa, Asia, and Latin America.

True, corporate globalization helps create new jobs in the developing world and can contribute to infrastructure development.[1] It also creates cost savings for giant global firms that contribute to efficiency in the short term. But over the long term, all poor nations will be subjected to the same outsourcing and surplus people production as the United States today. Companies are outsourcing not to help the desperately poor masses of the world, but to exploit their vulnerability and squeeze grotesque profits through abuse of sweatshop workers who will accept horrific labor conditions to avoid starvation.[2] Most of these workers will work during their youth and then be disposed of for even younger and cheaper workers, often in yet other countries.

The long-term effect is not to elevate workers in the rest of the world or build their economies in a sustainable greater good. Quite the contrary. The foreign investment of US transnationals will extract the cheapest labor and the most valuable natural resources in poor nations while subjecting them to US corporate dominance and policies, deeply compromising their sovereignty. This form of globalization—often called "neoliberal"— will create in the Third World countries dependency in the short term, vast inequalities in the mid-term, and abandonment and collapse in the longer term.

While the argument of global benevolence on the part of US globalizing companies is a self-serving myth, it leads to our second caveat: the current "surplus strategy" is not rooted in some perverse new demonic motivation by US elites. The 1 percent knows what it is doing—creating an American mass surplus population—but this is all in the service of their historic commitment to profit maximization. The 1 percent also knows that in abandoning US workers it is not creating paradise for the poor workers and nations of the world. But today's elites are not greedier or more sociopathic than their predecessors. Their new actions simply reflect new conditions that make mass surplus people production a prime condition of profitability today. This willingness to subordinate the well-being of the mass populace to profit is hardly new; it is simply taking place on a larger and more dangerous scale.

Third, this is not an elite conspiracy. It is not a fully conscious strategy, nor are executives the all-knowing possessors of the consequences of their own individual or even class-wide economic strategies. The elites are following a semi-conscious plan that appears to ensure major short-term profits and long-term effects that are largely ignored. They are prepared to grab the profits at hand even as the long-term risks, especially for US society itself, appear increasingly ominous. While hardly morally laudatory, this is no major deviation from the historical strategies US elites have embraced since the beginning of the nation.

Nonetheless, let's not underestimate the elite hypocrisy involved. The elites never acknowledge their surplus strategy even as they downsize and outsource with frenetic enthusiasm. Their talk is all about creating jobs, jobs, jobs. While their motives may not be new, the gap between rhetoric and action could not be higher.

In our emerging surplus nation, all elites claim to be totally united in the production of jobs for US workers. The jobs mantra dominates the business rhetoric of executives and the political leaders of both main parties. Meanwhile, all the leaders are carrying out precisely the policies that are undermining the prospects for job creation at home. They are destroying jobs in the name of creating them. And this will remain the case, since to admit the truth would create a social revolution.

·⟡·

4

The Four Roots of Surplus People Production

The new surplus strategy, with its lethal long-term social consequences, is connected with four major forces that in the past actually created productive jobs rather than destroying them. They are globalization, technological innovation, the intensification of corporate control over politics and economic policy, and the erosion of national stewardship that might protect the US economic infrastructure from terminal destruction and US society itself from the ruins of a surplus mass populace.[1]

All four forces grow out of a new economic phase, in which corporate and political elites seek to maximize profits by disengaging from the US workforce. More broadly, this phase represents a decision to disinvest in the US itself, leading to the rotting of American infrastructure and the decline of the nation, but saving elites the costs of rebuilding it. Greater profits can be realized by investing in new technologies that dispense altogether with the need for workers as well as investing abroad in a cheaper and more compliant global workforce. Elites hunger for and help build the more modern, gleaming infrastructure that supports cheap labor in Shanghai, Abu Dhabi, or Rio.

All of this reflects the inherent tendency toward stagnation and declining profits within mature capitalist economies such as the United States. Markets become saturated, infrastructure ages and erodes, technological innovation slows, regulations increase, and domestic workers become more expensive and less compliant than their counterparts abroad. Domestic profits can still be generated at home from domestic labor, especially as anti-labor and anti-regulatory policies are implemented, but the real money is in labor-saving machinery and foreign investment and production. The profit centers of the world have moved east and south, to Asia (especially China and India)[2] and to Latin America (think Brazil).[3]

This points to the core role of globalization. Corporate globalization is at the heart of the American surplus crisis. The threat posed by neoliberal globalization to the jobs of US workers is widely understood, leading to mass discontent on both the Right[4] and Left[5] with "free trade" treaties and with the entire corporate globalization agenda. Polls show that millions of Americans fear that their jobs may be outsourced and downsized in favor of production abroad.[6] US unions have understandably made reform of neoliberalism and "free trade" a top priority.

But even opponents of today's globalization have not grasped fully its new dimensions. It is not just that jobs today are being outsourced faster than anyone imagined a few decades ago. It is that the loss of such jobs will be more permanent than anybody in the United States wants to believe.

This is because outsourcing jobs is connected with the bigger change of dismantling the US economic and social infrastructure. Might this be the first time in history that economic elites have abandoned their nation's own physical and social foundation? In a sense, globalizing elites today are burning their own nests because they have new homes everywhere across the globe. The cost of maintaining the original declining nest has been abandoned in favor of creating new nests everywhere else.

Globalization has been happening for centuries, largely under the umbrella of colonialism's self-legitimating civilizing project. But globalization today takes a new form. In earlier stages, globalization was part of a project of developing the domestic infrastructure of the globalizing home country. Looting colonies provided the raw materials to build early capitalist countries into models of capitalist prosperity, never seen before.

Such earlier colonial globalizations thus were a way of creating domestic jobs and building the home nation. They involved "in-sourcing" rather than outsourcing. When the British Empire conquered India, England did not outsource its budding textile industry to its new Indian colony. Instead, it shut down India's relatively advanced textile business, thus opening the door for its own domestic industries and workers.[7] Globalization in the eighteenth and nineteenth centuries was part of a larger strategy to fuel domestic development and absorb surplus people at home.

Many orthodox neoclassical and neoliberal economists argue that corporate globalization today will ultimately also turn out to be a form of insourcing rather than outsourcing. As foreign nations develop, they will presumably create great demand for high value-added products and services that only advanced countries can create. But this orthodoxy overlooks the fact that nations such as China and India already have millions of highly skilled workers and many high-tech industries, capable of producing components for Intel, Microsoft, and similar companies at far lower wages than highly skilled US workers.[8] Investment funds to promote the high-tech infrastructure in such nations—both from their own governments and from the US companies—are booming, even as disinvestment in the US infrastructure by both the US government and US companies accelerates. This helps explain why the head of Intel has said that his company could thrive with no US workers at all.

Surplus people are being created at all skill levels. This grim reality punctures the orthodox fantasies of both conservatives and liberals, who argue that education will resolve the current surplus people problem. American educated workers may do relatively better than the nation's uneducated workers, but both will see their fates suffer. Education, as a panacea held up for all surplus people, is a myth.[9] The rise of the Occupy Movement, bulging with highly educated students who can't find jobs to pay back their bloated student loans, is testimony to that reality.

Technology is a second force driving the new crisis. Mainstream wisdom is that technological innovation is actually a solution rather than a cause of the surplus problem. However, while innovation can create jobs and absorb surplus people, current forms of innovation are now eliminating more jobs than they are creating, particularly in the United States.[10] Between 2000 and 2009, more US manufacturing jobs—numbering 6 million, or one of every three—were eliminated through technological displacement than all the manufacturing jobs created in the United States in the previous seventy years.[11]

This has not always been the case. Earlier waves of technological innovation—creating the steam engine, the locomotive, or the automobile, for example—displaced people from the land and threw out of work hordes of earlier transport and craft workers, but they also created huge numbers of new jobs in the nascent oil and steel industries and textile factories. Technologically driven displacement and job creation were more balanced, with technologically inspired economic growth creating millions of new jobs to absorb those displaced.

Things have changed. This is partly because financial and electronic innovation helps free corporations to move offshore and pluck cheaper workers. The Internet, arguably the greatest innovation of recent decades, is unquestionably one of the great drivers of globalization, thus contributing to mass outsourcing and surplus people production.

The globalization of technology is an important factor here. New technologies in the United States are now rapidly diffused to other nations, partly because they are essential to the production of US companies abroad. Moreover, the decline of US economic hegemony makes it very difficult for the United States to protect its own technological innovation. As China's strength grows, it has insisted on technology sharing as a precondition of accessing its vast market. Even if new American technologies create jobs, they are more likely to be utilized to produce jobs in China than in the United States.

Another factor is the nature of the new technology. Robotics serves as the paradigm case. Obviously, robots replace workers; but robotics take technological innovation in a new direction, threatening to eliminate the majority of workers of all skill levels. This leads to entirely robotized auto plants at Toyota that create cars without a worker (or manager) in sight. And to forms of medicine and education and accounting that allow far fewer professionals at home to carry out services online to any corner of the world, while outsourcing much of the actual work to offshore producers or online consumers who may be part of the surplus masses.

Robotics offers spectacular possibilities of labor-saving social advances but leaves in its wake vast numbers of surplus people. This reflects not just the awesome power of the inventions but also the new determination by corporations that profit is greater when human workers are disposed. Robots are more efficient, more reliable, and less rebellious than humans, the paradigm innovation for a "surplus nation."

Of course, if such labor-saving technology could be linked to social redistribution permitting a good life for all, this could be a major advance in human society. Liberation from work, even Karl Marx[12] argued, could end the cold alienation of capitalist society. But all depends on the people in power who design and implement the new technology and determine the social consequences. The intention of American leaders is anything but to allow the surplus masses to get a piece of the profits.

This brings us to the third surplus-creating force: the corporate takeover of Washington, D.C. There's a good reason we talk about "political economy." Economics is never separate from politics. In twenty-first-century America, corporations and government, business and corporate elites have never been closer, joined at the hip, a corruption at the heart of concern among both Tea Partiers and Occupiers.

The economic forces producing surplus people are not inevitable consequences of either globalization or new technology. Far more humane models of globalization and new technology are easily imaginable. But they seem utopian or out of reach because people with wealth have gained increasing control over government, and thus over the design and implementation of both globalization and technological innovation.

Corporate takeover of Washington drives the crisis in multiple ways. Corporate politicians design and implement the neoliberal policies, offshore incentives and subsidies, and trade policies that send jobs abroad. They carry out the foreign policy and regime changes abroad that create friendly low-cost environments abroad for US business. They aid and abet the disinvestment in American infrastructure by describing the infrastructure itself as socialism.

They also block the prospects of domestic reconstruction that might reverse the surplus crisis. Massive domestic public investment, which would require controls over the flow of capital and vast government involvement in the economy and taxation of the rich to fund new US infrastructure and jobs, is impossible in a corporate-run state. A Green New Deal has no realistic political future in the US corporate regime, since it would threaten the hegemony of the fossil-fuel corporate establishment, the military, and the ideology of laissez-faire.

The disinvestment in the US infrastructure has been so prolonged and deep that even if the political will to reconstruct could be created, success would be dubious. Keynesian liberals and members of the Obama administration argue for renewing America through public investment and incentives for private-sector domestic job creation, with substantial attention to twenty-first-century energy infrastructure. This could help create some jobs in the short term. But the reality is that the infrastructure has been so degraded already, Keynesian remedies that are sufficiently large to make an enduring difference will never be accepted by political elites. And even with major progressive political change empowering liberals, public investment advocated by Keynesians—though far preferable to current policies—are unlikely to solve the surplus people crisis, for reasons we discuss later.

This leads to the fourth driving force of the crisis, the erosion of any sense of national stewardship among elites. Global US-based elites have largely abandoned national loyalties, despite their dependence on the US government for their survival and profits, through massive corporate welfare, tax subsidies and giveaways, assault on labor, globalization policies, and so forth. This is arguably the American elite with the greatest dependence on the US government and the least sense of commitment to the government or the tax-paying workers who support them.

Rejecting the nation for a global perspective could be a liberating global policy. But corporate elites look to other nations simply as profit-making opportunities, a form of leveraged buyouts. Their policies may help create jobs abroad in the short term, but each nation and foreign workforce will be abandoned as soon as offending foreign workers seek dignified, well-paying work or the offending foreign country seeks regulation and respect for its sovereignty or environment. The corporate rejection of nationalism is not an embrace of global humanity but an escape from the need to conform to civilized codes of behavior enforced by any country.

Stewardship is the other abandoned virtue. We suffer from the rule of the most myopic, short-term obsessed elites in the history of recent centuries. The United States has historically had business leaders, particularly in the financial sector, that looked out for the longer-term interests of the national economy. No longer.

In fact, the concept of the long term is vanishing. Money travels too fast, financial markets demand immediate return, the future is too precarious to believe in or care about, and time itself has accelerated and telescoped into a disregard for anything beyond tomorrow. Executives know their tenure is short and want to cash in now. There is nothing in place to support the longer-term vision that would create a passion for rebuilding the degraded infrastructure, revive the nation, and solve the crisis of mass surplus people.

·‿·

5

How Many Surplus People Are There in the United States?

The US government has no official records of "surplus people." For obvious reasons, it is not a legal or official category, since just to discuss it would create mass discontent. Even if elites wanted to collect such data, it would be difficult. There are, of course, data on the number of unemployed people, but even these are flawed. Accurate data on many of the other categories of surplus either do not exist or are hard to operationalize and count accurately. Nonetheless, since our whole argument rests on the notion that the United States is moving toward a majority of surplus people, we shall proceed with a conservative approach—one that clearly understates the real surplus population but offers validation of the huge size of those surplus populations that are counted in government reports.

We can offer official records or relatively reliable estimates of the number of Category 1 surplus: the unemployed, under-employed, and marginally attached workers. We will also report numbers of Category 2 surplus populations: prisoners, soldiers, and conservative estimates of the percentage of students and retired people who should be counted as surplus. Because the other categories are not reported by official agencies, we will not include them in our count of the surplus workers.

The following chart is one estimate of the total number of surplus people in the United States in 2010–2012, relying only on official numbers reported by government agencies and not counting the surplus populations in Categories 3–6.

Category 1
Unemployed   15.3 million[1]
Underemployed (involuntary part-time)   8.2 million[2]
Marginally Attached Workers
   (including discouraged)   2.8 million[3]

Category 2
Prison and Jail Inmates   2.3 million[4]
Probation and Parole   4.9 million[5]
   (by conservative estimates, 25 percent are
    surplus = 1.25 million)
Active Military   1.5 million[6]
College and University Students   19.7 million[7]
   (by conservative estimates, 25 percent are
    surplus = 4.9 million)
Retirees   34.4 million[8]
   (by conservative estimates, 25 percent are
    surplus = 9.3 million)

The total of our conservative estimate is 45.6 million. It represents 34 percent of the civilian nonfarm labor force, which was slightly more than 132 million[9] as of December 2010. Because it does not include four of our six categories of surplus people, all of whom are officially counted as employed, this total radically under-states the true surplus people population.

6

Introducing the History of Surplus People

The surplus crisis of the 2010s was a long time in coming. Its roots were planted in the very foundation of capitalism—maybe even earlier. Capitalism is notorious for going through cycles of boom and bust, which may cause the expansion and contractions of surplus population throughout history. Or perhaps, depending upon how you define it, the surplus population doesn't really contract, but sometimes, surplus status is disguised and surplus people are allowed to live in moderate comfort. Other times, their situation is made blatant and they face misery.

One of the biggest problems for the 1 percent is how to contain and control the surplus population. We can refer to two approaches as "the carrot" and "the stick," although throughout history there has usually been a mixture of the two, with some surplus people getting more carrot and others more stick. However, depending on circumstances, there will be periods of greater seduction and others with more brutality. To understand the surplus crisis of the 2010s, we need to trace the history of surplus people and how they have been treated, beginning with the very emergence of capitalism. The fate of surplus people is not determined in a vacuum; it is a reflection of broader circumstances, which vary when the state and the 1 percent feel threatened and secure. Therefore, we will not be able to present this history by referring to surplus people alone; instead, we have to discuss the relevant historical contexts, including the birth of capitalism, the age of the robber barons, the appearance of a consumer economy in the 1920s, the Great Depression and the New Deal, the world wars, the height of American prosperity in the 1950s and 1960s, and the beginnings of America's decline in the 1970s.

Indeed, examining the fate of surplus people is actually a window for understanding the entire history and structure of capitalism. We cannot look at recent traumas alone, but instead must write about political economy, economic history, and political, economic, and social theory. In a past crisis, particularly around the time of the Vietnam War, people on the left routinely thought and wrote about such issues. They were prominent concerns among college students and in university courses. Scholars such as Paul Baron and Paul Sweezy[1], in books like *Monopoly Capital,* tried to update Marx and account for how capitalism was transformed since his death. The loss of this tradition is a tragedy that we hope to overcome.

Among the most important changes since the 1970s is the Reagan counterrevolution, which shifted the discourse and squelched discussion of fundamental problems within capitalism. As a consequence, it became difficult for anything more critical than Keynesian liberalism to get an audience in mainstream academia and the mainstream media. Organizations such as URPE, the Union of Radical Political Economists, carried on, but were seldom heard. It is our hope to help bring their perspective once again above ground. It appears a time for a revival is ripe, and we are not acting alone. The Occupy Movements of 2011 suggest the torch has been passed to a new generation, and we offer our understanding as a tool they can use in their classrooms, their living rooms, and their demonstrations.

7

How Capitalism Created Surplus People Right from the Very Beginning

How Early Capitalists Got Their Opponents, the Feudal Aristocracy, to Create a Surplus Population

Capitalism began by creating surplus people. Capitalist logic requires making a profit by keeping costs to a minimum. It applauds efficiency. Usually the greatest single cost is labor. People are a cost of production: employees are a tool to use and then abandon when no longer needed. Capitalist ideology, at least in the neoclassical or laissez-faire form, proudly proclaims this. All people are inherently self-interested, but rational. Everyone is in competition with everyone else to maximize their own benefit within the market. Everybody uses whatever resources they have for whatever advantage they can gain. Some people have property, but others just have their bodies and must sell their labor to survive. To compete and increase profit, capitalists are expected to continually innovate, a process that renders some people obsolete. If nobody needs their labor, they are cast aside—but the ideology claims there is unlimited opportunity and that if no one wants you, you must be lazy or incompetent. If you fail, you ain't got nobody to blame but yourself and nobody owes you nothin'.

Capitalism produced surplus people from its origins in the late Middle Ages, an integral part of the new system's DNA. Over time, it created growing masses of surplus people and blamed them for their fate.

Precapitalist societies, like feudalism, made different ideological claims. They were more brutal in many ways than capitalism, but they did not incorporate an inherent drive to create surplus people. On the contrary, medieval feudalism

27

was organized on economic and ideological principles that, in theory, prevented surplus people production. The feudal moral commitment was to allow peasants to maintain their station and work their land in perpetuity. The feudal system rested on a promise to prevent the creation of a mass surplus population.

The feudal lord presented himself as the guardian of his peasants within a self-contained commonwealth in whose bounty everyone shared, although it would require complete blindness to believe everyone shared equally. The manor was not trying to produce commodities to sell for profit on the market and therefore had little need to create goods simply to make more money. Allegedly, production was for use. Everyone was bound together as links in a Great Chain of Being[1] in which God had assigned everyone a fixed place that could not be questioned. The goal was to maintain the chain, to provide order and stability. Progress, advancement, certainly striving to rise above your station, was shunned. The chain required a network of mutual obligations. The peasant owed the lord labor, submission, and obedience. The lord supposedly owed his serf protection in health and in sickness, in youth and in old age, in plenty and in scarcity. If the manor was productive and required lots of labor, great; but if crops failed and there was little for the peasant to do, the lord was still supposed to provide for him. So the peasant was either assured a right to work or cared for by the lords if deprived of this right, thereby spared the fate of surplus people in postfeudal societies.

As capitalism emerged in the shadow of feudalism, feudalism itself was transformed, with the production of surplus people both an initial mark and a consequence of this great transformation.[2] Prosperous merchants, the early capitalists or the bourgeoisie, gave the lords access to ever-greater luxury. Consequently the gap in lifestyle between lord and peasant grew. Paying for their lavish lifestyle required the lords to shift to commodity production for the market. Often, the lords were in debt to the merchants. Although generally hostile to the bourgeoisie and professing a very different worldview, the lords started to behave more like capitalists. In the search for greater efficiency, fewer peasants were needed to work the land. Land, which the lords previously claimed was a common trust held for the benefit of all, including the peasant, was declared to be the lord's private property. It was enclosed, fenced off. Peasants would have to pay taxes and rents in hard currency—gold and silver—to stay on the land. Many who could not pay were expelled, and thus transformed into a surplus population: vagabonds, wandering aimlessly, who to survive turned to crime, vice, prostitution, and begging. Some did not survive; many were hung.

The aristocrats and bourgeoisie labeled each other parasites. The nobles called the capitalists upstarts, lacking refinement, grace, honor, and pure blood. They would destroy order and tradition for the sake of money and profit and would not care whom they hurt in the process. The bourgeoisie thought the aristocrats were stagnant, wallowing in luxury, claiming wealth and status that they did not earn, and standing in the way of progress. They used the growing number of vagabonds as proof that the nobles' concern for the poor was a lie that they would disregard when there was money to be made.

The aristocrats claimed that a fundamental biological essence, difficult to define, separated people. Because they lacked this alleged essence, the bourgeoisie presented themselves as representatives of the masses. In France, the richest capitalist could call himself a member of the "third estate," comprising 95–98 percent of the population. In Britain, the wealthiest lawyer, industrialist, or banker would be a "commoner" along with the poorest vagabond, peasant, or factory worker. To rally the support of the very people whom they exploited or displaced in their struggle against the aristocracy, the capitalists spoke of democracy and suggested that all people were equal because biological barriers separating people did not exist and everyone was entitled to an equal opportunity to prove their merit on the market. Those who failed deserved their fate. Capitalist democracy would offer freedom—freedom from a network of obligations; freedom to fend for yourself, perhaps uplift yourself; but also freedom to become surplus, and freedom to starve. Promised democracy, equality, and freedom, the masses provided foot soldiers for the capitalists in their revolutions against the aristocracy in Britain, America, and France. But many of these foot soldiers would end up becoming the first generation of capitalist surplus people.

· ⁓ ·

8

How the First Truly Industrial Society, Britain, Used Surplus People

As a reward for their service to the bourgeoisie, the starving vagabonds were forced into workhouses, little different from slave labor and extermination camps. The workhouses were the first major "surplus people retention centers," meant to warehouse the surplus population. Many of the residents were children, abandoned by their parents who lacked the means to support them. Lacking ventilation and heat, the workhouses were frigid cold in winter and stifling hot in the summer. Diseases like tuberculosis, cholera, diphtheria, and typhoid were rampant. Not only to save money, but also fearful that too rich a diet, including meat, would make the inmates feel overly entitled and spark their rebellious spirit, the workhouse guardians deliberately underfed them. Whereas life expectancy for a feudal peasant had been about thirty-five years, by the 1850s it fell to about twenty-five for the poor in Liverpool and Manchester.[1]

The suffering, even the deaths, among the poor were proclaimed by the authorities as part of a natural winnowing process necessary to separate the worthy from the unworthy. The unworthy lacked stamina, would happily wallow in minimal subsistence, and would enjoy sloth if given enough to get by; the worthy understood their degraded condition as an inspiration to uplift themselves by their bootstraps. Misery and mortality for the unworthy were a necessary cost for creating unprecedented prosperity and improving the quality of the race. It might bring a tear to the bleeding heart, but the Victorian British GDP was the highest the world had yet seen, although it was hardly evenly distributed. The surplus population whom the workhouses could not absorb would be hung or shipped off to colonies like Australia, in essence a "surplus people nation."

The English managed their own surplus population largely by creating a surplus population in the colonies, especially India. As has been mentioned, the British destroyed the native precolonial Indian textile industry, calling it primitive and inefficient. The Indians then could no longer compete with the British, and their land was used to grow cotton that would service the English mills. Rather than outsource industry and jobs, as the United States has recently been doing, the British "in-sourced" Third World resources to build their domestic infrastructure.

·⚊·

9

How American Capitalists Controlled the Surplus Population before World War I

The 99 Percent Were Both Promised the "American Dream" and Threatened with Destitution

Although not as brutal as the British workhouse, American manufacturers tried to control their workers by constantly threatening to make them surplus. They were forced to live in "company towns," where not only the factories but the housing, stores, and even the churches and schools were owned by the corporation. Although robber barons like Francis Cabot Lowell, George Pullman, and Andrew Carnegie spoke of free labor, they treated their workers almost like feudal serfs, forced to live on plantations, with their lifestyles and morality policed by their bosses. Many of these "serfs" were destined to become surplus people when they broke the bosses' rules or when the economy tanked. Almost like enclosing the manors, when profits fell, the robber barons lowered wages and fired workers, expelling them into the surplus population. Carnegie threw 1,100 employees at his Homestead factory town out on the street.[1] When the workers struck, he built a barbed-wire fence around the factory, sent in the private Pinkerton army, and then got the governor to mobilize the national guard to break the union.

Having the national guard and federal troops attack the unions and protect the factories are examples of how dependent the bourgeoisie are upon the government. Nineteenth-century capitalist ideology, laissez-faire, which has had a resurgence since the 1980s, insists the private sector thrives best with minimal state involvement in the economy, but the private sector itself may be a myth. The ideology claims the government is inherently incapable of creating wealth; it can only destroy it. All wealth must be created by the private sector. However, private industry can exist only because the state is there to support it. The early industrialization of the northeast was sparked by state-built canals, the most famous of which was the Erie Canal. As another example, the federal government handed over huge tracks of land to the private railroad companies.

Among the most important services the government gives to the very rich is controlling the surplus population, through both brutal and soft means. The genocide the US Army conducted against the Native Americans provided Western land for white settlers or homesteaders, including returning Civil War veterans, many of whom could not find jobs in the East. Much of the land was unfit to farm and would eventually degenerate into "dust bowls" in the 1930s. In the meanwhile, the homestead farmers would provide customers for Eastern capitalists as they pored over their Montgomery Ward and Sears mail-order catalogs to buy farm implements and dry goods. Many of the farmers found themselves heavily in debt to the railroads and banks, to whom they had to mortgage their farms.

One reason why homesteaders would have faced unemployment in the East was federal encouragement of immigration. Immigrants were used to displace native-born workers, who joined unions, demanded higher wages, or wanted better working conditions. Each at risk of becoming surplus, immigrant and native-born workers would often fight against each other rather than against the bosses.

Governmental assistance to the employers was often disguised as a benefit for the working and surplus populations. Compulsory public education acculturated the children of both immigrants and native-born into American capitalist values and disciplined them to become an obedient controllable working population who did not question the privilege of living in a free country. The grading system would get them to accept a hierarchy in which everyone gets what they deserve. Placing children in school removed them from the labor market. Although they were made surplus people, they were taught they were preparing for the American dream, which often did not come, and children and their parents usually would not identify themselves as surplus.[2] Ending child labor was a short-term blow to many employers, for children will work for lower wages than adults and are easier to intimidate. However, it was less dangerous to push children into the surplus population than full-grown men. It is harder to hide the surplus status of unemployed and underemployed men, who are apt to become bitter and resentful and might become disruptive. They could challenge authority and turn to crime or maybe even revolutionary movements.

· ⸂⸃ ·

10

World War I and the Roaring Twenties

How American Capitalists Came to Be the Richest and Most Powerful in the World By Turning Their Workers More into Consumers than Producers

One of the best ways to eliminate the surplus population, especially among young grown men—the most dangerous element—is to send them off as cannon fodder to war. The problem is, what to do with them when peace comes? Immediately after World War I, unemployment hit 12 percent and GDP fell 17 percent.[1] Angry veterans, who felt they sacrificed for their country but could not support themselves when they returned home from Europe, could be especially dangerous as they shifted from warrior to potential surplus civilian. (And the same is true today!)

Nevertheless, wars provide enormous subsidies to armament industries, including textile mills that make uniforms and agribusinesses, which feed the troops. At the onset of World War I, the United States was the world's largest debtor and owed the rest of the world, primarily Europe, $3 billion[2] (about $65 billion in 2010 dollars). However, the debt was a sign of economic health. It stemmed from rapidly expanding industries: steel, oil, and cars, which needed foreign capital to flourish. By 1914 the US economy had grown to rival Britain's, which had gone to war with its other rival, Germany. Before the United States entered the war, Britain and Germany pretty much wiped each other out, but American financiers, especially the J. P. Morgan banks, lent so much to Britain that a German victory would have devastated the US economy. By the war's end, America more than paid off its debts and became the world's greatest creditor, with $6 billion[3] in the black.

Although the war destroyed the infrastructure of every major country in Europe, it left America's more than intact. "By 1920, the United States national income was greater than the combined incomes of Britain, France, Germany, Japan, Canada, and seventeen smaller countries."[4] To arm, supply, and feed its troops along with its allies, the United States built an industrial base that overwhelmed the rest of the world. It was an infrastructure so large that when peace came, the civilian economy could not sustain it, even though the factories, which had expanded to build armaments during the war, converted to domestic consumer goods. Markets had to be found to absorb this new capacity, but Europe and the rest of the world were now too poor to buy America's products and American workers were not paid a wage high enough to purchase the very things they made. From 1923 to 1929, factory output per worker grew 43 percent, corporate profits rose 62 percent, and corporate dividends climbed 65 percent—but workers' wages only increased by 8 percent, while the income of the richest 1 percent of the population was enhanced by 75 percent.[5] The economy of the Roaring Twenties thus gave rise to a gap between the 1 percent and the 99 percent resembling the 2010s. But the very rich can only eat so much or buy so many cars. They will save much more and leave many products without customers.

From a capitalist point of view, much of the American population had become surplus by the 1920s. Not everyone was needed to produce; many millions might no longer be needed as workers. But for corporations to make a profit, almost everyone, including the surplus people, needed to consume. The solution to the dilemma was to create a credit economy. It would be anachronistic to call it a "plastic economy," but people went in debt to buy new inventions like cars and radios on the installment plan, whether or not they could afford them. Sixty percent of automobiles and eighty percent of radios were purchased through the installment plan. From 1925 to 1929, consumer installment debt rose from $1.38 billion (about $17 billion in 2010 dollars) to $3 billion (about $38 billion in 2010 dollars).[6] The advertising industry, whose primary function is to get people to buy for the sake of buying, spiraled. Cars marketed for their appearance, like GM's Chevrolet, outsold cars marketed for their utility, such as Ford's Model T.[7] As debt surpassed wages, the economy became a bubble bound to pop. While the bubble held, unemployment was low, remaining at about 3.2 percent from 1925 to 1929.[8]

As early as 1914, Henry Ford recognized the "wage paradox"—namely, that unemployed or underpaid people do not make good customers. No matter how cheaply he could make Model Ts on the assembly line, he could not sell them and make a profit if wages were not high enough for workers to buy his cars—or if enough workers were not actually employed. Accordingly, he hired generously and instituted a minimum wage of $5 a day[9] in his factories (about $115 a day in 2011 dollars). In effect, Ford was setting wages not on the value of what employees produced, but on the anticipated yield from their consumption. Some employees were paid more than what their labor was worth to Ford; they would have worked for less. To encourage consumption, he subsidized their lifestyle, almost implementing a private welfare system. This was impressive because Ford was among the staunchest followers of laissez-faire, an opponent of unions and government involvement in the economy. Work on his assembly line was brutally tedious and boring. Nonetheless, thanks to the wages he paid, there were lines outside his factory gate. Ford, as a private citizen (albeit a very powerful one), was trying to make social economic policy, largely because he was so hostile to state regulation. But setting social economic policy—including the ability to create stimulus that can absorb surplus workers across the national economy—is something only the government can do. There was a limit to how many men Ford could hire whom he did not need to produce cars, especially cars he could not sell. The result was that he ended up subsidizing his rival capitalists. His workers could buy radios and refrigerators, but employees of other companies could not buy Model Ts.

By the 1920s, the shift from a production economy to a consumption economy was in full force, but it was soon to implode and create a tidal wave of new surplus people. Not only was the American consumer dependent upon credit, but so was Europe as it tried to recover from World War I. To maintain a viable European economy capable of buying American goods and paying its American debts, the United States continued to lend Europe ever more money throughout the 1920s. Not only consumer goods but investment instruments like stocks were purchased on credit or margin, with the investor putting as little as 10 percent down. With both the international and domestic economies so dependent upon credit, any decline in lender confidence could bring the entire system to virtual collapse.

·‿·

II

The Great Depression Begins

The Consumer Economy of the Roaring Twenties Implodes and Leaves Millions of People as Surplus

And the collapse came in October 1929. The Dow Jones Stock Market Average achieved a record high, 381.17, on September 3. By November 13, it had fallen to 198.60, a loss of 48 percent. From 1929 to 1932 the US national income dropped from $87.4 billion (about $1.1 trillion in 2010 dollars) to $41.7 (about $659 billion in 2010 dollars), industrial productivity fell 44 percent, construction declined by 78 percent, and investment was down 98 percent. Stock values in 1932 were barely 20 percent of their 1929 peak. Of the roughly 25 thousand American banks in 1929, some 11 thousand had failed by 1933. The surplus population spiraled. Thirteen million Americans—at least 25 percent of the official labor force (to say nothing of the unofficial force)—was unemployed by 1932.[1] This resulted in an extremely volatile situation, for the growing surplus population could turn rebellious. Rural sheriffs were prevented from foreclosing mortgages at gunpoint. In 1932 an assembly of 150,000 World War I veterans—many unemployed—and their supporters marched on Washington to demand payment of bonuses they had been promised. After they built a tent city, the army was sent in to disperse them.[2] The rich still lived well, but profits were down because few could afford to buy products and services. The huge new mass of surplus people made selling all the more difficult. Capitalism could collapse. For the sake of the capitalist class, capitalism had to be saved from itself.

In the 1920s under the Harding, Coolidge, and Hoover administrations (the direct ancestors of the Reagan and Bush regimes), laissez-faire ideology was dogma. With few exceptions, the 1 percent were unwilling to accept state policies that could raise their taxes or interfere with their prerogative to manage their fortunes any way they chose. Despite insisting the economy was sound, President Hoover was willing to create the Federal Reconstruction Finance Corporation, a federal agency that lent to banks, who then underwrote private industries as well as public works projects for dams, roads, and bridges.[3] Hoover produced the largest federal peacetime deficit until that time, and his Democratic opponent, New York governor Franklin D. Roosevelt, attacked him as a "spend-thrift."[4] However, the scale was too small to stimulate recovery. Hoover refused to have the federal government intervene directly to aid displaced people, but by 1932 many state and municipal funds to relieve poverty as well as private charities were exhausted. Under these circumstances, Roosevelt overwhelmingly defeated Hoover on a vaguely contradictory platform that simultaneously called for a balanced budget and spending whatever was necessary to alleviate suffering, both among the surplus population and those in danger of becoming surplus. The New Deal was born out of the desperation of the new surplus masses and the fear that they could destroy capitalism itself.

·⤚·

12

Roosevelt, Keynes, and the New Deal

How the Government Tried to Save Capitalism from Itself by Relieving Misery among the Surplus

After several years of experimentation, Roosevelt's New Deal settled on the economic policies of British theorist John Maynard Keynes, although Roosevelt and Keynes held each other in personal contempt. Roosevelt used Keynesianism to reintegrate surplus people into the economy, rebuild their capacity to consume, and sometimes mask their surplus status. Keynes was no Marxist or revolutionary. He was an adamant supporter of capitalism and an investor who died with a personal fortune of about £500,000 (about $16.5 million in 2009 dollars).[1] He believed that stabilizing capitalism required abandoning the laissez-faire model and accepting the reality that the capitalist class and the so-called private sector had always been intimately dependent upon the government.[2] The market cannot be trusted to regulate itself. It is subject to fluctuations—periodic booms and busts—that could end in catastrophe. Capitalism can only survive with a planned social economic policy managed by the government.

In laissez-faire theory, the fundamental unit of analysis is the individual, in competition with all other individuals. Among those individuals are the corporation and the state. In the zero-sum Darwinian struggle, any resource going to the government is removed from the private sector, the source of all productivity. Keynes shifted the unit of analysis to a single integrated system upon which everyone, rich and poor, depends. The government was to act almost like the maestro of an orchestra, directing resources wherever they may be needed, sometimes to the 1 percent, sometimes to the 99 percent, or even to the lowest 10 percent. Unlike Marxism, which seeks to heighten class struggle—that is, the struggle of the 99 percent against the 1 percent—the goal of Keynesianism is to achieve class harmony. Everyone either shares in the economy's bounty or suffers from its failures. As John F. Kennedy later put it, "A rising tide lifts all boats."[3]

Wealth is valuable only if it circulates. Money stuffed in mattresses and factory inventory rotting in warehouses does no one any good. The 99 percent spends a much larger proportion of its income than the 1 percent. Corporations can only make a profit if people can buy their products. The 1 percent may no longer need the surplus populations for their production, but they still need them for their consumption. Keynes proposed a "trickle up" theory. Give to the poor (the core surplus population) and money will float to the rich while benefiting all. For the sake of the rich in a depression, resources must be directed toward the poor and other surplus and the government must spend to stimulate growth.

But how is the state to pay for its spending? If it raises taxes, it takes money out of circulation, and that may defeat the whole purpose. The solution: deficits. In the laissez-faire paradigm, the government, as an individual like everyone else, must keep its house in order. Borrowing should only be for emergencies and is destructive in the long run. Keynes, in contrast, saw the state as the embodiment of the entire society, and when it borrows (unless it borrows from other countries), the economy is only borrowing from itself. He envisioned a "multiplier effect," whereby government spending could stimulate consumption. With increased demand, industry would have an incentive to produce more and employ more people, who in turn would buy more. State consumption is really an investment. If the government borrows properly and encourages growth, it can pay for this year's loan with next year's income. But how long can debt be sustained? Eventually, years later, maybe decades later, the bill will be due.[4] We will see what happened in subsequent decades later in our history. To borrow, you need collateral. For an entire economy, infrastructure is the collateral. During the Great Depression, infrastructure was deteriorating, lying fallow, unused, with a huge surplus population incapable of consuming its produce. If the goal is to preserve capitalism, relieving the misery of the surplus by giving them the confidence to buy may be the best investment when the economy is in the doldrums.

Keynesian policy is intended to maintain capitalism, and capitalism needs surplus people. Keynesianism has a professed goal of full employment, but full employment is defined as 4 to 6 percent unemployed, not 0 percent. Thus, guaranteeing that a certain percentage become surplus is systematically and intentionally built into Keynesian policy as conceived by business and political elites, at least in the United States (in Europe, Keynesianism sought to reduce the unemployed surplus to 2 percent). Underneath this Keynesian logic is the capitalist fear that if not enough people are desperate for jobs, workers might feel entitled to demand higher wages and better working conditions. In the interests of bosses, US economic planners declare an economy approaching full employment "over-heated" and deliberately induce a "recession" or mini-depression, which will throw people on the street.

Keynesianism and the New Deal had a complex relationship to surplus populations. Many Keynesian New Deal programs, such as Social Security, served real needs of older workers and were a major achievement. But Social Security also had the effect of expanding and absorbing the surplus population. It incentivized exit from the labor force since it provided a soft landing for people who retire, usually at age 65. Until 1986, retirement was not a choice; it was compulsory.[5] Social Security, like unemployment insurance, serves capitalism by sustaining the ability of people who no longer produce—that is, the surplus population—to consume.

The most obvious way to maintain people who are removed from the labor force is to give them money directly. However, that carries the danger of undermining the work incentive. If you can support yourself without an alienating job, why bother? Accordingly, capitalists would want direct welfare to pay less than the worst jobs and be so unpleasant that hardly anyone would choose it voluntarily. As welfare bills worked their way through Congress, the laws that emerged, constrained by capitalist influences, were more limited than Keynes or Roosevelt might have wanted.

Welfare also exemplified the contradictory effects of Keynesian policy on surplus people. As finally enacted, Aid to Families with Dependent Children (AFDC), the main welfare program from the New Deal to the 1990s, provided real support for the poor. But while servicing the most vulnerable of the surplus people, it forced recipients to essentially surrender control of their private life to state-supported social workers.[6] A social worker could enter the apartment of an unwed mother and demand that she account for an extra pair of pants. The welfare mother and the social worker were actually both dependent upon the state, but the social worker, educated and middle class, was the worthy guardian; and the welfare mother was the unworthy poor, who had to be made deliberately miserable for her own benefit. This distinction among worthy and unworthy surplus people was essentially the same one found in the British workhouses of the 1800s.

Another reason why it is unwise to allow the poor to starve to death is that employers need to maintain a "reserve army of labor"[7] as a whip to prevent workers from becoming too demanding. New Deal welfare policies thus provided a service to capitalists that FDR may not have intended. As long as there are desperate people, bosses can say, "If you don't want to work here, I can find someone who does." Thus the worthy worker, who is often a disguised or near surplus person, and the unworthy poor, who is hardcore surplus, are pitted against each other. The employed are told, "You work hard and pay taxes to support lazy sluts who lounge around and have babies. They are lazy and they want your jobs." The lazy over-indulged unworthy poor committed "welfare fraud" by working "under the table" for pay below the legal minimum wage at jobs that workers within the official labor force will not take, such as harvesting crops, cleaning other people's houses, and taking care of their children. Anger toward the unworthy poor—that is, the core surplus population—deflects hostility away from the very rich. Seeing how their modest income is taxed, the employed think of lazy parasites instead of government support for the 1 percent, what is sometimes called "corporate welfare." The war between the 1 percent and the 99 percent becomes a war within the 99 percent (mostly employed or partially employed) who think they have escaped surplus, and the other portion of the 99 percent (the wretched folks on welfare) who can't deny their nakedly surplus position.

To uphold the work ethic and defuse the discontent that stems from not having a job and a social role, the rich often used another tactic that could be masked as a kind of benevolent Keynesianism: seek to disguise welfare as employment.

Unlike private corporations such as the Ford Motor Company, the government can afford to employ people for the sake of employing them. Efficiency has a different meaning for the state and for private industry. The government's goal is not to make a profit but to maintain social stability and build the "favorable investment climate" that capitalists crave. Employed people will feel a stake in the existing capitalist society that the blatantly idle will not. However, "workfare" has its problems. It is more expensive than the dole. You must pay people who work more than those who don't, and most jobs require expensive infrastructure to support them. You can't have factory workers without factories, road crews without roads, teachers without schools, and doctors and plumbers without equipment. Recall our earlier discussion of make-work; it may be cheaper to give more money to the poor than hire social workers to police them. Meter maids and toll takers may not bring in that much more revenue than their wages warrant.

As part of his Keynesian New Deal, Roosevelt initiated extensive public works programs. Many had real social value that we should applaud, but their primary purpose was to give surplus people work. Projects included building dams, roads, schools, hospitals, civic buildings, and bridges. Special effort was made to employ idle artists, writers, and actors through such means as publicly supported theaters. The Civilian Conservation Corps established camps for unemployed youth, who planted trees, made reservoirs and fish ponds, built dams, dug diversion ditches, raised bridges and fire towers, fought tree diseases, restored historic battlefields, cleared beaches and camping grounds, and protected and improved parks, forests, watersheds, and recreational areas.[8] Much of this Keynesian government employment created socially useful work; some was pure make-work (ditches to refill, bridges to nowhere) to prevent open revolt from the surplus masses.

When the government actually does create productive work and real wealth, capitalists panic. Consider the Tennessee Valley Authority (TVA). In the days before the TVA was created, the Tennessee River frequently flooded. Throughout the valley, average income was barely half the national level, half the families were on relief, and barely 2 percent of the farms had electricity. Despite this, if the river was properly dammed, not only would flooding be prevented but cheap electricity could be generated. Moreover, millions of surplus workers could be absorbed, in this case, by productive Keynesian intervention—a surplus-absorption strategy that works, at least in the short term.

But, political realities in capitalism prevent such productive Keynesian anti-surplus strategies from reaching a scale that can truly solve the mass surplus crisis. If the TVA succeeded it would be in direct competition with Commonwealth and Southern, the largest private electrical utility in the area. As we have seen, laissez-faire dogma asserts the state is an inefficient parasite that can only destroy wealth, never create it. But the real danger was that government enterprise might be too efficient and wipe out smaller private competitors. Commonwealth and Southern's CEO, Wendell Willkie, was so outraged at the threat from TVA that he ran against Roosevelt as the 1940 Republican nominee. He received 22 million votes, more than any previous candidate except Roosevelt himself.[9] Because of the threats that public enterprise posed, the energy sector remained overwhelmingly private, and few new projects like the TVA were created, thus minimizing help for the surplus population.

Some capitalists, nonetheless, gravitated to the security they got from the Keynesian New Deal. Boston retail magnate Edward Filene was one; he mused, "Why shouldn't the American people take half my money from me? I took it all from them."[10] A universe of capitalist Filenes would have reduced the surplus population and alleviated its misery, at least in the short- to medium-term. But most of the 1 percent resisted increased taxes, regulations, and governmental competition.[11] A long list, including the DuPont brothers, Alfred Sloan, William Knudsen and Jouett Shouse of General Motors, Nathan Miller of US Steel, Ernest Weir of National Steel, Sewell Avery of Montgomery Ward, and Howard Pew of Sun Oil, formed the Liberty League.[12] Like the Tea Party of the 2010s, it was designed to defeat a liberal president or at least force him to accept a conservative agenda. Roosevelt may have been maligned as a "traitor to his class,"[13] but he was constrained from too aggressively investing in social services that might serve the surplus at the expense of the 1 percent. He was also unwilling, or perhaps unable, to pursue policies that would challenge the Southern gentry within his own Democratic Party and threaten the Southern racial hierarchy. To not interfere with them and keep blacks dependent, welfare benefits for the most vulnerable surplus population were kept under the control of the states; and agribusiness, a traditional sector filled with people on the edge of surplus, was exempt from minimum wages and other new regulations that applied to Northern industries.[14]

The bottom line? Keynesianism, as used by corporate elites, was a strategy designed to absorb surplus people through state intervention to prevent open revolt from the surplus masses and to divide and conquer the worthy and unworthy surplus. It had modest success in the short term but proved unsustainable in the long run, partly because of the overwhelming resistance of the 1 percent.

·～·

13

America at Its Height

War, Keynesianism, and How People Who Were No Longer Needed to Produce Came to Believe They Had Achieved the American Dream

From 1933 to 1939, President Roosevelt spent $41 billion (about $637 billion in 2010 dollars), mostly on social services and public works. That is almost as much as the total amount the federal government spent from its formation in 1789 to 1932, $45 billion, a number that includes the Civil War and World War I.[1] Everything Roosevelt spent on his New Deal was not enough for the economy to fully recover from the Great Depression. In 1939, US GDP reached $92.2 billion, well above its 1933 nadir, $56.4 billion, but still below the 1929 total of $103.6 billion. By 1945 the federal deficit reached $259 billion (about $3.1 trillion in 2010 dollars), but GDP achieved $223 billion[2] and unemployment was near zero. It was World War II, not Roosevelt's New Deal, that ended the Great Depression and solved the immediate crisis of the huge surplus population.

War can be the ultimate corporate welfare and the ultimate surplus-eliminator. It kills off many of the surplus population and indirectly employs them in producing for death. The 1 percent uses war and related nationalism as one of its most powerful tools to absorb surplus people and win their allegiance.

War does not necessarily compete with private industry, actually helping deal with the crisis of surplus population in a way most beneficial to the 1 percent itself. That helps explain why the corporate elite does not object to Keynesian state deficits as long as taxpayer money is spent on guns, not butter. War can be presented as a national emergency for which parochial concerns would have to be forgotten. Social services benefit only a few, the working class and the surplus, but everyone has a stake in defense. Government contracts for tanks, ships, and bombs can serve as an economic stimulus, just like schools and food stamps. Money from military contracts may "trickle down" through increased employment, thus absorbing surplus people, but the money first goes to the corporations. It would be cheaper to have the government build weapons directly as a public works project because the state does not have to take a percentage out as profit, but that would seem anticapitalist.

During World War II, the United States expanded its industrial apparatus far more than it had during World War I. There was a such a shortage of young civilian men that women were recruited to staff the weapons factories. With peace, there was once again a problem of what to do with returning veterans, going from war heroes to surplus. Immediately after the war, GDP fell 12.7 percent.[3] The Great Depression was showing signs of a relapse. Some economists argue that the depression never ended; the US economy has been propped up by armaments spending ever since. War dollars are arguably utilized mainly as domestic weapons to soak up surplus workers and prevent surplus people from launching a class war at home.

Following World War I, a potentially large surplus warrior class emerged as the armed forces fell from 5 million to 250,000. As discussed in a previous chapter, an artificial burst in consumerism, based on unsustainable debt, allowed many of these surplus warriors to get jobs temporarily. After World I, France and Britain, while also heavily in debt to the United States, continued to police the world, with economic benefits accruing to America. The European debt sustained the surplus US soldiers who now worked on products sold to Europe. But this all ended with the 1929 crash.

World War II left the United States even more clearly the world's dominant economic power, as Britain and France were now too weak to serve as the world police force. US corporations could gain from perpetual military contracts, as well as the army protecting foreign investments and markets and securing access to Third World resources and cheap labor. Rather than reducing its military, as it had done at the conclusion of World War I, [4] the United States would now become a permanent garrison state, a long-term strategy for dealing with the surplus people crisis. This shift to permanent warfare was symbolized by renaming the Department of War as the Department of Defense. *Defense* may sound softer, but war is sporadic whereas the need for defense never ends. The Soviet Union, the ally who had borne the overwhelming cost of defeating Adolf Hitler, was now declared an eternal enemy as brutal as Nazi Germany. Containing Russia required weapons capable of killing every person on this planet, many times over. While the discourse was all about the Communist threat, the aim was partly to cope with intensified surplus people crises.

The 1 percent might benefit from a country locked in cold war, but what about the returning GIs who felt especially entitled for their sacrifice? Keeping them in the surplus population would be risky, but many would be reabsorbed by the military as the United States fought Korea. A permanent draft after World War II continued to absorb hundreds of thousands of potentially surplus Americans.

Arms factories also absorbed potentially surplus men, but many would not get jobs in the expanding armament industries if women stayed in the factories. A "togetherness family values" campaign encouraged female workers to leave the labor market, marry the returning veterans, purchase houses in newly built suburbs, have babies, and buy, buy, buy! The veterans and their wives got their homes through mortgages underwritten by the federal government through the GI Bill,[5] which set aside billions of dollars to help returning veterans readapt to civilian life. The GI Bill effectively subsidized not only veterans but also banks and the construction industry. "Homeowners" might be heavily in debt, but they would identify themselves as part of the propertied class. When they did get jobs, their mortgages would restrain them from doing anything that might put their income at risk. And turning Rosie the Riveter into a housewife opened up jobs for returning warriors who otherwise could plunge from hero to surplus person.

The bill actually encouraged GIs to postpone their reentry into the labor force and disguised being surplus, at least temporarily, as a privilege. Before 1940, barely 5 percent of the population attended colleges, but through grants offered by the GI Bill, almost half of World War II veterans received higher education. The GI Bill did not increase the number of jobs requiring advanced specialized training, such as doctors, lawyers, and scientists. Instead, college graduates took jobs for which previously a high school diploma was sufficient: sales manager, nurse, even cop. However, rather than feeling like surplus people, they would now identify themselves as educated, middle class, and professional. A highly educated population carries risks for bosses, though. They may feel entitled, competent to challenge authority, and resentful if not given positions commensurate with knowledge or, worse, relegated to surplus for the long run. This would prove to be a problem during the Vietnam War and the Occupy Movement of 2011.

To get the veterans, some now with degrees, to buy into the newly formed suburbs with their newly formed families, with women nobly redefined in the sacred role of motherhood rather than as surplus workers, infrastructure was intentionally dismantled. Viable inner-city neighborhoods and downtowns were reduced to enclaves of poverty and boarded-up buildings, as downtown department stores were replaced by monotonous strip malls, which ringed the metropolitan areas. Neighborhood movie theaters closed down as suburbanites bought newly invented televisions, through which they watched commercials intended to get them to consume all the more. Central city public transportation was destroyed. The streetcar became a relic of the past.[6] Standard Oil and General Motors jointly bought the Los Angeles Transit system, then one of the finest in the world, and closed it down.[7] They then pressured the California legislature to build freeways. Homes, stores, businesses, even schools and recreation centers, were now so far from each other that they could only be reached by automobile. Life in Los Angeles became almost impossible without a car. All of these policies undermined the existing infrastructure and threatened a new major surplus people crisis, with jobs in public transit and those related to public services more broadly threatened with obsolescence. As one example of the desperate need to confront this new looming surplus people crisis, President Eisenhower undertook a public works project to build a network of multi-lane interstate highways that now crisscross the nation.[8] This created the fiction that the dismantling of public space and the rise of suburban America would create jobs and prosperity for all.

World War II left America's competitors in Europe and Japan decimated, so American industry had little incentive to innovate, with serious consequences to come for the rise of surplus populations. In as early as the 1920s, automobile companies changed the appearance of their cars regularly, even annually, but the actual technology remained essentially the same. Cars were marketed by making people's sense of status depend upon having this year's look. If people drive last year's car, their neighbor will think they are poor or "not with it." They may have become poor to look rich, but that increased profit for the auto companies. By the 1950s, Ford and GM had adopted "planned obsolescence."[9] They decided it was self-defeating to make well-built cars and focused on appearance, not quality. The sooner cars fell apart, the sooner people would replace them. From a corporate point of view, cars with life spans of three to five years was not a bad idea; it was a way of absorbing workers who would be hurtled into the surplus population by certain job-eliminating innovations. Technological innovation was actually squelched. American auto companies held patterns for engines that were more efficient and less ecologically destructive than the internal combustion. However, these alternatives would compete with existing technology, and developing them would require paying to retool plants that were yielding adequate profit, at least for the time being. The patterns were locked in vaults to prevent other companies and countries from using them. Oil companies gave solar and other green energy technologies a similar treatment.[10]

With little competition from abroad, American auto, oil, and steel companies could afford to pay their employees enough to buy houses, cars, and televisions and perhaps send their kids to college. In the 1950s and 1960s, workers typically identified themselves as middle class and often felt they had attained the American dream. Industrial corporations signed an armistice with unions, and together, they worked to preserve industrial peace. The practice Ford began with his $5 day was becoming standard nationally. By 1955 the average autoworker made $90 a week (about $725 in 2010 dollars). [11] Wages were set to maintain consumption and social stability, not necessarily on the value of what the worker produced. Families could sustain a middle-class lifestyle on one income. Although outside the labor market, housewives and children did not feel themselves to be surplus. However, the real surplus population hardly vanished; it was just hidden. If you traveled to the South, to Appalachia, or to northern inner-city black ghettoes, you would see a different picture. [12]

One reason why industrial corporations could afford to pay their workers well and employ so many people was that they were subsidized by the government, largely, as noted earlier, through weapons contracts. Armaments became America's staple product, the foundation of the rest of the economy. [13] It supported aerospace, chemicals, energy, mining, communications, and transportation. For many corporations, the Department of Defense was their largest customer, even outweighing the private consumer. Keynesian public works projects, ones that offered butter as well as guns, were sponsored under the Pentagon. Military money built the interstate highways, and federal loans to college students were called National Defense Loans. After World War II, when the United States was the world's economic engine, military research sparked most innovation—transistors, computer circuits, and plastics among them. However, American industry so dominated the world that American corporations felt little motivation to apply these innovations to civilian consumer goods. But, as we shall see in the next chapter, the effect of these military-driven policies was to undermine the civilian infrastructure, leading to US decline and the most recent and catastrophic stage of the US surplus people crisis. [14]

14

America Enters Decline

How Other Countries Used America's Discoveries to Create Wealth while America Dismantled Its Industries and Wasted Its Prosperity on Weapons and Consumer Debt

Understanding the surplus people crisis of the 2010s requires an unflinching view of US decline. Forced to rebuild their industries, which had been destroyed in World War II, from scratch, Europe and Japan adopted the latest technologies. They took the discoveries from American military research and used them to improve televisions, tape players, and cameras. Because their populations were too poor to afford American cars (which were big, ostentatious, inefficient, and short-lived), they built small, durable, more ecological ones. People in other countries didn't purchase American cars, but by the late 1960s Americans regularly bought foreign goods, with obvious consequences for US auto workers and other employees destined for surplus.

By the early 1970s, Europe and Japan had recovered from the war. Their populations no longer felt poor, desperate, and in awe of the United States. They had stronger unions, better social services, and more efficient public transportation than America. Rather than destroy their inner cities, they rebuilt them.[1] By sacrificing civilian infrastructure to military domination, the United States had squandered its advantage. While American corporations hardly used weapons technology to improve the quality of civilian consumer goods, Toyota, Sony, Fuji, Volkswagen, LG, and, later, Samsung and Hyundai most certainly did. America's borrowing to buy guns may have bought several decades of prosperity, but by 1970s the loan

51

was being recalled. United States domination in the 1950s and 1960s had stemmed from one specific historical fact: the world wars had left America's infrastructure intact but decimated those of its rivals. By the late 1970s, ironically, continued military spending had undermined the US infrastructure, proving there was no inherent reason why the United States should rule; American exceptionalism is a myth.

The war in Vietnam played a central role in US decline and the coming of the next great crisis of surplus people. When you build the world's largest arsenal, as America did, eventually you must use it. Saber rattling poses no credible threat unless you occasionally stab someone. With the United States and the Soviet Union each holding a nuclear arsenal capable of destroying the entire biosphere many times over, a direct war with Russia would be too perilous. Instead, the actual shooting wars took place in the Third World periphery, the most serious being Vietnam. The war served some functions; it turned youths who did not do well in high school and might have become dangerous surplus, into cannon fodder. Recall that the military is and has always been one of the main surplus-absorption institutions.

Of course, schools are equally important as surplus absorbers, and the Vietnam War drove many youth into colleges to avoid the draft. However, young people, whose surplus status was disguised as college students, were educated to think more critically. They wondered if the nation they were told was a peace-loving democracy was really a militaristic empire intent upon world domination for the sake of its 1 percent. The civil rights movement revealed to them the extent of poverty and racism—the core of the surplus population at home. Seeing a country that would sacrifice much of the 99 percent to the dustpan of surplus, they turned to radical left movements and a counterculture that rejected capitalism and militarism. Ironically, one reason why they had the luxury to shun mainstream American society was that they were confident that their surplus status was voluntary and temporary. If ever they chose to seek a professional career, marry, and buy a home in the suburbs, they could. But as the 1970s progressed, there were signs that the US economy might permanently wane. As we shall see, though, economic anxiety could serve the 1 percent.

Nevertheless, from a capitalist point of view, the costs of the war in Vietnam, unlike the World Wars, may have outweighed its benefits, ultimately accelerating the decline that would create a new mass surplus population and making it harder to control the existing surplus people, both educated and not. Keynesianism may embrace state spending and deficits that build an economy, but Keynesianism also warns that some debts may undermine it. In the long run, militarism is counterproductive. Either weapons are never used and are pure waste, or they are used, only to destroy. Vietnam War armaments were draining America's resources.

With politicians fearful of raising taxes in the midst of an unpopular war, the conflict produced rampant inflation. Loss of faith in the nation's goodness spread from the college campus to the Vietnam frontline. Drugs were everywhere. Junior officers had an exceptionally high death rate; many were killed by their own troops.[2] There was a malaise throughout the country, largely stemming from a sense that the government and the 1 percent did not really care about the 99 percent. On the factory floor, this resulted in "Monday morning cars," made by workers who came in drunk from the weekend.[3] With American workmanship deteriorating, even the American people preferred foreign goods, thus inadvertently using their buying power to undermine their employment prospects and thus speed their path into the surplus population.

With their profits declining, American industrial corporations became less willing to offer the high wages and secure employment to which their workers had become accustomed. They broke their accommodation with the unions and deemed American workers lazy and greedy. One advantage of having the United States act as the world's police force is that it supports puppet governments who make their countries available to American corporate investments. When President Salvador Allende of Chile tried to nationalize mines owned by American corporations Kennecott and Anaconda Copper, the CIA had him overthrown and replaced by General Augusto Pinochet.[4] Third World dictators opened their countries for factories with low wages, few regulations, low environmental standards, and minimal worker protections. American corporations could say to their employees, "If you won't work on our terms, we can just close the factory and move to other countries. You'll be out on the street and we'll keep making money." Formerly thriving metropolises like Detroit were reduced to rows of boarded-up factories, offices, and houses—hence, the beginning of global outsourcing rather than insourcing, and the first stages of the new globalization that would create a tsunami of surplus US workers. What was called the "deindustrialization of America"[5] was the 1 percent's new strategy to maximize profits by turning the majority of US workers into both disguised and naked surplus people.

Industrial jobs were not coming back. Real wages fell to the point that it was no longer possible to keep a middle-class lifestyle on one income. Housewives returned to the workforce in low-wage pink-collar jobs. People who had thought they achieved the American Dream found themselves desperate surplus, who would be lucky if they could find low-paying service jobs.

Production declined, but low-level consumption continued. Eventually, Wal-Mart replaced General Motors as the world's largest corporation.[6] In retail, optical scanners took away whatever skills cashiers had. Workers became truly interchangeable and replaceable. Someone in Brooklyn wanting a phone number in Manhattan would get a recording; if he were persistent, he might eventually get a human voice from India. Even service jobs got eliminated. McDonald's got customers to act as janitors and throw away their own plastic wrappers. One military technology that American industrial corporations did adapt for civilian use was robots. Robots can work without pay twenty-four hours a day without unions or health insurance. However, one thing that humans, even humans reduced to surplus, can do that robots cannot, is consume.

Despite the alliance between the US military, American corporations, and Third World dictators, the visible decline of the United States made other countries feel freer to challenge it. Vietnam was not essential to the American empire; originally, it could have been sacrificed with little cost. However, it became a test case to demonstrate American power, to show improvised Third World countries what would happen if they dared defy the United States. To galvanize support for the war, policy makers spoke of a "domino effect."[7] If Vietnam were allowed to fall, so would all of Indochina. But this militarism served, we shall see, a crucial domestic purpose: creating a new global environment to dismantle much of the US economy, with its overpaid workers and regulatory New Deal environment, and creating a frightened domestic workforce, rightly terrified of becoming a surplus majority.

Abroad, the Vietnam debacle did indeed show what happens if you challenge the United States with enough will; you win. It may have exposed the American empire as the "paper tiger" Mao Tse-Tung called it.[8] Sure enough, when the United States was driven out of Vietnam, the rest of Indochina—Laos, Cambodia—did go communist. In the Middle East, oil sheikdoms did not go communist, but they formed the Organization of Petroleum Exporting Countries (OPEC). From the 1920s through the 1960s, Western oil companies like Exxon, Mobil, and Shell could treat Middle Eastern oil almost like their private property.[9] Around the time of the American defeat in Vietnam, OPEC began to demand much higher payments. The result was a direct assault on the lifestyle dependent upon cheap oil to which Americans had been accustomed. By the late 1970s, there were mile-long lines to get gas, if you could get gas at all.

If the United States was in decline, then who should bear the burden? Admitting that America could no longer police the world alone, David Rockefeller, CEO of Chase Manhattan Bank and grandson of John D. Rockefeller, and fellow 1 percenters formed the Trilateral Commission. He and his followers determined that three areas—the United States, Europe, and Japan—must jointly dominate the globe. The 99 percent must be brought to recognize that their prosperity cannot be sustained indefinitely. Actually declining expectations might not be a bad thing; people, especially educated youth, were feeling too entitled and challenging authority. Anxiety that they might become permanently surplus and never achieve the standard of living of their parents might make them more docile. "Excessive Democracy" or "democratic distemper"[10]—a favorite slogan of conservative Trilateralists—was interfering with the prerogatives of the state, the military, and the 1 percent. The détente between the 1 percent and the 99 percent achieved by the Keynesian New Deal paradigm was no longer working. Although there was not an economic collapse comparable to the Great Depression, a crisis could be looming. An alternative paradigm had to be found.

·⤳·

15

The Age of Reagan

How Reaganism Accelerated the Outsourcing and Destruction of Infrastructure, Widened the Gap between the 1 Percent and the 99 Percent, and Made More and More People Surplus

Ironically, the alternative regime was implemented by someone hostile to the Trilateral Commission's sense that "America's best days are behind us,"[1] President Ronald Reagan; and as of 2012, we still live in the Age of Reagan. Reagan dismissed the Trilateralists' message as "doom and gloom."[2] Of all the possible solutions to the crisis of the time, Reagan may have chosen the worst one, the one most likely to yield a permanent majority of surplus US workers. Although an aggressive militarist, he tried to restore the domestic economic paradigm of the Roaring Twenties, the one that brought about the Great Depression. He undid the Keynesian New Deal and gave the 1 percent virtually a license to do whatever it wanted. He blamed all of America's problems on what one of his heroes, Ayn Rand, called parasites[3]: parasites in the government who steal resources from the productive private sector, parasites within academia and the media who undermine the nation's will, and parasites who choose to wallow on welfare rather than uplift themselves by their bootstraps.

As president, Reagan declared, "Government is not the solution to our problem; government is the problem."[4] For decades, détente between the 1 percent and the 99 percent had been preserved through a Keynesian promise of "butter and guns." Reagan kept the guns but eliminated the butter. Rather than mitigating the problems of the 1970s, he intensified them: a growing gap between the 1 percent and the 99 percent, a military-sapping civilian infrastructure, factories dismantled and jobs and industry outsourced to other countries, and spiraling government debts without the collateral to support them. Reagan's most important legacy was a growing crop of outsourced, downsized, and redundant Americans.

Unlike Keynesianism, which gave to the poor to help the rich, Reaganism blatantly gave to the rich. Reagan's administration eliminated regulations to protect the environment and workers' health and safety. The 1 percent and corporations enjoyed huge tax cuts. Reagan called his policies "supply-side economics."[5] His vice president and eventual heir, George H. W. Bush, a member of the Trilateral Commission, called it "voodoo economics."[6] The claim was that high taxes discouraged rich people from investing, innovating, producing, and employing Americans. A lower tax rate would presumably cause the GDP to grow so much that there would more revenue to tax. In this post-Keynesian fantasy, the result of reduced taxes would not be government deficits but a balanced budget, maybe a surplus. With more money in the hands of the 1 percent, who have proved their productivity in the market, there would be more jobs with higher pay. Wealth will "trickle down," and everyone, even the poor, will prosper. Another way to help wealth to trickle down was to lower, if not eliminate, the minimum wage. Minimum-wage laws ignored the market and artificially set salaries above what surplus people's labor was worth, so no one would hire them. The main cause of poverty was welfare programs, which allowed the unworthy surplus to get by, rewarded sloth, and undermined their desire to achieve. One of the architects of trickle-down theory, Budget Director David Stockman, admitted that he never believed it made sense and feared that it could blow up.[7] The growing surplus population would soon discover the truth of Stockman's nightmare.

There were no conditions on Reagan's corporate tax cuts and deregulations, and thus there was no real incentive to invest the windfalls in the American domestic economy. Rather than using them to rebuild industry in the United States, corporations used them to close down factories, displace workers, and build plants in Mexico, Singapore, and the Philippines. Unions were threatened to choose between lower wages, benefits and security, or few jobs, if not boarded-up plants. Oftentimes, even when the unions acquiesced, the factories still closed. Reagan, who had once been head of the Screen Actors' Guild,[8] was intent upon undermining unions, both private and governmental. One of his first acts as president was to respond to a strike among federal air traffic controllers by firing them all.[9] Eliminating jobs, both private and public, in the name of efficiency, was presented as a good thing; "down-sizing" became the mantra. A corporate rationale was imposed on the state, ignoring the Keynesian assumption that the government is supposed to be an employer of last resort and provide jobs, when the private sector does not, for the sake of providing jobs. Creating surplus workers become an economic virtue rather than vice, the key to maximizing both domestic and global profits.

Under the guise of reawakening the motive to achieve, Reagan eliminated or substantially reduced welfare benefits, barely disguising his contempt and indifference to the plight of the growing surplus masses. Homelessness, to a degree unseen since the Great Depression, reappeared.[10] Hunger and malnutrition became commonplace. Programs to foster the health of poor schoolchildren, like school lunches, were routed. The Reagan regime declared ketchup to be a nutritionally adequate vegetable.[11] As the welfare rolls contracted, prisons expanded, in effect becoming the new welfare. From 1980 to 1992, the prison population went from 500 thousand to 1 million; by 2000 it exceeded 2 million, the highest in the world.[12] Among young black men, there were more prisoners than college students (by 2000, 791,600 vs. 603,032).[13] Most were jailed as victims in a "war on drugs." The motive for replacing welfare with prisons was not to save money. In 1985, it cost about $16,000 annually[14] to keep someone in jail, but AFDC provided a family about $4,200 a year.[15] The reason was to change a palatable system to a punitive one, to keep the surplus population in its place and make dependency so distasteful that almost anyone would try to avoid it.

Treating the unworthy surplus as criminals also established that they are not victims deserving sympathy but evil threats who should suffer. The Reagan regime strove to turn the worthy against the unworthy, make people barely getting by believe that parasites were the source of their problems, and deflect hostility against the 1 percent to the destitute. There was a contradictory message: in the land of opportunity, any assault on the rich is an attack on you, because 100 percent can become 1 percent. On the other hand, as long as there is desperation, the anxiety that you could fall into surplus status would make you reluctant to challenge authority. The Reagan regime used that fear to squelch the left and the residues of the 1960s/70s radicalism and counterculture. Also, in order to prevent another generation from interfering with the preroga- tive of the corporations and the military, the Reagan regime encouraged a "back to basics" movement in education; rote memorization replaced critical thinking.[16] In the end, Reagan moved the political spectrum way to the right; Keynesian liber- alism, which had been the mainstream, became the "L word," and the real left fell off the edge. The ultimate victim was the US workforce, which was hurtling toward permanent surplus.

As we have seen, Keynesian liberals accept restrained state deficits, which stimulate production and economic growth. However, they worry that excessive misdirected debts are destructive. Reagan preached resurrecting laissez-faire ide- ology. Big government is an assault on freedom and prosperity. He said he would shrink the state and strive to balance the budget. He did cut the social service safety net that protected the surplus and provided a buffer, which prevented the middle class from falling into the surplus. However, under Reagan, military spending spiraled, along with forms of domestic state violence and brutal forms of domestic surplus people absorp- tion like prisons, as taxes for the 1 percent were slashed. Reagan debts were undermining, not building, infrastructure. When Reagan ran for reelection in 1984, his opponent, Walter Mondale, a Keynesian liberal, focused his campaign on the premise that the deficit had gone out of control and taxes must be raised.[17] In the 1988 campaign against Reagan's anointed heir, George H. W. Bush, Democratic vice presidential candi- date Lloyd Bentsen offered this critique:

> You know, if you let me write $200 billion (about $364 billion in 2010 dollars) worth of hot checks every year, I could give you an illusion of prosperity, too. This is an administration that has more than doubled the national debt, and they've done that in less than eight years. They have taken this country from the No. 1 lender nation in the world to the No. 1 debtor nation in the world. And the interest on that debt next year, on this

Reagan-Bush debt of our nation, is going to be $640 [about $1,164 in 2010 dollars] for every man, woman, and child in America because of this kind of a credit-card mentality. So we go out and we try to sell our securities every week, and hope that the foreigners will buy them. And they do buy them. But every time they do, we lose some of our economic independence for the future. Now they've turned around and they've bought 10 percent of the manufacturing base of this country. They bought 20 percent of the banks. They own 46 percent of the commercial real estate in Los Angeles. They are buying America on the cheap.[18]

Despite this critique after Reagan left office, even Democratic presidents could not, or would not, challenge his paradigm, one lifting the 1 percent in the short term but assaulting the 99 percent and especially the surplus core of poor people within the 99 percent. Bill Clinton hammered the final nail in the AFDC's coffin. He signed a welfare bill that forced welfare recipients, even mothers with young children, to return to work after two years and set the time someone could receive benefits to a five-year lifetime maximum.[19] The number of homeless and hungry—not just homeless men but homeless families with children—grew.

Soon after Reagan left office, the Soviet Union collapsed, largely because it destroyed its economy trying to compete with the United States in the arms race. As the cold war against communism ended, there was talk of a "peace dividend" in America. The money spent on weapons could be used to rebuild civilian infrastructure and reintegrate surplus people, but the peace dividend never came.[20] Corporations just made too much profit from weapons. Instead, communism was replaced by a new eternal enemy, "terrorism," something even more abstract, vague, and elusive. The new fight against terrorism resulted in at least two shooting wars, in Afghanistan and Iraq. Perhaps $4 trillion[21] were spent to destroy rather than build, as the 99 percent became even more apprehensive about their future. However, corporations made profit and surplus young men and, now, women could be sent off to fill equal-opportunity body bags in the struggle to maintain access to foreign oil.

Job security deteriorated; real wages declined; the gap between the 1 percent and the 99 percent mushroomed, as did the surplus population. In the largest corporations in 1965, the average CEO made 24 times the average worker;[22] that number ballooned to 343 times the average worker's salary by 2011.[23] The surplus people ended up in schools, in prisons, or on the streets. To defuse the surplus crisis bomb, it was necessary to create the appearance of no assault on the average consumer's standard of living. People lucky enough to work were reminded to take pride in being above the unworthy surplus. People were seduced to use credit cards to maintain a lifestyle they could no longer afford; total credit card debt exploded from $54 billion in 1980 (about $140 billion in 2010 dollars) to $214 billion in 1990 (about $352 billion in 2010 dollars) to $793 billion in 2011.[24] Fewer and fewer of the things they bought were manufactured in the United States. Reaganism, by design, had demolished the US infrastructure, encouraging a total migration of US capital into either foreign production or financial speculation. The US share of the world's GDP declined from 27.3 percent in 1950 to 20.6 percent in 2003.[25]

To say the United States had evolved into a paper economy would be to suggest it was producing something more tangible and real than it was. Even calling it a plastic economy would imply it was more industrious than it was. The United States had become a virtual economy, where most money existed as electrons on a computer screen, which could be instantly transferred to anywhere in the world. Instead of productive assets, investors bought mutual funds and derivatives, which bought shares of funds which bought shares of funds which bought shares of fund which ... bought stocks, bonds, and real estate.

Members of the so-called middle class, despite being downsized and outsourced, could identify themselves as property owners with a stake in the economy by buying homes with mortgages. A house is a consumer good that, like anything else, deteriorates over time. When a used home is sold, nothing new is produced; there is no real economic growth, yet housing costs spiraled. The cost of the average home went from about $72,000 in 1980 to $314,000 in 2008.[26] During housing booms, some mortgagees saw the value of their home grow more in one year than their total income for that year. Yet they could only touch their new-found wealth when they sold their house—at which point they would have to find someplace else to live, which might cost them more than the house they just sold. The housing market, like the credit card market, the stock market, and the derivatives market, was a bubble that had to burst.

Americans, corporations, governments, and even banks and individuals, including the vastly growing surplus population, maintained the illusion of prosperity through borrowing, but this was a very different borrowing from the one Keynes advocated. It did not stimulate productivity. Keynesianism states that debt is not a problem as long as a country borrows from itself, but the United States had deliberately destroyed its infrastructure, its collateral. It no longer generated enough revenue to lend to itself, so it had to borrow from other countries. That meant that interest and revenues, as well as jobs, went abroad. As Lloyd Bentsen pointed out, in eight years, the Reagan regime transformed the United States from the world's largest creditor to the world's largest debtor. Earlier, we noted that America had been the world's largest debtor before 1914, but that was a sign of a dynamic, growing, productive economy. The new debt is different; it represents a country in decline, trying to cling to a standard of living that is no longer feasible. The largest holder of US debt is China, a nominally communist country whom the United States had formerly regarded as a backward enemy. As of 2011, China has lent Americans $1.16 trillion[27] to enjoy a lifestyle that eludes its own people. China, among other countries, now manufactures what America no longer produces. The United States may soon find itself eclipsed, and unable or unwilling to support its people, who face permanent surplus status.

When the United States adopted Keynesianism in the 1930s, it may have been in the midst of the Great Depression, but it was the world's unqualified dominant economy. The world was so dependent upon America that its collapse created even greater misery abroad. America's infrastructure may have been unused, but it was not dismantled. The collateral to borrow and respark the economy existed; the world needed America. As poor as Americans may have been, they would still be the best potential customers for the world's industrial goods. As of the 2010s, the Europeans and Japanese can buy whatever Americans can, if not more. Soon, the Chinese and Indians may be able to as well. The rest of the world may need the United States less than before. Other countries have not supported America in its wars. Many sense the world does not need a police force and that domestic consumer goods are a better investment than weapons. If the United States tried to rebuild its infrastructure and reemploy its people through Keynesian public work projects, it is not clear it could raise the money. Its industries may be too far gone to resurrect. Even if reconstruction were economically possible, the political will may not exist. The 1 percent shows little sign of accepting reduced militarism, higher taxes, increased regulation, and governmental competition. America's prognosis may be more and more boarded-up industries and displaced people, who will face misery rather than an artificial prosperity beyond their means. America has become Surplus Nation, with a majority of its population already surplus people or destined to become so.

The lesson of the 1 percent to the 99 percent: "You're fired!"

·⌒·

16

Does Our Theory Hold Up?

The Role of Bubble Jobs, Low-Wage Employment, and Students and Retirees in Explaining Unemployment Rates since Reagan Left Office

Our history suggests that the US surplus crisis has accelerated dramatically since the 1970s, particularly since the Reagan revolution. It reflects systemic changes now baked into our current political economy. We have tried to make clear that we are not describing short-term variations due to the capitalist business cycle, but longer-term structural and political changes difficult to reverse.

But the high levels of surplus people at this writing in 2012 might reflect something far more simple: the temporary effects of the Great Recession that began on Wall Street in 2008. In discussing unemployment, the single most important indicator of surplus people levels, mainstream economists tend to suggest that current high levels of unemployment are, indeed, temporary, reflecting the severity of the Great Recession but not a structural shift toward a permanently high unemployment rate. Economists acknowledge that the percentage of the long-term unemployed after each recent recession has increased, and that it takes longer after contemporary recessions to return to historically "normal" unemployment levels of 4–5 percent. And many Keynesian economists acknowledge some of the structural problems linked to globalization and technology we have discussed, as well as the deep political obstacles to create investments to reboot growth and the economy. But most economists expect the US economy to eventually move beyond recession and to return to traditional levels of unemployment seen since World War II. They do not see evidence that the US is moving inexorably toward permanent surplus or ever-higher unemployment.

This line of thinking represents a serious challenge to our argument, and there is reason to take it seriously. If you consider unemployment levels as the best surrogate indicator of surplus people numbers, our argument would appear to predict a trend toward ever-increasing unemployment since the 1970s. But the evidence since the 1980s does not appear to support our argument, as seen in Figure 16.1.[1]

As Figure 16.1 indicates, the US unemployment rate does not rise as a secular trend over the past several decades. As we predicted, we do find the beginnings of an important rise in unemployment in the 1970s, and significant periods of high unemployment in the 1980s, 1990s, and the first decade of the twenty-first century. But these seem to be temporary rises—spikes associated with downturns in normal business cycles. In each period prior to the cyclical downturns, unemployment since Reagan has declined to historically "normal" rates between 4 and 5 percent. This was true in the Clinton era between 1996 and 2000 and in the George W. Bush era between 2004 and 2007.

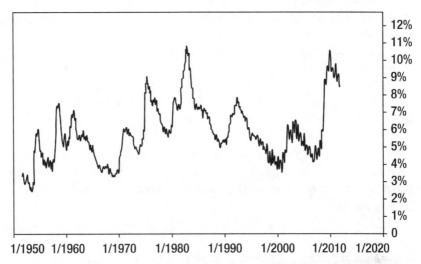

Figure 16.1 Unemployment Rate from 1950 to 2010 and Beyond
After: "USA Unemployment Rate Graph," http://forecast-chart.com/
graph-unemployment-rate.html.

If our thesis is correct, how can we explain these periods
of return to low unemployment? There are at least three factors
at play. The first has to do with what might be called "bubble
jobs." Bubble jobs—soaking up millions of workers—arise in
eras of speculation just before a bubble bursts. The most obvious case was the housing bubble, as we mentioned before,
that floated the entire US economy in the period between 2003
and 2007. The housing market boomed as speculators and
other investors watched the price of houses skyrocket. Millions of Americans became euphoric and used the easy credit
made available by Wall Street to buy bigger and most expensive houses, and to go to the malls and spend, spend, spend.
The construction industry boomed, and the housing bubble
helped fuel growth in the overall economy. Unemployment
dropped as employers rushed to hire, while corporations took
out more loans to produce and consumers used their houses
as ATM machines, confident of ever-rising housing prices and
housing-driven prosperity.

Of course, all of this was unsustainable. When the finance
companies trading in bubble housing stocks collapsed, panic
spread through Wall Street and the broader economy. The

markets collapsed. Credit evaporated. And companies stopped hiring and started firing.

This offers a different view of the drop in unemployment in the 2003–2007 period. The jobs created were bubble jobs, soon to disappear. If the housing bubble hadn't happened, hundreds of thousands of workers would not have been hired, and unemployment in the mid-Bush years might have increased rather than decreased. The bubble workers were actually disguised surplus workers, and the bubble artificially reduced the unemployment rate. The true, higher rate would have been consistent with our structural argument of rising unemployment.

The "bubble jobs" effect masked surplus crises in many earlier periods of history. In the mid- to late 1920s, before the 1929 crash, unemployment fell to extremely low rates of about 3.2 percent.[2] The financial speculation leading to the crash floated the economy and created unsustainable bubble jobs, absorbing into the labor market millions of returning veterans and other potentially surplus workers. A similar dynamic occurred in the Clinton years preceding the 2000 dot-com bust. Unemployment fell from between 6 and 8 percent to between 4 and 5 percent as a result of the bubble jobs produced during the dot-com tech-sector mania (see Figure 16.1). The bubble again artificially reduced the unemployment rate, disguising increases in surplus workers who otherwise would have been unemployed.

Beyond the "bubble effect," a second factor explaining periods of artificially low unemployment in the post-Reagan era is the "low wage" effect. Beginning in the 1970s, as US corporations faced increasing competition from Japan and Europe, a major corporate goal became breaking US unions and reducing wages and benefits. Reagan delivered on all fronts. The Reagan revolution successfully redefined good wages as a barrier to US competitiveness while redefining unions as an abuse of power and liberty.

As we previously observed, prior to the 1970s, and especially after World War II, US corporate leaders were able to deliver on Henry Ford's premise that high wages were essential for US prosperity. US global dominance permitted workers to be paid at a level commensurate with rising labor productivity. US corporations, feeling like they faced no real competition in the 1950s from Europe or Japan—since both were destroyed in World War II—could put their "high road" on display. The US corporate elite accepted unions and the "fair wage" bargain that led to reconciliation between corporations and unions in the 1950s and 1960s.

But in the 1970s, things changed. Europe and Japan, with US help, resurrected their economies and, without the burden of military spending, became serious economic rivals of the United States. The 1960s had produced the "distemper" of democracy, leading to more demands for popular social welfare programs. Corporate leaders decided to crack down. They decided that unions had to go and wages had to be slashed. As we noted, when Reagan was elected, his first act as president was to fire all the striking air traffic controllers and destroy their union. This was the beginning of the thirty-year era designed to produce a union-free America and a low-wage nation.

Low wages for most Americans, along with extremely high income and concentrated wealth among the richest, became the new normal. Over the thirty years since 1980 and 2010, inequality rose dramatically, as the rich got much richer and everyone else stagnated or declined. At the heart of the inequality crisis was lower wages for the great majority of US workers, who were no longer paid commensurate with labor productivity. Wages fell, creating a deteriorating condition of life for the vast American working and middle classes who worked longer hours and went deeper into debt.

Low wages had a direct effect on the surplus crisis and the unemployment rate. When wages are pushed down to low rates, more workers can be hired. That is, if workers in the post-Reagan years had continued to be paid at the relatively high rates characteristic of the 1960s, commensurate with their high productivity, fewer would have been employed. Low wages meant that a shrinking pool of jobs could be distributed among a wider number of workers.

Corporations were up-front about the new equation. They told workers they either had to accept lower wages or get laid off. In fact, corporations did both. They cut both workers and wages. But if they had not cut wages so much, they would, as they promised, have cut even more workers. The cost of having a job at all in the post-Reagan years was accepting low wages.

In this respect, low-wage jobs, much like bubble jobs, artificially reduced the unemployment rate and disguised the surplus crisis. If workers had been paid a fair rate, many more would have been downsized and seen their jobs outsourced or robotized. By accepting a low wage, often through cuts in union contracts forced by global corporations, some workers were able to keep their jobs who otherwise would have lost them. The relatively low unemployment rate of 4 to 5 percent in the mid- to late 1990s and from 2004 to 2007 would have been higher, reflecting a true rising unemployment rate consistent with our argument.

A third factor explaining the contradiction of low unemployment in the mid-Clinton and mid-Bush years has to do with the large and steady rise since 1980 in the numbers of other surplus populations, including students, retirees, and prisoners. The vast expansion in these groups sucked out of the labor force many young people and many seniors. The expansion of higher education, the new norms of retirement, and the drastic rise in the numbers of prisoners artificially lowered the unemployment rate, a third major factor masking a true rising unemployment rate.

Consider college and university students first. The rate of enrollment in higher education after graduating from high school steadily increased between 1959 and 2009. In 1959 only 45.1 percent of high school graduates went on to matriculate in higher education. By 2010 a steady rise over fifty years led to a record high of 70.1 percent of high school graduates enrolled in colleges and universities.[3]

This is a good thing, since more educated students gain tools for better citizenship and a better life. But our point here is that higher education sucks young workers out of the labor force and thus they are not counted as unemployed. If not in school, some of them would be employed but many would not be, as youth unemployment has been growing. So the rise in the percent of people ages 18–24 in schools reduces unemployment and masks what might otherwise be a higher unemployment rate.

Does higher education thus artificially push down unemployment rates? Students who need school for skilled jobs and obtain those jobs after graduation should not be considered surplus. But those in school simply to avoid unemployment, or who expect that a degree will help them get a job and then find the contrary, are more reasonably considered part of the surplus population. This group of college students artificially reduces the unemployment rate, and the growing numbers of such young people can help explain the relatively low unemployment rates in the mid-Clinton and mid-Bush years. The growth of "surplus students" not only explains unexpected lower unemployment but also suggests that the overall surplus population is growing, even with lower unemployment rates.

A similar argument can be made with regard to retirees. As in the case of students, the number of retirees has grown dramatically in the past fifty years, reaching 34.4 million in 2010.[4] As baby boomers begin retiring en masse, the numbers and percent of retirees in the population will mushroom even more.

As with students, retired people are defined as out of the labor force and are not counted as unemployed. This is reasonable for those who retired voluntarily and do not want to work. But for those forced out because of their age, and who may want to continue to work, it is irrational to not count them as part of the unemployed population. As this group of retirees grows—and it is growing substantially—it artificially depresses the unemployment rate, since it undercounts the true number of unemployed people.

Employers have economic reasons to force seniors out. The latter tend to be paid more than younger workers, and they may also be less physically capable of withstanding the longer hours and intense pace of work that employers increasingly expect. But seniors have increasing need to stay in the workforce or find a job because their retirement incomes have declined, both because of the shift from defined benefit to defined contribution plans and also because their nest eggs have been depleted by the 2008 financial meltdown. Within the growing retired population there is thus a higher percentage of involuntary retired, who would be counted as unemployed if they were in the labor force and looking for work.

A third group of surplus people is the number of prisoners, which has grown every year between 1978 and 2009. Like students and retirees, prisoners are neither counted as part of the labor force nor counted as unemployed. As the number of prisoners grow, the true unemployment numbers are artificially reduced further.

The trend in the startling growth of prisoners can be viewed in Figure 16-2. At year-end 2009, US federal and state prisons and county jails incarcerated 2,292,133 adults—about 1 percent of adults in the US resident population.[5] Additionally,

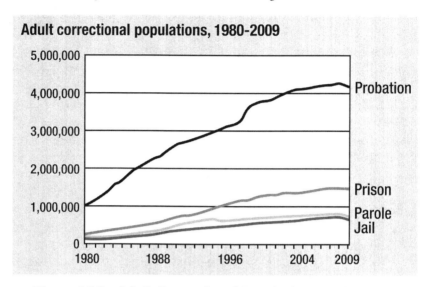

Figure 16.2   Adult Correctional Populations, 1980–2009

After: Correctional Population Trends Chart, US Bureau of Justice Statistics, http://bjs.ojp.usdoj.gov/content/glance/corr2.cfm.

4,933,667 adults at year-end 2009 were on probation or parole.[6] In total, 7,225,800 adults were under correctional supervision (probation, parole, jail, or prison) in 2009—about 3.1 percent of adults in the US resident population.[7] In addition, there were 86,927 juveniles in juvenile detention in 2007 (and a presumably similar total in 2009).[8]

It is difficult to say how many of the roughly 7 million people on probation and parole are part of the US surplus population. Some individuals on probation are certainly surplus, some are already outside the labor force, and others never leave it. Some individuals on parole readily reintegrate into the labor force whereas others never rejoin it. A conservative estimate would be that one-quarter of the probation-and-parole population is surplus. In 2009 a vast number of mainly black and other minority young men were locked inside the prison system and therefore outside the labor force, helping mask the true unemployment and surplus population numbers; their huge numbers help explain the decline in official unemployment in some of the Clinton and Bush years.[9]

When we take into account the huge bubble and low-wage effects in masking high unemployment levels, along with the drastically growing number of other surplus populations, we can conclude that the true unemployment rate is substantially higher than that reported in Figure 16.1 and more consistent with our prediction of elevated unemployment in all phases of business cycles in the post-Reagan years. We also have shown that the rise of other surplus populations indicates significant increases in the numbers of all surplus people, even if the true unemployment rate has fallen less than we anticipated.

17

What to Do? The Tea Party and the Occupy Movement

In 2011 a few hundred people gathered in Zucotti Park, near Wall Street, pitched tents, and called themselves the 99 percent. Their aim, they said, was to "occupy" Goldman Sachs, J. P. Morgan Chase, and other gigantic Wall Street banks until they were held accountable for the economic catastrophe they had caused by their global profiteering and looting.

This, of course, was the beginning of the Occupy Movement. It spread immediately across the country and the world, capturing the imagination of millions of people.[1]

While it surprised almost everybody, it was virtually inevitable that such a movement would explode into existence in a surplus nation. The crisis of surplus people that we have described is not part of the typical capitalist business cycle. It is not just another spike in unemployment. It is a revolution, reflecting the relentless dismantling of the US economic infrastructure and the specter of permanent loss of work and meaning for the majority of the US population.

What happens when 99 percent of the population face a future of dwindling jobs and shrunken wages and life prospects, engineered by the 1 percent for their own profit? What happens when the 99 percent wakes up to the possibility that they will become increasingly redundant in the calculation of those running their own economy? What happens when the majority realizes that they are no longer needed and face a lifetime of seeking a meaningful social role that may not exist?

Both common sense and history suggest that while a certain percentage of the 99 percent may remain passive, blame themselves, or be brutally repressed, social unrest will break out within sectors of the surplus majority. Revolutions breeding mass surplus, engineered by the top 1 percent, will always breed counterrevolutions by the traumatized 99 percent.

Such counterrevolutions, though, are not predictable or necessarily liberating. Before the Occupy Movement, the Tea Party revolt burst on the scene. It, too, was in large measure a populist response to the revolution designed by the 1 percent. It, too, included a large sector of people whose livelihoods and way of life were threatened by corporate globalization, the calculated demolition of Main Street, and the threat to jobs and a meaningful social role. And, even though it received funding from sectors of the 1 percent, the Tea Party, much like the Occupy Movement, also carried righteous and existential rage against the "Establishment."

The Tea Party and the Occupy Movement are windows into the politics of a surplus nation, a politics that reaches beyond conventional visions and strategies. Ordinary politics and mainstream parties may become the target of surplus people movements, as when the Tea Party colonized the Republican Party; the Occupiers, too, have begun to penetrate and change the Democratic Party's discourse. But conventional electoral politics does not typically offer the possibility of transformation that surplus people require. The 99 percent thus inevitably generates new political groups and movements that challenge everything, because for the surplus population everything is at stake.

The Tea Party and the Occupy Movement offer totally different visions, reflecting the huge diversity of the surplus population. Large sectors of both the Tea Party and the Occupy

Movement are already surplus or fear becoming it. But they do not come from the same economic, ethnic, or ideological backgrounds and thus see the crisis through different glasses. Thus the politics of the 99 percent may end up pitting one part of the sector of the surplus against the other, precisely the aim of the 1 percent. Yet the 1 percent themselves cannot perfectly orchestrate this outcome, nor can they defuse the rage that all sectors of the 99 percent may come to direct at them.

The Tea Party and the Occupy Movement reflect the two great historical trends of political response by surplus populations to surplus crises. The Tea Party reflects the revolutionary politics of reaction, rooted in a right-wing vision of restoration of an earlier world in which now-surplus people were privileged or at least had jobs and social respect. The Occupy Movement is not reactionary but progressive, seeking to create a new economic system that puts people before profit. In our view, the Occupy Movement offers the more hopeful prospect for solving the surplus crisis in a humanistic mode, and we thus focus more attention on it. But we start with the Tea Party, because right-wing populism, the politics of reaction, has proved potent and dangerous during all surplus crises.

· ⌖ ·

18

The Tea Party and the Dangerous Politics of Reaction

The Tea Party emerged with enormous force shortly after the Great Recession began. By 2010 it had already become the most visible new player in US politics, winning banner headlines as its angry activists called for restoration of the

Constitution and government by and for "the people." The Tea Partiers stormed town hall meetings and condemned "big government," Obama "socialism," and the bailout of the big banks. In the fall 2010 midterm elections, the Tea Party ran a slate of ultrareactionary Republican congressional candidates who won, took over the House, and changed the dynamics of America.

The Tea Party is right-wing populism, a politics of reaction with a long history in the United States, flourishing during severe economic downturns among surplus peoples.[1] In the Great Depression of the 1930s, right-wing populist movements led by figures such as Father Charles Coughlin became a fixture on the landscape.[2] They attracted a significant chunk of the new surplus masses during the Depression, rooted mainly in the South and in rural areas, but also attracting from all around the country conservative workers, small businessmen, and religious conservatives, all thrown out of work or frightened by the prospect of economic collapse. The Depression-era right-wing surplus populists had the same demographic coloring as the groups now making up the Tea Party, which tells us something about its roots and dangers.

The right-wing populists had various agendas, but they all sought a return to tradition: traditional small business or traditional family values rooted in the sacred value system of the white-dominated Old South. Even before the Depression, many of the groups attracted to the politics of reaction had seen the new corporate capitalism built by the Rockefellers and Morgans and their government sponsors as a threat to their way of life. They were hardly anticapitalist, but they wanted the stability of the older agrarian and small-town order, where the small farmer or small businessman was king and white folks and Bible Belt religion ruled the roost. The federal government was the enemy, since it paved the way for the large-scale corporate development that threatened their jobs and their control over local and state government run by "good ol' boys."[3]

The emerging corporate capitalist 1 percent of the early twentieth century thus laid the ground for the politics of reaction even before the Depression, since it threatened to turn so much of the traditional small business and small-town folks into roadkill. When the Depression hit, these groups became part of the huge surplus masses that made up the 99 percent

of the 1930s. But they were a distinctive segment, with a different response than the Northern urban manufacturing workers
thrown out of their jobs. They wanted a return to the "good old
days" and ferociously attacked the governing federal corporate
and political elites of Washington, D.C., and the North, the 1
percent of the era whom they saw as responsible for turning
them into a permanent surplus population. These "Tea Partiers" of the time were dangerous because they embraced racist
and authoritarian groups, which under the name of states'
rights and individual liberty sought to reinforce a white Jim
Crow order and destroy the social welfare and state regulations
built up during the Progressive era and by the New Deal itself.[4]

Fast-forward to the Tea Party, today's wake-up call for the
dangers posed by movements of reactionary surplus people. The
Tea Party, like the Depression-era right-wing surplus movements, is made up overwhelmingly of conservative white older
people, mainly male and from the South and rural areas. Many
are evangelical Christians. And they are drawn most heavily
from a middling strata of small farmers or business owners,
small-town lawyers and insurance men, and other conservative
rural, small-town or suburban craftspeople, such as "Joe the
Plumber," the iconic figure who emerged as an early symbol of
the Republican politics of reaction in the 2008 elections.[5]

These groups have continued to be deeply threatened by
the advancement of corporate capitalism. Big corporations
marginalize or swallow up small businesses, with Wal-Marts
colonizing the southern and prairie landscape, and threatening to make mom-and-pop stores and small businesses an
extinct species. Entire small towns are often threatened by
large corporate development that takes their land for huge
agricultural projects or suburban real estate projects, often
backed by the federal government.[6]

In the Great Recession that hit in 2008, the threats to the
rural, small-town, and small-business Tea Party groups hit
the proverbial fan. Suddenly, slow-developing threats to their
existence materialized into massive unemployment and the
collapse of the "fly-over" economies in the South and Midwest.
The Great Recession pushed these groups over the edge, into
what appeared to be permanent surplus, with their jobs wiped
out and their way of life extinguished by the federal corporate
juggernaut.[7]

The fear and rage of this conservative sector of the surplus population exploded. They created the Tea Party and spouted a reactionary and angry agenda, endangering, ironically, their own jobs and future. Seeing President Obama as the symbol of the new federal threat to their existence, the Tea Party fought for a radical dismantling of the government (except the military and corporate welfare), blaming it for taking their jobs and transferring their tax dollars to the urban poor. In the name of personal liberty, they called for the shutting down of the very federal programs that could help them in need and the short-term stimulus that might help reboot their local economies in the short- to mid-term. And they focused their hatred on the poor, immigrants, and other scapegoats—including social service workers, teachers, unions, and other liberal groups. The Tea Party viewed them all as parasites sponging off the "productive workers"—themselves—and the nation.

In 1920s Germany, known as the Weimar Republic, an economic collapse led to the rise of huge numbers of fringe far-right groups, which included the Nazi Party. Many of these groups had the same demographics as the Tea Party—largely rural, religious, small-business folks. The German economic collapse wiped out the jobs and rural economies of these groups, making them a vocal part of a new massive surplus population. While urban surplus groups—made up of workers and intellectuals or artists—began to support socialists and Communists, the rural, small town, and small business surplus turned to the Nazis.[8]

We have written elsewhere of a "Weimar Syndrome," a far-right politics of reaction, typically driven by economic downturns and mass new surplus people.[9] The Tea Party is but another variant of the Weimar Syndrome. What happened in Germany is evidence enough that surplus people can create a frightening new kind of far-right politics—and that any leftist who believes that surplus crises in capitalist societies are the automatic or inevitable ticket to a more progressive, socialist, or liberating future is smoking weed.

·᠊ᔓ·

19

The Occupy Movement and the Politics of Hope

But if there is no inevitability of a new progressive politics, the sudden surfacing of the Occupy Movement shows it can happen, and in exciting and promising ways. The Occupiers exploded on the scene in 2011, one of the most creative and hopeful US social justice movements in decades. While it brought together many types of Americans, surplus people and those who feared becoming surplus were at the core of the Occupy Movement. Anybody who wants to understand the Occupy Movement needs to understand our new surplus nation. And anybody who wants to understand the politics of a surplus population—and especially its potential to launch a liberating politics of people over profit—has to take a good look at the Occupiers.[1]

The Occupy Movement is the biggest explosion of progressive social protest since the 1960s. Within a period of a few months, Occupiers had taken over public squares not just in Wall Street, Boston, San Francisco, and Los Angeles but in thousands of cities across the country—and, in fact, across the world. They also "occupied" campuses, homes that banks are trying to foreclose, the headquarters of banks and other global corporations, Fox News and offices of other big media outlets, congressional offices, governors' offices, and campaign headquarters or rallies of political candidates running in the 2012 races. It's hard to identify places that have actually *not* been occupied.[2]

Most important, the Occupy Movement has occupied the minds of millions of Americans and changed conversation. The "1 percent" and "99 percent" are now part of mainstream vocabulary. Concern about the power of the 1 percent and the gap with the 99 percent has exploded, with Pew Polls in early 2012 showing that over 65 percent see the inequality gap and struggle between the rich and everyone else as very important and serious.[3] Public concern has shifted from the conservative obsession with cutting government to progressive concerns with inequality, unemployment, corporate dismantling of the US economic infrastructure, and global outsourcing of US jobs. The Occupy Movement may have no single ideology, political party identification, or precise policy agenda, but it is creating a new national mindset consistent with the conditions of a surplus nation and the desperate needs of a majority surplus population.

Occupiers defy easy description. They are predominantly young but include millions of middle-aged and older people. They are white, black, and brown; male and female. They include some rich people, many middle classers, and a core of low-wage workers, unemployed, and—perhaps the largest contingent—students with substantial student loans and no jobs in sight. They are the legions of the surplus population, and they are speaking for the US majority, which is either already surplus or destined to become so.[4]

The Occupy Movement brings together social movements that have largely been isolated from each other: student activism, labor unions, environmentalism, feminism, anti-globalizationism, African American and Hispanic communities, immigrant rights movements, single health-care provider advocates, and so on. What unites all the groups in the Occupy Movement is that they now see their struggles interlinked. Occupy creates a shared focus on the power of the 1 percent, that is, the ruling class of US capitalism. They all speak to empower the 99 percent, who have been disenfranchised and made increasingly surplus.

All the Occupiers seek to transform power and values in America, away from the corporate regime run by the 1 percent to a more authentically democratic society, which they try to model in the rituals of the General Assembly. Anybody who has been in the General Assembly—the daily general meetings of the Occupy groups—and witnessed the "mike-check" supportive repetition of each member's comments, rotation of leaders, commitment to consensus, and communal finger-waving to express solidarity, will see that Occupiers, often in hilarious ways, are struggling to create a democratic process that exemplifies the larger democracy they want to create. There is no 1 percent elite leadership in the Occupy Movement, a situation detractors argue suggests a hopeless, leaderless anarchism. But, in fact, the Occupiers have been well-organized, showing remarkable creativity in hewing to innovative practices of participatory democracy. There is no "surplus" in the community of the Occupy Movement itself, because all have a role and share leadership, and all can claim a voice, a tent, a place in the medical, media, outreach, organizing, or General Assembly; in other words, a meaningful part of "Occupy society."[5]

The Occupiers do not share a single solution, despite intense debate and conversation about participatory democracy, cooperatives, socialism, localism, anarchism, democratic globalism, or a Green New Deal. But they all feel the social fabric is being destroyed by the 1 percent as they transform the 99 percent into surplus and uses the government to disempower the mass surplus population. The critique of corporate looting and destruction that is ruining the country—which got expression in the 2012 elections when Mitt Romney was accused of being a corporate raider looting factories for "vulture capitalists" such as himself—is not based on a dogmatic leftist ideology but on the lived experience of masses of people who are losing their jobs and any meaningful place in America. The Occupy Movement is fundamentally a movement to reintegrate the surplus 99 percent back into a democratic community and support their constitutional right to govern their nation.

·⤙·

20

The Past and Future of the Occupy Movement

Where is the Occupy Movement going? Will it endure or morph into some new form? Will it change the nation? One way to answer this is to look at history. This is not the first "occupy movement." Each time corporations have mobilized successfully to change the Constitution and reengineer their control of government and the country, in what we have called a series of domestic regime changes, occupy movements of surplus people have arisen. They have never fully succeeded, but they have always made a difference.

The first modern major Occupy Movement came during the robber-baron era of the late nineteenth century, when John D. Rockefeller, J. P. Morgan, and Andrew Carnegie, among others, were at the core of a particularly ruthless 1 percent. By 1890 Rockefeller had become America's first billionaire, while 90 percent of Americans were poor and many found it impossible to find work or keep the miserable jobs they had. Farmers, then a majority of the nation, were being squeezed into ruin by the Wall Street credit system, and the majority of farmers fell into unsustainable debt, virtual slaves of the bankers. As economic conditions worsened for masses of farmers and immigrant workers, a movement arose among the 99 percent. They called themselves "populists" and they focused on the power of the 1 percent on Wall Street.[1]

These Occupier forerunners developed new conversations around kitchen tables and in churches and town squares all over the country. They debated, protested, and organized in a movement involving hundreds of thousands of surplus people. There were marches and rallies on Wall Street—with denunciations of the financiers that make today's Occupiers look tame—that might be seen as the first Occupy Wall Street protest. As today, they occupied not just Wall Street but their own churches and town halls, calling for a local and national movement to kick the 1 percent out of power. They demanded nationalization of the big banks and a social transformation of the financial and credit system, shifting finance to government banks and local credit unions. They demanded social ownership, agrarian and worker cooperatives. They sought to kick the plutocrats out of Washington, give jobs and political voice to the surplus masses, and take back the government for the entire 99 percent. Some historians, such as Lawrence Goodwyn, call it the most radically democratic movement in American history.[2]

In 1892 the populist movement turned itself into a new "People's Party." They ran a presidential candidate in 1892,

James Weaver, who lost to the Democratic candidate, Grover Cleveland, but won a million votes, 8.5 percent of the total vote, carrying four states and twenty-two electoral votes.[3] By 1896 the populists had "occupied" the Democratic Party and William Jennings Bryan became both the populist and Democrat candidate for president. He lost to Republican William McKinley, getting 6.5 million votes, 46.7 percent of the total, running on his own smaller version of populism, which shrunk famers' debts by inflating currency with silver. A radical grassroots movement that initially disdained politicians and electoral politics turned to more pragmatic politics. It lost its radical edge, and Jennings was buried by the money the 1 percent gave to his Republican opponent, William McKinley.[4]

The populists, however, not only left a legacy of a democratic and cooperativist vision but also seeded the twentieth-century progressive movement that sought to rein in big business, even though it didn't challenge capitalism itself as the early populists had. With Teddy Roosevelt as their mainstream leader, and with muckraking journalists and social workers such as Lincoln Steffens and Jane Addams educating and preaching their message from the brutal meatpacking factories and slums of Chicago, the new Progressives fostered democratic reform and at least the rhetoric of a more democratic and inclusive society. The unemployed, poor children, dispossessed workers, indebted farmers, and others all got, if not revolution or even a New Deal, a set of reforms in the name of reintegrating everyone into a fairer society. Roosevelt was an ally of business, but he also called for a new Bureau of Corporations that, by some accounts, could lead to government control of banks and companies and was viewed by many in the business community as American socialism. The most persuasive scholars have shown that TR actually used these proposals to save capitalism by ushering in a new regulated system offering a sense of public legitimacy, as well as ushering in a new order of corporate welfare.[5]

America's first great Occupy Movement of populists and early progressives failed in its loftiest democratic goals, but it showed that the 99 percent could organize itself and give voice to the surplus population. It made clear that a politics to rein in the 1 percent could catch fire from the plains of Kansas to the shirtwaist immigrant factory district of Manhattan. The populists and early progressives proved that the 99 percent could demand justice for a huge surplus population that was already surfacing as the roadkill of American capitalism, and begin to reshape the political dialogue and the economic system with calls for democracy and a job and voice for the immigrant, the factory worker, and the surplus masses.

Historically, the rise of new corporate regimes in America, in which a newly reconstituted 1 percent take over the government to serve the big corporations, has always produced surplus people crises leading to new Occupy Movements. A second example came in the wake of the Roaring Twenties, when corporations took over Washington, threw out the progressives, and went wild with greed. Capital shifted from Main Street to Wall Street in a regime change that concentrated power and wealth in Wall Street, aided by three Republican presidents who were in the pocket of the new corporate 1 percent.[6]

The 1920s 1 percent, like the earlier robber barons from whom they descended, created their own destruction. Just as the chiefs of the Gilded Age had created massive speculation and financial panics, the corporate elites of the 1920s produced a huge financial bubble, quadrupling in eight years the value of the stock market before it finally crashed in 1929. The crash would give rise to the second Occupy Movement, which began in riots of millions of newly unemployed workers in the streets of America's great cities and led to the election of Franklin Roosevelt. Like his cousin Teddy Roosevelt, FDR once again co-opted the spirit of the Occupy Movement on the streets but also institutionalized reforms to integrate and protect the mass surplus population and limit the unfettered power of the corporations.

The Great Depression created the greatest mass of surplus people since the construction of the national capitalist system by the robber barons. Some 25 percent to 30 percent of Americans were unemployed, and a much larger number were on the edge, looking over the precipice. And so a second Occupy Movement of sorts took to the streets. New Yorkers and other city dwellers around the country began to block police from evicting their neighbors, and people jammed into churches and town halls to curse a Wall Street that had left them jobless and indebted. Within a few years, workers began to "occupy" their workplaces, refusing to leave until they got their jobs back and the right to industrial unions that would speak for the surplus population.[7]

The heart and lasting legacy of this second Occupy Movement was the national labor movement. Workers' occupation of their factories changed the country forever. It was a spontaneous uprising of surplus people who knew that everything was at stake. They had to act because if they didn't, there would be no food on the table, no work on the horizon. This was life or death for millions, as is the case with workers today facing the job genocide of global outsourcing and technological obsolescence.

The spontaneity of the Depression-era factory occupations gave rise to and was bolstered by the new industrial labor movement led by the fiery coal miner John Lewis and coalescing into the Congress of Industrial Organizations (CIO). The creation of a bold new labor movement changed the fate of the 99 percent and the surplus population for decades to come. The labor movement became the most important countervailing power to big corporations and the main protector of not just the American wage but the American job.[8]

This second Occupy Movement, like the first, developed a complex relation with electoral politics and the federal government. The earliest Depression-era Occupiers came before FDR, fighting police on the street who were trying to foreclose them or their neighbors. People without work or homes congregated under bridges, in parks, or on the streets, essentially "occupying" as their only option, their only way of creating a new social survival.[9]

FDR was elected and created the New Deal only because of the desperation of these very public surplus masses. Herbert Hoover's failure to feed the hungry, house the homeless, and create jobs for the mass surplus, including jobless veterans, created the prospect of both total economic collapse and a "surplus people" revolution. The New Deal evolved as a strategy to both save capitalism and rescue politically crucial sectors of the surplus population. FDR would contain and co-opt the anger of the surplus people on the streets, as TR had done before him. But he also did something real for them, creating the reforms that would give many surplus people hope and a job. He delivered soothing fireside chats that promised all Americans that the 1 percent and the surplus masses could live peaceably in a new social contract.

Because of the surplus rioters on the streets and the workplace occupiers in the factory, FDR shifted the compass of the federal government. For the first time in decades, the government became a cautious ally of the surplus population and the 99 percent rather than the 1 percent. Direct job creation by government in FDR's first two terms, through the federal Works Project Administration and the Civilian Conservation Corps, put masses of surplus people to work planting trees, constructing libraries and schools, and building roads. The Occupiers on the streets awakened FDR and his advisers to the need to build the economic infrastructure that would absorb the surplus and lay the groundwork for the giant manufacturing behemoth that the United States became during and after World War II. Likewise, the anger and activism of factory Occupiers led to Roosevelt's legalization and support of the labor movement through the 1936 Wagner Act. The New Deal Occupiers thus helped create the institution that promised to save the American worker in perpetuity from falling into surplus. The unions gave the 99 percent a bridge to somewhere, namely from the chronic nightmare of surplus to the promise of a secure job and place in America.[10]

At the same time, these second-wave Occupiers, like their predecessors among the 1890s populists and early twentieth-century progressives, ultimately failed in creating a long-term transformation of 1 percent rule or in banishing the long-term specter of surplus. Roosevelt's support was a lifeline for the surplus workers but undermined their more radical visions and deeper structural changes. After all, FDR helped the surplus workers to save capitalism from itself; the New Deal elites sympathized with the surplus workers but feared they might destroy the capitalism they wanted to save. They were hardly revolutionaries. They wanted to absorb the surplus within the capitalist machinery, and would turn against an occupy or labor movement that challenged the larger economic system. This helps explain the current Occupy Movement's ambivalence toward electoral politics. Occupiers need power in the White House, but the price they pay for presidential alliance is sacrifice of their deepest democratic aspirations and loss of permanent protection against the inexorable US capitalist march toward a surplus nation.

The third great Occupy Movement took place in the 1960s. African American civil rights activists launched the occupation of segregated buses, diners, and voting systems that ended

Jim Crow. Anti–Vietnam War activists occupied the streets, the campuses, and the military companies and recruiting stations that kept the war machine alive. This Occupy Movement would change the nation, creating a new generation of Americans who learned to question authority, fight for equal rights, challenge the American Empire, and fight for a new economic system of people over profits.[11]

Like the current Occupiers, those in the 1960s grew from a new generation of young people, many highly educated. Higher education has proved to be a fertile soil for occupy movements, particularly when students face the prospect of surplus or unsustainable debt. Yet this helps to define a crucial distinction between the Occupiers of the 1960s and today. Then, student Occupiers, even some of the African American civil rights activists risking their lives, believed their future was hopeful and, for many, secure. They thus had the freedom to fight for their ideals. Feeling immune from surplus, they could experiment with radical visions of liberation.[12]

Today's young Occupiers, while many are privileged and feel secure, know that their future could slip away. And the majority of today's young people, including elite college students, are facing the toughest job market in years while burdened with debt that is unsustainable. This marks the biggest distinction between the two generations of Occupiers, and it explains why today's young Occupiers may admire the 1960s protests but also see themselves as a new breed.

With the exception of many African American civil rights activists, the Occupiers of the 1960s were not experiencing or fearing surplus. This makes clear that occupy movements do not necessarily arise from surplus people or crises; in fact, the 1960s suggests that it may be freedom from fear of surplus that fuels some occupy movements, and can help explain why many of the most privileged young people—and even very rich people like Warren Buffet, Bill Gates, and George Soros—can feel sympathy with and support the Occupy Movement.

Of course, while the 1960s Occupiers were not mainly surplus themselves, their movements were directed to helping the millions of poor and marginalized people, black and white, gain jobs, power, and dignity. They also tried to protect the surplus people abroad, in Vietnam and around the world, who were being deprived not only of jobs but of their own nation and their lives. The 1960s Occupiers may have personally been privileged and secure, but their entire movement aimed to empower the American and global 99 percent and provide them jobs, power, and hope.

The boldness of the 1960s Occupiers reflected partly their own perceived immunization from surplus status. Abundance and prosperity for themselves seemed permanent; the question was how to distribute the pie and turn abundance into a meaningful and joyful life. This led Occupiers to visionary philosophical, political, and personal experimentation, unconstrained by the fear of economic hardship and confident that they could create an idealized future. Nothing could prevent new feminists from occupying male bastions of power; new environmental activists from occupying corporate development mega-projects; new peace activists from questioning the entire purpose of US wars and occupying the Pentagon; or new economic justice activists occupying corporate headquarters of the "military-industrial complex" and calling openly for the end of capitalism and the creation of socialism, cooperativism, or economic democracy.[13]

Like previous Occupy Movements, the 1960s Occupiers had a tangled, ambivalent relationship with electoral politics. They viewed the Democratic Party as hopelessly trapped in the politics of American Empire and the 1 percent. At the same time, some maintained hope that they could infiltrate the Democratic Party and turn it in their direction, as the Mississippi Freedom Democratic Party, led by newly enfranchised blacks, flocked to the 1964 Democratic Party convention and demanded their rights to political voice. In the end, the Democratic Party embrace of the Vietnam War in 1968 turned most Occupiers against the Democrats, and they built their movement largely outside electoral politics, although in 1972 some turned to the Democratic presidential candidate George McGovern, who spoke for elements of their peace-and-justice concerns. Their presence on the streets and their militant antiwar, new economic justice, gender, and environmental movements pushed the Democratic Party to the left, led ultimately to the end of the Vietnam War, and created parts of what Lyndon Johnson called a new "Great Society," protecting surplus people with voting rights, new welfare programs, Medicare, and more jobs, many protected by a strong industrial labor movement.[14]

The 1960s Occupiers, like their predecessors, had an ambiguous legacy. Because they didn't fully or successfully "occupy" the political system, they left an opening for a new right that laser-focused on politically mobilizing an ultraconservative southern and western base, funded by the 1 percent, leading to the Reagan counterrevolution. This would undo much of the gains created by the 1960s (and early 1970s) Occupiers.

On the other hand, the 1960s Occupiers changed the country by laying the foundation for new movements and visions of all hitherto surplus people. Poor people, racial and ethnic minorities, women, environmentalists, peace activists, and those fighting for economic justice would remain forever inspired by the 1960s Occupiers. Much of what was radical in the 1960s has become common sense, and without the 1960s, we would not have a black president, a majority in America favoring gay marriage, or a labor movement fighting side by side with today's Occupiers against the 1 percent.

Today's Occupy Movement, even for its most privileged members, takes place in an entirely different environment. Nuclear weapons and climate change have created existential questions about the very existence of a human future. US economic hegemony and global dominance are in decline, as powers in Asia and Latin America are the new dynamic engines of a twenty-first-century global transformation. US corporations have taken over control of the US government and eviscerated the labor movement and most challengers to corporate rule. The 99 percent now face surplus as their own biggest challenge, and the confident idealism and security of the 1960s Occupiers must give way to a measure of fear, caution, and even hopelessness.

But while this may seem to put enormous brakes on the current Occupy Movement, it also inspires both new boldness and radical vision. The systemic challenges are about the survival of humanity itself, and without radical change everything may be lost. When the great majority face the loss of work and a meaningful social role, despite the need to put millions to work building a new sustainable infrastructure that saves the planet, the zeitgeist changes; everyone must take part in a reexamination of society, the economic order, and our basic values. Saving ourselves now requires willingness to question everything about our culture and the rules of our economic and political regime.

The Occupy Movement in a nation-become-surplus is thus playing for the highest stakes. This is, in fact, the unique situation of the current Occupy Movement, differentiating itself from all prior Occupy Movements. *Everything* is in question, and the movement will lose if does not have the revolutionary spirit to challenge the entire economic, political, and cultural regime constructed by a predatory and existentially suicidal 1 percent and embraced by many in the 99 percent itself. The Occupiers face not only personal surplus but also the prospects of both the complete dismantling of the economic infrastructure and, more important yet, human extinction. How can they then abandon the revolutionary spirit that is required to save both themselves and the world?[15]

The strength of the Occupy Movement is its astonishing creativity, diversity, decentralization, and inclusiveness. It has none of the dogma of historical leftist movements and may, in fact, represent a new kind of movement. It cannot be easily destroyed because it has no headquarters, no central telephone number, and no leader or dogma, constantly adapting and evolving as it responds to dire threats we haven't faced before.

The Occupy Movement faces a number of huge challenges going forward, should it survive the increasing attacks against it and the decision by mayors around the country to evict occupiers from the public square, the first of many steps intended to destroy the movement. One is how to define its aim and whether to embrace more specific visions, ideologies, and policy goals. Another is how to reach out to the 99 percent and gain more support among both unaffiliated surplus and the majority on the precipice of surplus. A third is what kind of leadership system and organizational structure it needs to sustain itself. A fourth is whether to engage in electoral politics.

The "vision thing" is the most important. Some call the Occupiers "beyond left and right," some call it "new left" or "new new left," some call it pro-democracy, some call it the politics of the 99 percent, some call it progressive green populism, and we could name many other labels. This sign of apparent ideological incoherence is only partially true, and it represents both strength and weakness.[16]

In fact, the Occupiers have no single political ideology or doctrine but share a democratic and egalitarian sensibility, as evidenced by the universality of the "1 percent" and "99 percent" taglines. All Occupiers see an America looted by a plutocratic corporate elite who are in the business of shredding not only US jobs and the US economic infrastructure but also American democracy and, ultimately, the survival of the planet. They share a commitment to creating not just the procedures of democracy, such as voting, but to the real substance, meaning a government and society in which people rather than profits rule. They also understand that this cannot be done without an assault on the extreme concentration of wealth in the 1 percent, sharing the view of Justice Louis Brandeis that "We can have democracy in this country, or we can have great wealth concentrated in the hands of a few, but we can't have both."[17]

The Occupiers all choose democracy and thus fight for the 99 percent to share the wealth now monopolized by the 1 percent, both for social justice and to create a regime change for a truly democratic, sustainable, and inclusive order. So the movement's supporters share core values and a broad vision. They even share strategic and tactical ideas, such as the necessity of getting big money out of politics, eliminating "corporate personhood," and creating jobs for all by creating a sustainable new economic infrastructure. Beyond this, there are a thousand conflicting ideas of how and what to do to achieve their aims. Go socialist. No, oppose the state and be an anarchist. Support global democracy. No, go localist and forget any form of globalism. Create a Green New Deal Capitalism. No, abolish any form of capitalism. Abolish Wall Street. No, nationalize Wall Street. Create a third party. No, take over the Democratic Party. No, stay out of electoral politics. No, occupy it.

At this early stage, this bloomin' buzzin' confusion may be more strength than weakness. It creates an invitational movement open to a thousand flowers and to a serious debate about visions rather than a sterile political correctness. The absence of visionary doctrine is essential to a revolution brewing against existential threats that we have never faced, including a new global and technological reality that threatens to create entire nations of surplus people. Nobody knows enough about what to do to claim a monopoly on truth.

Moreover, the ideological and strategic differences may prove to be more compatible than they appear, with plenty of room for overlap. A movement of the 99 percent does and should have enormous ideological diversity. What it needs is tolerance and the search for the overlapping issues and values that can guide the majority. You can support nationalizing some of the big Wall Street banks, dismantling others, and building up entirely new financial institutions—whether local barter systems, national credit unions, or state banks. You can be a supporter of global community and global institutions to stop climate change and tax the global 1 percent while still being a localist who prioritizes local food and artisan production. Movements too frequently fall on the swords of their own false dichotomies. A movement as big as the 99 percent should welcome contradictions in its own practice. After all, no less than Karl Marx argued that contradictions are the life-blood of history and revolution.[18]

Nonetheless, Occupiers must move in the direction of greater clarity of vision and strategy. The movement could splinter and die from hyper-fragmentation and confusion, as began to happen with the proliferation of single-issue identity movements in the 1970s. It takes more clarity and unity than the Occupiers currently have to prevent the 1 percent and the far right, which have unbending doctrines of God-given dogma, from holding on to power and destroying everything in their path.

The problem of how to reach the majority is related to the "vision thing." The Occupiers already have a core vision that speaks to the basic needs of an America in which the majority are becoming surplus people. If they can communicate their core values of democracy, inclusion, sustainability, and equality, they will speak to the needs of the population. But they must invite all the 99 percent to the conversation about specific policies and strategies. People are attracted by core values but repelled by dogma; they want to be part of the dialogue about the solution. So the openness and lack of dogma is a bridge and invitation to the non-Occupiers. It says you face the same surplus-creating predatory corporate system that we do, but we need your help in figuring out how to solve the disasters tied to "vulture capitalism," extreme inequality, and massive surplus people. Join us because we need you to solve our shared problems.

Beyond invitation and openness, humor may be an underappreciated weapon of the Occupiers. Haven't political comedians such as Bill Maher, Michael Moore, Jon Stewart, and Stephen Colbert been some of the greatest critics of the 1 percent and advocates for the 99 percent? Michael Moore, for one, was out on the streets of Wall Street, openly speaking for the Occupiers with characteristic comic relief. Even if they don't join the movement, aren't Stewart's *Daily Show* and Colbert and Maher doing heroic work in laying the groundwork for the movement? Humor disarms opponents and humanizes while keeping Occupy Movement politics from becoming the divisive and ugly spectacle that it is in Washington.

Occupiers have a lot of humor, perhaps because so many are young and experimental and not afraid to embarrass themselves by wiggling their fingers in funny democratic rituals, painting their faces, sleeping in tents, and drawing funny graffiti or performing silly skits. They are theatrical and tech-savvy, and thus have a variety of skills for reaching out, even in the midst of doctrinal semi-chaos. Dancing or doing puppet theater or singing in the streets or sleeping in trees may appear to be trivializing themselves, but it shows humanity, builds community, and displays a certain vulnerability. If it is linked to respect for outsiders and a serious sense of purpose to save the majority surplus and the species, the levity and community-building on the streets will attract others to the Occupy Movement cause.[19]

Attracting the majority, in the end, is a serious matter, with everything at stake. Getting to the majority means moving from occupying public space to occupying spaces where the majority actually lives and works and studies. Holding public space is important because it symbolizes that the Occupiers will not permit the 1 percent to privatize every square foot of this precious and vulnerable planet. They should never abandon their occupation of the public square. But they need to move to new spaces as well.

Specifically, we need the local town hall occupations of the Gilded Age, the workplace occupations of the Depression, and the campus occupations of the 1960s. In every prior Occupy Movement, the Occupiers moved to the turf of people's daily lives. That is the great challenge of the current Occupy Movement, and they have begun to respond. Occupy groups now exist on hundreds of college campuses. They are joining forces with unions to occupy factories, offices, and hotels. And they are moving into town hall meetings, church gatherings, and community centers.

A majoritarian Occupy Movement must live, study, and work with the majority. In a privatized society, public space is often distant from the public. So the Occupiers must migrate into private spaces (workplaces and campuses in particular) and fight for what the 99 percent is looking for where it lives: jobs, security, empowerment, and dignity. Success is more likely when Occupiers rub shoulders with a population either surplus or fearing surplus, one that shares a visceral distrust of the 1 percent.

Every workplace and campus and community organization tends to have its own 1 percent. The Occupiers must find a way to help the 99 percent in each of those locations to empower itself and protect itself from the scourge of surplus and disempowerment. Occupiers can find common cause in this struggle with traditional progressive groups that already occupy or organize within these privatized sites of work, study, and community, leading us to the question of how the movement should be organized and "led."

Do Occupiers need leaders and organizational headquarters? That remains unclear. What *is* clear is that the more organized traditional progressive movements—the labor unions, environmental organizations, and civil rights and feminist and gay organizations—are picking up a new head of steam by affiliating loosely with the far less organized but more dynamic Occupiers. There may be a division of labor here. The Occupies stay decentralized and "disorganized," with a minimum of formal leadership. But the Occupiers change the terms of discourse, move the political spectrum, and bring the mainstream and traditional progressive organizations to consider policies and ideologies that were previously beyond the pale. They provide the juice to animate and build the more organized forces in the progressive universe. In just a few months, for example, scores of major unions, including the national AFL-CIO, poured money, volunteers, and passion into the Occupier campaigns. The Occupiers revived a moribund labor movement while the labor movement provided the funds and organization to spread the Occupier message far and wide.[20]

This division of labor may apply to electoral politics as well. The Democratic Party has kept its distance from the

Occupy Movement, and vice versa. This may be a strength rather than a weakness. It allows the Occupiers to maintain a radical vision and practice, and to maintain independence from the corporate politics of Washington. But the Occupiers have already influenced the national political debate, helping to create new debates about vulture capitalism and jobless or surplus people in both Republican and Democratic Party conversations. If they had joined the Democratic Party, the Occupiers might have lost their originality and revolutionary ideas. Yet even at a distance from Democratic Party head-quarters and the Obama campaign center in Chicago, early in 2012, they helped turn President Obama to a focus on mass joblessness, inequality, corporate greed, climate change, and a populist agenda of fighting for the 99 percent. The Occupiers have already moved both the Democratic Party and the nation to a new set of questions about capitalism, wealth concentra-tion, and the clash between the 1 percent and the increasingly surplus 99 percent, issues that were off the table before the Occupiers appeared.

Previous Occupy Movements have straddled the divide between movements on the streets and electoral politics. That seems the right place for today's Occupiers. Their best way to influence the political system, especially in Washington, may be to agitate from the outside while making unexpected forays into various political campaigns and building sustain-able alternatives to predatory capitalism from local community bases. It's too early to jettison movement politics for traditional electoral politics, but that doesn't mean the Occupiers should ignore the very real disasters that will accompany a Republican takeover of Washington in 2012 and beyond.

Occupiers need to "occupy" the electoral process in their own creative fashion. The New Right and the Tea Party dra-matically revived the Republican Party, a potent lesson of how social movements can transform electoral politics. The 1970s New Right helped enshrine the Reagan counterrevolution and fueled the Republican takeover of Washington, while more recently the Tea Party created a new Republican congressio-nal majority in 2010. This has been a national disaster that Occupiers must help reverse.

The Democratic Party will never solve the surplus crisis or overthrow the 1 percent, but the Occupy Movement will not be able to do it without some help from the Democrats. The tangled relationship between Occupy Movements and electoral politics remains deeply frustrating but impossible to avoid. Engagement with Democrats does not mean joining the party or eschewing third-party politics. But just as Karl Marx, in his day, argued that revolutionaries must be part of electoral politics while also organizing on the streets for more radical change, the same path is essential for Occupiers and their fellow progressive movements. If Occupiers cede Washington to the Tea Party and the vulture capitalists, there will be little possibility for solving the surplus crisis or saving the planet.

It all boils down to a simple equation. The 1 percent is seeking to make money at the expense of the people. Rule by the 1 percent is the economic neutron bomb, saving property by killing unnecessary people. It takes rule by the 99 percent to dismantle the economic bomb and solve the surplus people crisis by restoring sustainable work and a meaningful role for all people.

·⟋⟍·

21

Why a Play Is an Effective Way to Discuss Politics and Economics

The rest of this book consists of two versions of the same play, a longer version that allows us to explore ideas without time and space constraints, and a shorter version, which has already been performed. A play allows us to communicate our ideas in a form that is comic, visceral, and speaks to the emotions. Historically, as we show shortly, political writers over many centuries have often turned to theater and other forms of art to reach the human spirit and move beyond the limits of the traditional book genre.

The play also helps flesh out the argument we are making. Thus far, we have been examining the forces that are creating a surplus economy and society, the responsibility of its perpetrators, the impact on its victims, and how the victims are responding. However, we have not addressed the inner thoughts of the 1 percent in their lust for profit and power. Fiction does not bind us to what they actually dare say publicly but rather allows us to project what could be their private attitudes that they would not want the 99 percent to know. We can represent the 1 percent through historical and contemporary individuals, fictional characters, or real people transformed into fictional characters. Although the 1 percent may think they are bitterly fighting with each other, they share a fundamental consensus: capitalism must be preserved and the 99 percent must be kept in their place. They disagree over the best tactic for achieving this—how much carrot and how much stick. Obviously, we cannot know all the details and conflicting feelings, but it is relatively easy to imagine, in the main, what goes on in their heads.

Even for we who are from the 99 percent, the 99 percent are much harder to caricature. Sometimes they are called the "masses," as if they converge into a single lump, but the differences among them are far more profound. One of the strategies of the 1 percent is to divide the 99 percent against themselves and bring them to believe that American capitalism is the freest, fairest, and most equitable society in the history of the world. Some Marxists say that any 99 percenter who believes this suffers from "false consciousness"[1]; Thomas Frank suggests this mass delusion is in fact "What's the Matter with Kansas."[2] There are people who resist the indoctrination of the state and the 1 percent. In 2011 many of them were actively involved in the Occupy Movement. And then there is a large number who carry ambivalent or contradictory beliefs. They sense something is wrong but are unsure how to interpret it; perhaps their experiences do not correspond to what the media and the schools tell them, but they do not feel the confidence to challenge the authorities, who supposedly deliver the American dream. Frank observed: "These people are tired of moral decay. They're tired of everything being wonderful on Wall Street and terrible on Main Street. . . . They're voting Republican in order to get even with Wall Street."[3] The 99 percent is conflicted and volatile; some may become Occupiers, but other may gravitate to movements like the Tea Party. Often the same people are torn and could go either way. The direction they choose may partly be determined by who approaches them and effectively guides them in interpreting their problems. The victor will probably appeal to their emotions as well as their intellect. A play can do that in ways a written text cannot. People are motivated not just by their rational material or economic interests but also by what and whom they symbolically identify with. Frank fears the right has been able to manipulate symbolic identity in ways that few on the left can understand.

Largely because it is so hard to present a clearly articulate ideology within the 99 percent, our play focuses on policy makers in the state and the 1 percent. We do not develop characters among the 99 percent. Instead, we present them as voices from the street, almost an undifferentiated mass, a moral conscience, something like the chorus in ancient Greek dramas.

Unlike text on a page (or a screen), theater appeals to multiple senses. If successful, it engages the audience, both intellectually and emotionally, and leaves them with a memory to reflect upon. It is active and thus could be part of a process that inspires action. A good play involves the audience and makes them feel part of the experience. It should entertain and make people want to be in the theater. Even if the message is serious, there should be humor and perhaps music.

There is a long tradition, going back at least to ancient Greece, of using theater to teach, provoke discussion, and inspire action. The powerful used plays to propagate their ideology. In the Middle Ages, the church used skits to teach the peasants the virtues of faith, obedience, and submission.[4] In the 1950s, children were taught that nuclear holocaust was manageable and survivable through cartoons of Bert the Turtle, telling them to "duck and cover."[5] Ayn Rand used fictional characters to expound the virtue of unbridled capitalism.[6]

Opposition groups have also used theater to mock and challenge authority. Sometimes it was light and disarming. The rulers would tolerate it, maybe even encourage it as a way of defusing discontent. The message: "We are not enemies; we can all laugh together." During the medieval Feast of Fools, peasants and vagabonds took on the roles of nobles and higher clergy and ridiculed them with irreverent, often sexual, innuendoes. It was understood that when the feast was over, peasants would return to being peasants and lords would return to being lords.[7] Other plays were far more biting and posed a much greater threat to authority. The powerful would try to suppress them. Eventually, the Feast of Fools was banned. While the Puritans ruled England they outlawed theater altogether, considering it sin and vice.[8]

Despite the pretense of free press and free speech, censorship certainly has existed in the United States. The 2011 Occupies (our term for the tent villages of the Occupy Movement) were attacked and eventually forced to close down, sometimes by politicians who claimed to support them, such as Mayor Thomas Menino of Boston.[9] Going back in time, Hollywood actors, screenwriters, directors, and producers suspected of not being adamant anti-Communist cold warriors were "blacklisted," or prevented from working; this was done with the support of then Screen Actors' Guild president Ronald Reagan. Eleven screenwriters and directors were considered to have ideas dangerous enough to be sentenced to jail.[10] One of them was writer Dalton Trumbo, who had to wait thirty years to be able to transform his 1939 novel *Johnny Got His Gun,*[11] which graphically illustrated the absurdity of World War I carnage, into a movie. Soon after the blacklist ended, Trumbo collaborated with director Stanley Kubrick on another movie, *Spartacus,*[12] about slaves struggling for freedom.

Kubrick then made *Dr. Strangelove,*[13] a counterpoint to Bert the Turtle. It was simultaneously acclaimed as absolutely hilarious and a provocative depiction of the most serious tragedy imaginable, nuclear holocaust. It provides a model for what we are trying to do as playwrights, bringing military officers and politicians together to say what probably goes on inside their minds but they would not want the public to know. The result is simultaneously funny and disturbing, leaving the audience both laughing and feeling vulnerable. Upon seeing *Dr. Strangelove,* you wonder if you can leave your life, indeed the entire biosphere, in the hands of such people. You may feel that the people with power are actually the ones who can least be trusted with it. The only way to be sane is to be insane.

You may react to the movie as a call to action, and in some circles, *Strangelove* may have been part of a paradigm shift on the cold war, one that reached maturity during Vietnam. Of course, it can't be denied that this paradigm shift also helped provoke the Reagan counterrevolution.

One of the playwrights sentenced to jail for resisting anti-Communist hysteria, Bertolt Brecht, fled the United States for his native Germany rather than go to prison. A proud self-proclaimed Marxist, his masterpiece *The Three Penny Opera*[14] was written in pre-Nazi Germany. Its plot revolves around this premise: the 1 percent dreads the surplus population, cannot bear to look at them, and strives to deny their existence. Deliberately didactic, Brecht continually interrupts the flow of the story with commentary, usually with songs by Kurt Weill. During one interruption, the surplus warns the audience:

> You gentlemen who think you have a mission
> To purge us of the seven deadly sins ...
> You lot who preach restraint and watch your waist as well
> Should learn, for once, the way the world is run
> However much you twist or whatever lies that you tell
> Food is the first thing, morals follow on ...
> What keeps mankind alive?
> The fact that millions are daily tortured
> Stifled, punished, silenced and oppressed ...
> For even honest men may act like sinners
> Unless they've had their customary dinners.

In a parody of the capitalist dream, the last scene elevates the main character, Mack the Knife (you would hardly call him a hero), from the gallows to wealth, status, and power. The audience is advised: this is the way operas end, not real life.

In Germany, when the musical was written, a culture war was raging that dwarfed the ones America would experience in the 1960s–1970s and the 2000s–2010s. The Nazis used art like the *Three Penny Opera* as evidence of urban, socialist, largely Jewish, sacrilegious decadence that was undermining the nation's moral will. Brecht and his comrades did not cower from the Nazi charge. Instead, they proudly proclaimed themselves as an avant-garde voice for justice and liberation. Social change requires people who feel empowered, and plays like Brecht's were signs of a vibrant left. However, as we have pointed out, in a volatile period there is no guarantee of who will win. The American counterculture of the 1960s–1970s culminated in Reaganism. In the German conflicts of the 1920s and 1930s, the Nazis prevailed with disastrous results.

The US protest movements that began in the 1960s relied heavily on art, music, and theater, much of it inspired by writers like Brecht and Weill. During demonstrations, folk singers like Joan Baez, Arlo Guthrie, and Pete Seeger provided musical interludes. Guerrilla theater troops offered skits. Improv theater actively involved and empowered the audience. Mimes created moods without words. At the height of the counterculture, one of us (Magrass) lived in a commune, which also served as a theater and regularly presented plays, musicals, mimes, and improvisations. In their conviction that they represented the emergence of a new society, musicians, artists, theater troops, and even cartoonists gleefully dubbed themselves "underground." Unfortunately, in the Age of Reagan, much of this was involuntarily driven underground.

If a new New Left is to emerge, it will need art, music, and theater to inspire it. A movement must uplift. Otherwise, it drains people of their energy and dissipates. As Emma Goldman declared, "If I can't dance, I don't want your revolution!"[15] In the Occupies of 2011, there were usually stage areas for speakers and entertainers. Plays could have been performed there. There are other places for performing plays to build a movement, including college campuses, schools, churches, temples, mosques, and community centers. We offer our play as a model and hope it will build the Occupy Movement. Derber's students, part of the Occupy Generation, assumed a creative role in the editing of the play, a role testifying to their talents and imaginations. Their names appear at the beginning of each version of the play. The students also performed one version of the play, included as Part III. We hope it will be presented at other venues, and we invite you to alter it so you can perform it ways that meet your needs.[16]

Notes

Notes for Chapter 1

1. George Kistiakovsky, "The Folly of the Neutron Bomb," *Bulletin of the Atomic Scientists* 34, no. 7 (September 1978):25.
2. Charles Derber, *Greed to Green: Solving Climate Change and Remaking the Economy.* Boulder, CO: Paradigm, 2010.
3. See Tom Friedman, "Average Is Over," *New York Times,* January 25, 2012, p. 25.

Notes for Chapter 2

1. Bureau of Labor Statistics, "Employment Situation Summary," February 3, 2012, posted on www.bls.gov/news.release/empsit.nr0.htm.
2. Mary Engel, "The Real Unemployment Rate," MSN Money, June 4, 2010.
3. Steven Camarota, Center for Immigration Studies, August 2010.
4. Jack Ewing, "The Apprentice: Germany's Answer to Youth Unemployment," *Business Week,* October 2009.
5. Betty Friedan, *The Feminine Mystique.* New York: Norton, 1963.
6. Robert Lekachman, *The Age of Keynes.* New York: Vintage Books, 1968.

Notes for Chapter 3

1. "The Pros and Cons of Globalization," *Business Week,* April 24, 2000.
2. J. Gray, *False Dawn: The Delusions of Global Capitalism.* London: Granta, 1999.

Notes for Chapter 4

1. Barry Bluestone and Bennett Harrison, *The Deindustrialization of America.* New York: Basic Books, 1984.
2. Mil Arcega, "Asia to Lead Global Economic Growth in 2010," *Voice of America,* January 21, 2010.
3. Deng Shasha, "Brazil's Economic Growth Hits Record High in 25 Years." Posted March 3, 2004, on http://news.xinhuanet.com/english2010/business/2011-03/04/c_13760668.htm.
4. Daniel Sayani, "Real Conservatives Oppose Nafta," *New American,* June 9, 2011.

5. Sam Marcy, "NAFTA: An Attack on the Working Class," *Workers' World,* August 26, 1993.

6. Catherine Rampell, "Job Insecurity Remains High," *New York Times,* August 31, 2011.

7. Ted Crawford, "The British Conquest of India," *New International* 8, no. 2 (March 1942).

8. Brian Dudley, "Microsoft Plans to Outsource More, Says Ex-Worker," *Seattle Times,* September 3, 2005.

9. "Unemployment Rate for College Graduates Highest on Record," *Mybudget,* 2009.

10. Jeremy Rifkin, "New Technology and the End of Jobs," in *The Case against Globalization,* Edmund Goldsmith and Jerry Mandler, eds. San Francisco: Sierra Club Books, 1999.

11. Cited in Tom Friedman, "Average Is Over," *New York Times,* January 25, 2012.

12. Karl Marx, *Grundrisse: Foundations of the Critique of Political Economy.* New York: Penguin, 1993.

Notes for Chapter 5

1. Jeannine Aversa and Christopher S. Rugaber, "Unemployment Rate Holds Steady at 10%," *Huffington Post,* January 10, 2010.

2. Bureau of Labor Statistics, "Employment Situation Summary," February 3, 2012, posted on www.bls.gov/news.release/empsit.nr0.htm.

3. *USA Today,* November 8, 2010.

4. US Bureau of Justice Statistics, "Correctional Population Trends Chart," posted on http://bjs.ojp.usdoj.gov/content/glance/corr2 .cfm. The chart is drawn from "The Annual Probation Survey, National Prisoner Statistics Program," "Annual Survey of Jails," and "Annual Parole Survey" as presented in *Correctional Populations in the United States, 2009, Prisoners in 2009, Probation and Parole in the United States, 2009,* and *Jail Inmates at Midyear 2009—Statistical Tables.*

5. Ibid.

6. US Department of Defense, "Active Military Personnel Strengths by Regional Area and by Country," September 30, 2010, p. 309A.

7. US Department of Education, National Center for Education Statistics, Integrated Postsecondary Education Data System, "Fall Enrollment Survey" (IPEDS-EF:94–99), and Spring 2001 through Spring 2009; Enrollment in Degree-Granting Institutions Model, 1980–2008; and First-Time Freshmen Model, 1975–2008, posted on http://nces.ed.gov/programs/projections/projections2019/tables/ table_20.asp.

8. Social Security Online, "Research Statistics, and Policy Analysis," December 2011, posted on www.ssa.gov/policy/docs/quickfacts/ stat_snapshot/.

9. Bureau of Labor Statistics, "Employment Situation Summary," February 3, 2012, posted on www.bls.gov/news.release/empsit.nr0 .htm.

Notes for Chapter 6

1. Paul Baron and Paul Sweezy, *Monopoly Capital.* New York: Monthly Review Press, 1966.

Notes for Chapter 7

1. Arthur Lovejoy, *The Great Chain of Being*. Cambridge: Harvard University Press, 1976.
2. Karl Polayani, *The Great Transformation*. Boston: Beacon Press, 2001.

Note for Chapter 8

1. Martin Daunton, "London's 'Great Stink' and Victorian Urban Planning." BBC History Trail, London, 2004.

Notes for Chapter 9

1. Jonathan Hughes, *The Vital Few*. Boston: Houghton Mifflin, 1986, p. 247.
2. Samuel Bowles and Samuel Gintis, *Schooling in Capitalist America*. Chicago: Haymarket Books, 2011.

Notes for Chapter 10

1. Thomas Woods, "The Forgotten Depression of 1920," Intercollegiate Review (Fall 2009).
2. Broadus Mitchell, *Depression Decade*. New York: Harper and Row, 1969, p. 6.
3. Ibid.
4. David Jarmul, "By 1920, America Had Become World's Top Economic Power." *The Making of A Nation,* Voice of America, July 12, 2006.
5. "Great Depression," *Encyclopedia of North American History*. Terrytown, NY: Marshall Cavendish, 1999.
6. Ibid.
7. Richard S. Tedlow, "The Struggle for Dominance in the Automobile Market: The Early Years of Ford and General Motors," *Business and Economic History* (2008): 9–62.
8. Bob McCaughey, "Unemployment in the US Labor Force, 1920–1941," in *History of American Civilization Since 1865*. New York: Columbia, 2007.
9. Bryant Sanchez de Lozada and Robert Armoush, "Henry Ford and the Five Dollar Day." Bryant University, 1999. Posted on http://web.bryant.edu/~ehu/h364proj/summ_99/armoush/index.htm.

Notes for Chapter 11

1. Arthur Schlesinger, *The Crisis of the Old Order*. Boston: Houghton Mifflin, 1957, p. 249.
2. Stephen Ortiz, *Beyond the Bonus March and GI Bill: How Veteran Politics Shaped the New Deal Era*. New York: NYU Press, 2009.
3. Schlesinger, *The Crisis of the Old Order*.
4. William Leuchtenburg, *Franklin D. Roosevelt and the New Deal*. New York: Harper and Row, 1963, p. 267.

Notes for Chapter 12

1. Robert Skidelsky, *John Maynard Keynes*. New York: Penguin, 2003, pp. 520–521.

2. John Maynard Keynes, *General of Employment Interest of Money.* New York: Harcourt, Brace, and World, 1965; Robert Lekachman, *The Age of Keynes.* New York: Vintage Books, 1968.

3. John F. Kennedy, "Remarks in Heber Springs, Arkansas, at the Dedication of Greers Ferry Dam," October 3, 1963.

4. James O'Connor, *The Fiscal Crisis of the State.* Piscataway, NJ: Transactions Publications, 2001.

5. Till von Wachter, "The End of Mandatory Retirement in the US: Effects on Retirement and Implicit Contracts." Columbia University, 2007. Available online at www.columbia.edu/~vw2112/papers/vonwa_mr_2009.pdf.

6. Frances Fox Piven and Richard Cloward, *Regulating the Poor.* New York: Random House, 1971, p. 123.

7. Karl Marx, *Capital.* New York: Penguin, 1992, vol. 1, ch. 25, sec. 3.

8. Arthur Schlesinger, *The Coming of the New Deal.* Boston: Houghton Mifflin, 1958, p.338.

9. Data on Wilkie votes posted on USElectionAtlas.org.

10. Edward Filene, *Speaking of Change.* Washington, DC: National Home Library Foundation, 1939, p. 270.

11. Yale Magrass, *Thus Spake the Moguls.* Cambridge: Schenkman, 1981.

12. Schlesinger, *The Coming of the New Deal,* p. 486.

13. H. W. Brands, *Traitor to His Class.* New York: Random House, 2008.

14. Piven and Cloward, *Regulating the Poor,* p. 115.

Notes for Chapter 13

1. Robert Lekachman, *The Age of Keynes.* New York: Vintage Books, 1968, p. 151.

2. Bureau of Economic Analysis, "Chart of US Gross Domestic Product, 1929–2004." Economics-Chart.com, 2007.

3. Victor Zarnowitz, *Business Cycles.* Chicago: University of Chicago Press, 1966, p. 229.

4. Richard W. Stewart, *The United States Army in a Global Era, 1917–2003.*Washington, DC: Center of Military History, United States Army, 2005, p. 54.

5. Glenn C. Altschuler, *The GI Bill.* New York: Oxford University Press, 2006.

6. Charles Siegel, *The Politics of Simple Living.* Berkeley, CA: Preservation Institute, 2008.

7. Jim Klein and Martha Olson, *Taken for a Ride,* a film produced by PBS in 1996. *Culture Change.* Arcata, California, 1996.

8. Stephen Ambrose, *Eisenhower, Soldier and President.* New York: Simon and Schuster, 1990, p. 573.

9. Vance Packard, *The Waste Makers.* New York: Simon and Schuster, 1978.

10. Chris Paine, *Who Killed The Electric Car?* Sony Pictures, 2006.

11. "Reuther's Guaranteed Wage," *Life,* February 14, 1955, p. 49.

12. Michael Harrington, *The Other America.* New York: Scribner, 1997.

13. Paul Baron and Paul Sweezy, *Monopoly Capital.* New York: Monthly Review Press, 1966.

14. Seymour Melman, *Our Depleted Society.* Concord, CA: Delta Books, 1966.

Notes for Chapter 14

1. Jeremy Rifkin, *The European Dream.* New York: Tarcher, 2005.
2. Robert D. Heinl Jr., "The Collapse of the Armed Forces: Bounties and Evasions," *Armed Forces Journal,* June 7, 1971.
3. Douglas French, "Is Sin City Turning into the Motor City?" Auburn, AL: Ludwig Von Mises Institute, 2011.
4. "The 'First' 9-11, the 1973 Overthrow of Salvador Allende in Chile," *The History They Didn't Teach You in School,* vi.uh.edu/pages/buzzmat/htdtisallende.html.
5. Barry Bluestone and Bennett Harrison, *The Deindustrialization of America.* New York: Basic Books, 1984.
6. "Fortune 500," *Fortune,* 2001. Posted on http://money.cnn.com/magazines/fortune/fortune500_archive/full/2001/301.html.
7. Dwight D. Eisenhower, "Domino Theory Speech," April 7, 1954.
8. Mao Tse-Tung. "US Imperialism Is a Paper Tiger." July 14, 1956. Speech posted on www.marxists.org.
9. Michael Tanzer, *The Energy Crisis.* New York: Monthly Review Press, 1974.
10. Samuel Huntington, Michael Crozier, and Joji Watanuki, *The Crisis of Democracy: Report on the Governability of Democracies to the Trilateral Commission.* New York: NYU Press, 1975.

Notes for Chapter 15

1. "Ronald Reagan:" Horatio Alger Association of Distinguished Americans. Posted April 25, 2011, on www.horatioalger.org.
2. Michael Schaller, *Reckoning with Reagan.* New York: Oxford, 1994, p. 66.
3. Ayn Rand, *Atlas Shrugged.* New York: Signet, 1992, p. 928.
4. Ronald Reagan, Inaugural Address, January 20, 1981.
5. Bruce Bartlett, "How Supply-Side Economics Trickled Down," *New York Times,* April 4, 2006.
6. "Reaganomics or 'Voodoo Economics'?" BBC News, June 5, 2004.
7. William Greider, "The Education of David Stockman." *Atlantic,* December 1981.
8. Reagan, Horatio Alger Association of Distinguished Americans.
9. Andrew Glass, "Reagan Fires 11,000 Striking Air Traffic Controllers Aug. 5, 1981." *Politico,* Aug. 5, 1981.
10. Martha Burt, "Causes of the Growth of Homelessness during the 1980s." *New Policy and Research Perspectives,* 1997. Posted on www.knowledgeplex.org/showdoc.html?id=1364.
11. "Now a Vegetable, Who Deserves a Break Today?" *Newsweek,* September 21, 1981.
12. "New Incarceration Figures: Thirty-Three Consecutive Years of Growth," Sentencing Project, December 2006.
13. "Beyond City Limits," *August Chronicle,* August 30, 2002, www.austinchronicle.com/news/2002-08-30/101266.
14. Douglas C. McDonald, "The Cost of Corrections," *Research in Corrections,* February 1989, p. 3.

15. Sanford Schram, "Welfare Spending and Poverty," *American Journal of Economics and Sociology*, April 1991, p. 138.

16. Alfie Kohn, "A Look at Getting Back to Basics," *Washington Post*, October 10, 1999.

17. Walter Mondale, Acceptance Speech, Democratic Convention. San Francisco, CA, July 19, 1984.

18. Bentsen-Quayle Debate, Omaha, NE, October 5, 1988.

19. Fred Goldstein, "Clinton's Cruel Legacy: Welfare Vanishes as Poverty Soars," *Workers' World*, New York, posted February 9, 2004, on www.workers.org/2009/us/welfare_0212.

20. Sanjeev Gupta, Benedict Clements, Rina Bhattacharya, and Shamit Chakravarti, "The Elusive Peace Dividend," *Finance and Development: A Quarterly of the IMF*, December 2002.

21. Susan Seligson, "Staggering Price Tag for Iraq, Afghanistan Wars," *BU Today*, July 8, 2011.

22. Lawrence Mishel, "CEO-to-Worker Pay Imbalance Grows," *Economic Policy Institute*, June 21, 2006.

23. Jennifer Liberto, *CNN Money*, April 20, 2011.

24. www.federalreserve.gov/releases/g19/hist/cc_hist_sa.html. July 2011.

25. Derived from Angus Maddison, *Contours of the World Economy, 1–2030 AD: Essays in Macro-Economic History*. New York: Oxford University Press, 2007, p. 379.

26. www.census.gov/hhes/www/housing/census/historic/values.

27. CBS, *Moneywatch*, February 28, 2011.

Notes for Chapter 16

1. "USA Unemployment Rate Graph," http://forecast-chart.com/graph-unemployment-rate.html.

2. Bob McCaughey, "Unemployment in the US Labor Force, 1920–1941," *History of American Civilization since 1865*. New York: Columbia University Press, 2007.

3. Catherin Rampell, "College Enrollment Rate at Record High," *New York Times*, April 28, 2010.

4. US Department of Labor, December 2010.

5. Correctional Population Trends Chart, US Bureau of Justice Statistics, http://bjs.ojp.usdoj.gov/content/glance/corr2.cfm. The figure is drawn from The Annual Probation Survey, National Prisoner Statistics Program, Annual Survey of Jails, and Annual Parole Survey, as presented in *Correctional Populations in the United States, 2009, Prisoners in 2009, Probation and Parole in the United States, 2009,* and *Jail Inmates at Midyear 2009—Statistical Tables*.

6. Ibid.
7. Ibid.
8. Ibid.
9. Ibid.

Note for Chapter 17

1. Sarah van Gelder, *This Changes Everything: Occupy Wall Street and the 99% Movement*. San Francisco, CA: Berrett-Koehler, 2011.

Notes for Chapter 18

1. For one of the best histories of US right-wing populism, see Michael Kazin, *The Populist Persuasion.* New York: Basic Books, 1995.

2. Ibid., chapter 5.

3. We have recounted some of this history in Charles Derber and Yale Magrass, *Morality Wars: How Empires, the Born Again, and the Politically Correct Do Evil in the Name of Good.* Boulder, CO: Paradigm Publishers, 2010, chapter 5.

4. Kazin, *Populist Persuasion,* chapter 5.

5. For a vivid journalistic description, see Thomas Frank, *What's the Matter with Kansas?: How Conservatives Won the Heart of America.* New York: Holt, 2005.

6. Karl Marx described this capitalist threat to small business and peasant life, even in his own lifetime, focusing on the right-wing politics of the peasantry that supported Emperor Louis Napoleon in the 1850s and 1860s. See Karl Marx, "The 18th Brumaire of Louis Bonaparte," *Die Revolution,* New York, 1852. For a brief summary of Marx's analysis that was prophetic of right-wing movements emerging in advanced capitalist downturns, such as the Tea Party, see Charles Derber, *Marx's Ghost.* Boulder, CO: Paradigm Publishers, 2011, pp. 103–121.

7. Derber, *Marx's Ghost.*

8. Derber and Magrass, *Morality Wars,* chapter 4.

9. Ibid.

Notes for Chapter 19

1. Books on the Occupy Movement are proliferating quickly. See Sarah van Gelder (ed.), *This Changes Everything: Occupy Wall Street and the 99% Movement.* San Francisco, CA: Berrett-Koehler, 2011; and Carla Blumenkranz, *Occupy: Scenes from Occupy America.* London: Verso, 2011. See also "What Is Occupy? Inside the Mass Movement," *Time,* December 6, 2011.

2. Ibid.

3. Pew Center Research Publications, "Rising Share of Americans See Conflict between Rich and Poor," January 11, 2012, http://pew research.org/pubs/2167/rich-poor-social-conflict-class.

4. Van Gelder, *This Changes Everything.*

5. Ibid.

Notes for Chapter 20

1. Michael Kazin, *The Populist Persuasion.* New York: Basic Books, 1995.

2. Lawrence Goodwyn, *The Populist Moment: A Short History of the Agrarian Revolt in America.* New York: Galaxy, 1978.

3. Kazin, *Populist Persuasion,* p. 42.

4. Ibid. See also Lawrence Goodwyn, *The Populist Movement.*

5. While he sees TR correctly as using these proposals to consolidate a new regulated corporate capitalism, Gabriel Kolko gives a good description of the Progressive era. See Gabriel Kolko. *The Triumph of Conservatism.* New York: Free Press, 1963. For another interpretation,

see Martin J. Sklar, *The Corporate Reconstruction of American Capitalism, 1890–1916*. Cambridge: Cambridge University Press, 1995.

6. For a discussion of corporate regimes and populist movements against them, see Charles Derber, *Hidden Power*. San Francisco: Berrett-Koehler, 2005.

7. William Leuchtenburg. *Franklin D. Roosevelt and the New Deal, 1932-1940*. New York: Harper and Row, 1963.

8. Ibid. See also Milton Derber, *The American Idea of Industrial Democracy, 1865–1965*. Champaign: University of Illinois Press, 1973. See also Milton Derber and Edwin Young, *Labor and the New Deal*. New York: De Capo Press, 1972.

9. Frances Piven and Richard Cloward, *Poor People's Movements*. New York: Vintage, 1978.

10. Leuchtenburg, *Franklin D. Roosevelt and the New Deal, 1932–1940*.

11. Richard Flacks, *Making History*. Princeton, NJ: Princeton University Press, 1988. Todd Gitlin, *The Sixties*. New York: Bantam, 1993.

12. Flacks, *Making History*. See also Richard Flacks, *Youth and Social Change*. New York: Markham, 1972.

13. Ibid.

14. Flacks, *Making History;* Gitlin, *The Sixties*.

15. See Charles Derber, *Marx's Ghost*. Boulder, CO: Paradigm Publishers, 2011.

16. Sarah van Gelder, *This Changes Everything: Occupy Wall Street and the 99% Movement*. San Francisco: Berrett-Koehler, 2011.

17. Louis Brandeis, cited in Louis D. Brandeis Legacy Fund for Social Justice, www.brandeis.edu/legacyfund/bio.html.

18. Charles Derber, *Marx's Ghost*.

19. Carla Blumenkranz, *Occupy: Scenes from Occupy America*. London: Verso, 2011.

20. Richard Trumka, Statement by AFL-CIO President Richard Trumka on Occupy Wall Street, AFL-CIO Media Center, October 5, 2011, www.aflcio.org/mediacenter/prsptm/pr10052011.cfm.

Notes for Chapter 21

1. Christopher Pines. *Ideology and False Consciousness: Marx and His Historical Progenitors*. New York: SUNY, 1993.

2. Thomas Frank, *What's the Matter with Kansas?: How Conservatives Won the Heart of America*. New York: Holt, 2005.

3. Ibid., pp. 23, 24.

4. Alice B. Fort and Herbert S. Kates, *Minute History of the Drama*. New York: Grosset and Dunlap, 1935, pp. 7–8.

5. Paul Tibbits, *The Atomic Café* (film). New York: New Video Group, 2002.

6. Ayn Rand, *Atlas Shrugged*. New York: Signet [1957], 1992.

7. Harvey Cox, *The Feast of Fools*. Cambridge, MA: Harvard University Press, 1969.

8. Henry Barton Baker, *English Actors: From Shakespeare to Macready*. New York: Henry Holt, 1879, pp. 27–35.

9. Metrodesk, "Hours After Raid, Menino Says He Sympathizes with Occupy Boston Protesters," December 10, 2011, posted on www.boston.com/; *Boston Globe*, October 10, 2011.

10. "The 'Red Menace' in Hollywood," 2008, posted on www
.terramedia.co.uk/reference/documents/red_menace_in_hollywood_
.htm.

11. Dalton Trumbo, *Johnny Got His Gun* (film). New York: Citadel,
1971.

12. Stanley Kubrick, *Spartacus* (film). Los Angeles: Universal Stu-
dios, 1960.

13. Stanley Kubrick, *Dr. Strangelove* (film). Los Angeles: Sony,
1964.

14. Bertolt Brecht and Kurt Weill, *The Three Penny Opera*. New
York: Penguin, 2007.

15. Emma Goldman, *Living My Life*. Claremont, CA: Anarchy Ar-
chives, 2011.

16. If you use our play to make money, you will need our permission.

Part II

I Like Firing People

By Charles Derber and Yale Magrass

With the assistance of Brittany Bieber, Phil Cushing, Hillary Marshall, Emily Morton, Colin Madigan, Alison Miller, Ivana Perez, and Roberto Schaefli

Dramatis Personae (in order of appearance):

Narrator
Yourall Fired, Secretary of the Department of Surplus People
Chamberpot Commerce, head of the biggest business association
Sendu Packing, CEO of Hacker-Packer Computer Co.
Goldman Sacker, leading banker
Larry Summit, former Secretary of the Treasury and former president of Ivy University
Worthy Surper, administrative director of the Surplus People Retention Centers of America
Donal Trumpcard, New York real estate mogul
Warren Buffer, top investor
Bill Gateskeeper, investor and philanthropist
Watchi Everywon, of the Mayors' Conference for Surveillance of Vagrants and Homeless People
General Fourstar Beatem, director of the Military Absorption Unit of Surplus People
Warden Custer, head of the Division of Surplus People in the Department of Prisons
Enrolle Anibody, Vice President of the Universities of America Responsible for Matriculating Surplus People

Maura Lee Bankrupt, CEO of one of America's largest banks
Guardian of Incarceration
Inmate/Surplus Resident
Guard with Southern Accent
Guardian of Emigration
Karl Marx
Guardian of Immigrant-Expulsion and Work Opportunity
Guardian of Therapy
C. Wright Mills, Leading American social theorist
Surplus Resident
Therapist
Michel Foucault, Leading French social theorist
Ghost of Surplus People Past
Occupy Wall Street participants: Protestors 1, 2, 3, and 4, and
   General Assembly
Mutt Banecapital, vulture capitalist and leading politician
Robber Rubiner, Wall Street banker and former Secretary of
   the Treasury Dept.
Paul Krupman, economist and *New York News* columnist
Ronald Reagan
Nelson Rockefeller, former Governor of New York and Vice
   President of the United States
Kochaine brothers, oil and coal barons who are among the
   largest funders of the Tea Party
Lyndon Johnson
Howard Zinn, left-wing author
Bill Benedict, Reagan's drug war czar and education guru
Duke of Leisure, victim of the French Revolution
Sir Edwin Chadwick, founder of the workhouse system
George Pullman, railroad developer
Andrew Carnegie, steel magnate
John D. Rockefeller, oil magnate
J. P. Morgan, financier
Henry Ford, auto maker
Max Weber, German social theorist
Franklin Roosevelt
John Maynard Keynes, economist
Adolph Hitler
Rosie the Riveter
Henry Ford II
William Levitt, founder of the suburban movement in America
Betty Friedan, writer of *The Feminine Mystique*

ACT I

Scene 1: Teleconference, Year 2020

Smoky amorphous images of crowds in different cities, with some on Wall Street sleeping in ragged tents. Fires are lit where people are cooking and eating scraps. Some people have set fire to trash cans and vehicles. Sounds of yelling and protest. Masses of protesters wandering around, talking to each other, shaking their fists up at the sky, yelling at the Towers of Power that line Wall Street.

Distant shouts:
We Want Jobs! Jobs Now! We Want Jobs! Jobs Now!
New image appears of a teleconference on a huge screen.

Yourall Fired: Ladies and gentlemen, Welcome to our annual dinner to discuss our national management of the surplus population. We have a lavish dining experience for you to enjoy as we talk. You are now being served a three-course luncheon with an appetizer of lobster bisque, a main dish of duck a l'orange, and a dessert of gourmet chocolate cheesecake with strawberries and whipped cream. Enjoy your feast!
Applause and smiles from participants. Videoscreen shows elegant waiters serving the lavish meal to the participants.

Chamberpot Commerce: Mr. Yourall Fired, I am sure I speak for all of us in appreciation of your feast for us. This firing business is hard work—we all know that.

Yourall Fired: Nothing harder, and you're all doing a remarkable job. Congratulations! We have some special problems to consider this year, as the number of parasites and unworthy surplus rabble is increasing. We have 8 million additional unemployed and surplus people this year.
Participants continue to eat. They show interest but not distress as they relish their gourmet lunch.

Yourall Fired: Over 2 million new surplus people have been created in the past month. This increase in volume has created overflow in some of our absorption centers of the surplus population. Just look at those mobs down there on Wall Street!
Return to a video image of the streets below, with people marching, looking like a ragged army, moving in an angry and determined manner. Continuing sounds of protests: JOBS NOW! JOBS NOW! JOBS NOW!
The teleconference participants look up with some interest.

Sendu Packing: What do they want with me? I suppose my name is a good excuse for these troublemakers. Why did my mother give me this name?

Goldman Sacker: Well, I'm sure they're thinking about me too. After all, my Tower of Power is next to yours. And my name doesn't help either.

Chamberpot Commerce: Packing and Sacker, don't be concerned. You know the entire political and economic establishment support you, as do all of us here. The rabble will be disciplined and controlled.

Yourall Fired: Now let me turn the meeting over to Worthy Surper, director of the Surplus People Retention Centers of America. He can offer details.

Worthy Surper: Ladies and gentlemen, 10 million new unemployed in the past year and the most recent numbers this year showing a sharp spike upward. This, of course, is consistent with our business strategies over the past decade, as we have moved to outsource rapidly to keep up with the global competition and increase our profitability. In fact, our outsourcing is even ahead of schedule!

Cheers and self-congratulatory applause among most of the participants in the Teleconference.

Chamberpot Commerce: Our Chamber's data indicate this helps to explain why our corporate profits went up more rapidly than expected last year.

Larry Summit: Yes, my National Economic Council examined the national data, and it demonstrates just how profitable our national outsourcing and surplus strategy has been.

Worthy Surper: Thank you, Dr. Summit. High profit levels are a clear indication of the wisdom of the approach adopted after the Great Recession ten years ago; it then became clear that outsourcing was the best way to increase profit for our corporations.

Goldman Sacker: Yes, and we on Wall Street have applied billions of dollars annually to help finance the shift in production abroad. We have also applied the same principles to our own industry, finding hundreds of thousands of surplus American workers on Wall Street. The more we can outsource our financial services and dispose of surplus workers, the more profitable our operations will be.

Appreciative nods and applause from others on the teleconference.

Worthy Surper: Thank you, Sacker, but our successes seem to have put us in quite a pickle. The more we transfer production abroad, the harder it is to absorb and pacify the surplus population.

Chamberpot Commerce: Are you are referring to the street mobs that we were discussing earlier?

Worthy Surper: Yes, Chamberpot, of course. The mobs are increasing in numbers, not only on Wall Street but in Washington, D.C., Chicago, Dallas, and other major urban centers. The unworthy elements of the surplus people, the parasites and freeloaders, are questioning the virtues of our national downsizing and outsourcing strategy. Some are even questioning the wisdom of the shift in our entire production system abroad. And the worst—the parasites and freeloaders—are joining the mobs out there.

Donal Trumpcard's toupee falls into his food; he dusts it off and places it back on his head nonchalantly.

Chamberpot Commerce: After all we have done for them in the Surplus People Retention Centers and in our other surplus-absorption institutions! Outrageous!

Donal Trumpcard [*as he continues to adjust his toupee*]: Never underestimate the ingratitude of those who fail in our great competition. They are inherently lazy and lack talent. They can only think about themselves and their "entitlements," forgetting that our entire system depends on winnowing out parasites like themselves.

Nodding of heads in ascent around the conference screen.

Warren Buffer: Wait, wait gentlemen ... do I have to remind you again that we are taking a dangerous and illogical course here? Haven't Gateskeeper and I been warning you of how these policies might upset the population? WE MUST CHANGE OUR STRATEGIES.

Bill Gateskeeper: I agree, Buffer, we are playing with fire. We need our business strategies to be embraced by the public. If the public begins to question these approaches, the entire transfer of production strategy could fail, and trigger massive revolts.

Donal Trumpcard: Buffer and Gateskeeper, stop being wussies! Didn't you all see my big-time TV show ten years ago, "The Upended." I made firing people the hottest thing on prime-time television, besides me, of course [*flicks his hair, toupee falls off again*]. Most can understand that firing is necessary and rational, even exciting. Let me show how we can get our popularity back. Unlike most of you who tried to be anonymous and let all the attention and hostility be directed against parasites in the government, I made myself a media celebrity [*takes his cell phone and gives instruction through phone*]: Send out the trucks.

Videoscreen shows a truck going through the streets where the crowds are gathered. On the sides of the truck are large signs with a picture of Trumpcard pointing his figure. Beside his picture is the slogan in enormous letters "You're Fired!" Voices from some ordinary people on the street, clapping and cheering.

Audience Member: Yeah! Trumpcard, Fire them!

One soft voice in crowd talking to the person next to her.

Audience Member: Who is them? We've already been fired.

Yourall Fired: Let's give our buddy Trumpcard a round of applause. He's taught America about the efficiency of firing the unworthy and transformed our national culture of human disposal from tragedy into entertainment.

A general round of applause from most of the participants.

Bill Gateskeeper: But just how large are the crowds? They seem far bigger than anything we have seen in recent decades.

Yourall Fired: I think Ms. Watchi Everywon can offer us some sense of the magnitude of the problem, since she has been central to our National Surveillance System.

Watchi Everywon: It's a pleasure to be here. As you know, as part of our surplus policy, we have installed hundreds of thousands of surveillance cameras in every US city and suburb. Huge numbers of vagrants and homeless drift on the streets, and because we value freedom so highly, we have not rounded them all up and imprisoned them as in so many other countries. Long live our American liberty!

Applause from the participants:

Here! Here!

Watchi Everywon: But, of course, our surplus population has grown massively, so in addition to our absorption and retention surplus centers, we developed an advanced surveillance system. Take a look at these bad boys [*points to camera*]! I want to thank the military again for their help, since they have shared with us their techniques for global surveillance of terrorists. These have worked beautifully for keeping the homeless rabble in line and our own streets safe.

Loud applause from the participants.

Watchi Everywon: But I must tell you that the mobs we are seeing over the past month confirm Trumpcard's concern that the ingratitude of the surplus parasites and free-riders can never be underestimated. It appears to be a national, spontaneous uprising of angry wretches, with no clear leadership and ridiculous demands about jobs and justice.

Sendu Packing: I keep hearing my name. Are they coming after my money?

Watchi Everywon: They do seem to talk about Packing a lot. We think these ignorant folk are just using Packing as a symbol of our national jobs-cutting strategy.

Goldman Sacker: Are they coming after me too? These rabble could use my name too for their demonic purposes.

Watchi Everywon: They do seem to be all moving toward New York, and our listening devices indicate that they are planning to meet up in Wall Street, where a few rabble have already arrived. Sacker, your name does come up in the mob jabber. Our surveillance devices are picking up all kinds of talk about "bank gangsters," "revolution," and "people over profit." But most do not seem to be armed except with posters, ladders, and tent gear.

Goldman Sacker: Say what? [*with attitude*]

Watchi Everywon: Well, they are building a tent city and talking about launching an assault on the Wall Street Towers of Power. The ladders suggest they are going to try to move up from the street blockades around the Towers of Power on the street and break and enter on higher levels.

Bill Gateskeeper: This reminds me of when the Occupy Wall Street protests began 10 years ago. Sounds like the same crowds are coming back to haunt us. In my view, they had a positive effect in starting a new conversation about the extreme inequality between the bottom 99 percent and the top 1 percent.

Warren Buffer: Yeah, and I was happy to help them by confessing that the government coddles me and my billionaire friends with low taxes. I supported their goals, if not their tactics.

Donal Trumpcard: I remember those crazy hippies and tree-huggers. This is an even more dangerous and demented group than the Occupy Wall Street idiots ten years ago. These are mobs pure and simple, and I'll bet a lot of them are armed.

General Beatem: Ladies and gentlemen, please don't let this alarm you. My colleagues in the Pentagon have the situation well under control. Law and order will prevail, I can assure you.
  Loud sighs of relief and appreciative nods from the participants.

Yourall Fired: Let me go around and get brief reports on the overflow and how our surplus institutions are coping. General Beatem, why don't we start with you.

General Beatem: Yes, sir, Mr. Fired, sir [*salutes*]. As you all know, the US military not only protects the empire and corporations but also serves a vital domestic economic function. We are the largest surplus-absorption institution in America, but we also build patriotism and belief in our great American system among our recruits.

Elites [Fired, Trumpcard, etc.]: Thank God, Thank God.

General Beatem: As we fight terrorists at home and abroad—and the new great threat from China and East Asia—we have been able to absorb many of the downsized and outsourced, along with those who never had a job, into our armies. In fact, the vast majority of our 5 million soldiers are drawn from the surplus population. We have the discipline and control and service ethos that turns these human failures into patriotic members of society, who feel loyalty and gratitude to America.

  Donal Trumpcard jumps up, salutes, and cries "Go Patriots!"

Yourall Fired: And what of the overflow crisis?

General Beatem: We have expanded our wars and interventions abroad to soak up more of the growing surplus people at home. But over the past year, I will acknowledge that we have had trouble keeping up. While we have expanded our military capacity into an "unlimited war" doctrine, we still aren't able to absorb all the potential recruits from the surplus population. This is partly a problem of technology. Our high-tech capabilities mean we can fight more wars with fewer soldiers. Our drones and robot-soldiers are much better fighters than humans. So while recognizing our domestic economic function in soaking up surplus people, we are now starting to downsize the military, without ending, of course, our long wars.

Yourall Fired: Thank you, General [*they salute each other, along with Donal Trumpcard*]. Let me turn to Warden Custer, who is the best person to talk about absorption capacity within the prison system.

Warden Custer: Thank you, Yourall Fired. We know that the unworthy surplus population includes millions of angry and violent parasites, who use their jobless status as an excuse to commit crimes against worthy American citizens. We have coordinated with many of the great corporations represented in this room to expand rapidly our prison-industrial complex and house many more of the surplus rabble. But, like the Pentagon, we are experiencing absorption problems; too many new criminals, too few government dollars coming into house them. We now put seven people in each small cell, and serve only two small meals of bologna sandwiches each day. But the crowding is causing uprisings in the prisons themselves, and we don't have the capacity to absorb more of the surplus rabble. We are in the process of coordinating with prison systems in allied countries to transfer prisoners to other countries as well as to local jails and nuthouses—I mean mental hospitals. This may help to alleviate the overflow crisis.

Donal Trumpcard: You know, at one time there was an alternative to the prison system for soaking up and pacifying the surplus rabble. There used to be a welfare system that gave unworthy parasites checks for not working. There are still some residues of this policy. They were able to have their own apartments with televisions and refrigerators, but they kept having babies and buying booze.

Elites groan.

Elites, in unison: Disgusting, disgusting!

Donal Trumpcard: Welfare was cheaper than making them suffer in prisons, which are quite expensive, but we were rewarding sloth. Through my media, we were able to get the worthy workers to hate welfare recipients and see them as their real enemy, not us billionaires. They didn't mind the trillions we spent on warfare or repression, but resented every penny given to the poor. It was a great way to divide and conquer, but now we make more profit from prisons, and the more we make the unworthy suffer, the more low-wage people, who think they are hardworking and productive, love us.

Elites, in unison: They love us, they love us, they love us!

Warren Buffer and Bill Gateskeeper [*in unison*]: Are you sure? Even those mobs down there?

Donal Trumpcard: Chill out, Buffer and Gateskeeper. The fact is that prisons are much more effective than the antiquated welfare system that we've mostly abandoned—and that you bleedings hearts want to restore. Locking 'em up gets the population to side with us moguls against the surplus rabble inmates, just as they sided with us against the welfare queens.

General Beatem: Trumpcard, I am sure you endorse not just our domestic prisons but our rendition program to transfer terrorists to CIA secret prisons in other countries. Don't you think Custer has a very good idea?

Yourall Fired: We wish you Godspeed in this prisoner-transfer-abroad initiative, Warden Custer. But let's hear now from Ms. Enrolle Anibody, who can report on the absorption functions of our schools and institutions of higher education.

Enrolle Anibody: Thank you, Mr. Fired. Our institutions of higher education realized at least a decade ago that absorption of the surplus population was becoming the major function of the academy. As our graduates found themselves without job prospects, we realized the need to keep them enrolled longer.

Prolonging education would siphon off discontent and maintain hope in the younger generation, who are facing life-long jobless-ness. What could be a better alternative than life-long learning? Corporations also saw this as a profitable venture, helping us build the university-industrial complex alongside the prison-industrial complex so eloquently discussed by Warden Custer. We also have been aggressively recruiting the middle-aged and older population as well who were losing their jobs and sinking into the surplus masses. Our program attracts the more mo-tivated and worthy surplus folks, and some of them are being trained to help manage the unworthy surplus people—with our new MBAs in Surplus Human Resource Management.

Donal Trumpcard: Long live the University of Phoenix! I think I'll buy it!

Yourall Fired: Are you also experiencing an overflow crisis, En-rolle Anibody?

Enrolle Anibody: Yes, we can't build fast enough to accommodate the need, and the government can no longer provide the grants and loans to help keep our university-industrial complex sus-tainable. Our students have little money, although the ones with working parents are still able to draw on family resources. So the student loan system has grown into a vast scheme, which our Wall Street friends have been generous in capitalizing.

Maura Lee Bankrupt: Yeah, we've made a lot of money off those loans.

Applause from elites.

Enrolle Anibody: But we are reaching our limits as student loans have become too risky; our bankers know that our graduates will likely join the surplus and be unable to pay them back. Nonetheless, we are committed to educating the worthy surplus people who we all know play a crucial role in managing and guarding the unworthy surplus masses. We realize that it is education that legitimates our surplus economy and cultivates the belief among the surplus masses that we elites are doing everything possible to sustain opportunity among all the worthy citizens of this great nation.

Chamberpot Commerce: You mean, opportunity for us in this room, hah hah.

Elites all laugh appreciatively.

Enrolle Anibody: To cut costs we have closed many of the weaker traditional universities, where students went to attend classes and become part of an academic community. Now most classes are conducted online via computer. Students watch lectures on television, input answers to multiple-choice test through the

Web. They think they are being educated, even though very few of them remember anything they were taught and the jobs they prepare for don't exist.

Appreciative loud applause from the participants.

Yourall Fired: Thank you, Enrolle Anibody. Let's now turn to the Surplus People Retention Centers (SPRC) where the worthy surplus play a major role in housing and guarding the unworthy. Worthy Surper, do you want to update us on the overflow problems?

Worthy Surper: Ladies and gentlemen, I have just received a call indicating major disruptions in the New Jersey SPRC, one of the largest in the country. I'm afraid I have to go there immediately, since the situation there is serious, and we are getting information about similar protests and revolts in other Surplus People Retention Centers around the nation. However, I should be able to rejoin this teleconference in two hours and update all of you on the situation in our SPRCs around the country.

Yourall Fired: It's a good time for us to take a break, anyway. Let's all take a nap after this hard work we've been doing. Good luck to you, Worthy Surper, and we'll be eager to hear the latest news, direct from the New Jersey Retention Center.

Scene 2: The New Jersey Surplus People Retention Center, two hours later

Narrator: Worthy Surper is now reporting to the teleconference from the New Jersey Surplus People Retention Center.

The teleconference resumes and lights focus on Worthy Surper at the New Jersey Surplus People Retention Center. The other teleconference participants are shadows in the background, but can still be heard. Loud noises and yelling can be heard in the New Jersey Retention Center, which appears filled with smoke.

Worthy Surper: Can you hear me now, Yourall Fired?

Yourall Fired: Yes, we can hear you, Surper. But it sounds like quite a ruckus going on there. Are you safe?

Worthy Surper: The worthy staff Guardians here are in the process of a lockdown. We will restore order, but we have had a major incident, with several thousand of our surplus residents breaking out and moving in a large group to escape the Retention Center—apparently these rabble are all headed towards you, Wall Street!

General Beatem: Permission to speak!

Worthy Super: Permission granted!

General Beatem: I have been getting similar reports from the Pentagon. Parallel break-outs are occurring around the country. The military, as we speak, has received an order from the president to set up blockades and disperse the unruly parasites.

Worthy Surper: The situation does seem not fully within our control, so we appreciate the president's call for the military to help stabilize the situation. Here in the New Jersey Retention Center, the situation is still up in the air, but our Guardians are playing an important role in pacifying the remaining rabble.

General Beatem: Permission to speak!

Worthy Surper [*annoyed*]: Permission granted.

General Beatem: Do you need military units in your New Jersey Center?

Worthy Surper: No, General, thank you. Our Guardians are trained in military-style and prison control protocols.

Donal Trumpcard: This is an outrage! We do so much for the surplus population in our national Surplus People Retention Centers. These parasites need to be subjected to the most severe discipline. I would think that once control is reestablished, forced emigration should be instituted for the ringleaders.

Worthy Surper: Trumpcard, I think we will soon have the situation under control.

Yourall Fired: Can you give our participants an overview of the Surplus People Retention Center in New Jersey and the various disciplinary and rehabilitation programs operated by your center? This can help us understand the motives of these unfortunate and ungrateful parasites and will help inform our decision making about how to respond to the surplus uprising.

Worthy Surper: Let me remind you that the centers were established by Congress and the president four years ago, in 2016. By 2015, the number of vagrants, drifters, and other surplus rabble on the streets and in our communities were growing so rapidly that they were undermining domestic security and stability. The failure of the economy to absorb the unemployed after the long Great Recession that began in 2008 was clearly taking its toll. Unemployment continued to grow rapidly for years. The corporations and banks, as you well know, realized that survival and profitability in the global economy required the transfer-of-production system, which dismantled productive operations in the US and ensured large-scale further growth in the surplus population because of permanent outsourcing and downsizing. The military, prisons, and universities helped absorb surplus people, but they could not handle the numbers.

Our retention centers were established to help set a model for how to manage the surplus population as it mushroomed out of control.

Sendu Packing: It's impressive how much you have achieved in only four years.

Worthy Surper: Thank you, Packing. The total surplus population in our Surplus People Retention Centers is 1,412,000. It is a large number but a small fraction of the estimated 150 million surplus people in the US. Most surplus folks, of course, continue to live in communities and drift on the streets or are sucked into the surplus-absorption institutions we have discussed.

Yourall Fired: Remind us of exactly what the centers do and how they work.

Worthy Surper: Yes, of course. Our central mission is to develop a long-term custodial service to warehouse a sector of the surplus population, while researching other national strategies for dealing with the much larger number of surplus people who are not housed in our centers. We seek to winnow the worthy from the unworthy. The unworthy, who are the majority, must basically be disposed of, controlled, expelled. The worthy are rehabilitated and trained for useful service, largely in the management of the Surplus People Retention Centers themselves. They also help manage the surplus populations in the military, prisons, mental hospitals, and universities. And the whole process turns the worthy and unworthy against each other, deflecting the rage they would obviously turn on us if they had the chance.

Donal Trumpcard: Mr. Surper, I take it you were one of the residents. I congratulate you because you have demonstrated that surplus people are responsible for their own fate.

Worthy Surper: All the Guardians were initially residents. They were chosen from the surplus people as capable and motivated, passing through a rigorous process of selection. In a sense, we initially carry out a kind of process similar to the winnowing process made popular by you, Mr. Trumpcard, in your "Upended" television series. Like Mr. Trumpcard in his business, we work very hard to select the small cadre of surplus people who will not be permanently fired or disposed of. All of the Guardians you will meet today have proved their worthiness, much like the finalists in Trumpcard's "Upended" show.

Guardian of Incarceration: Incarceration is the final solution for our most unworthy surplus residents. These are the rebels and drifters, over-entitled and lazy, who are not willing to acknowledge their responsibility for themselves. Many are criminals who once served sentences or got away with their crimes. Some did robbery to feed themselves and their families, but the most common offense is using marijuana and other drugs, which actually don't have any victims other than the users themselves. They blame the system rather than themselves for their unemployment and uselessness, and none of our other treatment options can change their basic mindset.

Goldman Sacker: This must be an expensive operation. Why don't you just send these vagrants, nuts, and criminals into the prison system?

Guardian of Incarceration: Actually, we are able to incarcerate them more cheaply than the prisons because we are not bound by the laws governing the judicial and prison systems. According to Supreme Court decisions in 2018, surplus people are not full citizens and are not guaranteed the constitutional rights of other citizens. The unworthy can be compared to the enemy combatants during the Guantanamo days, who could be held without cause and subjected to enhanced interrogation.

Donal Trumpcard: Thank God, since the Patriot Act was passed, many of those liberal so-called Constitutional rights that actually protected nuts, weirdoes, and traitors were eliminated.
Video image of a cell bloc. The camera zooms in on one small cell about 10 feet by 15 feet. Twelve people are squeezed into this room, with a toilet in one corner. Inmates are sitting or lying on the floor, looking pale, thin, and sickly. Some are trying to sleep.

Narrator: Here is a scene going on right now from an incarceration bloc.

Inmate [*stands up, grabs the cell bars, and yells*]: You barbarians! All we want is a good job. And you lock us up for the crime of wanting to work. You separate us from our families and take away all our freedom. We will never surrender our inner dignity, the one thing we have left.

A Guard with Southern Accent [*appears with mace spray*]: What we have here is a failure to communicate! [*Sprays the mace in the inmate's eyes.*]

Inmate [*falls down*]: OOoooooooo, owwwwwwwww. I can't see! I can't see!

Guard [*turning to other prisoners*]: Now, I can be a good guy, or I can be one real mean sum-bitch. It's all up to you. [*Turns to camera, speaking to teleconference participants:*] I am sorry you have to see what we are dealing with here. These are the worst of the parasites housed here. Only brute force works with them. I will admit that some will die, but this is an unfortunate side of our national mandate to keep the surplus population in check.

Everyone in the conference moves back to the main stage.

Donal Trumpcard: If they won't recognize the law of the survival of the fittest, then this is their inevitable fate. They had a chance to show their worthiness and rehabilitate themselves. Some deserve the ultimate firing—a firing squad!

Trump wildly waves around a pistol; toupee falls off again.

Worthy Surper: We offer many rehabilitation programs here for those who can prove their worthiness. But the unworthy truly cannot be coddled. We have studied the history of the poorhouses and workhouses in nineteenth-century London. The workhouses were where the British capitalists housed their surplus population, and it is a model for us. They realized that you couldn't go soft on the surplus folks. If we gave them good food and comfortable sleeping quarters and let them watch television, these freeloaders would just be happy to live here forever.

Chamberpot Commerce: Those Brits really knew what they were doing!

Worthy Surper: Right, Chamberpot! The British workhouses also separated husbands from wives and children, and showed no mercy to those who didn't respond to rehabilitation or make-work. They provided little food and no comfort. This sent the message loud and clear: we are in charge and we have no mercy for freeloaders. Many who couldn't adjust, simply died. Believe me, those outside the retention centers as well as our residents get the message and do anything to try to keep a job, no matter how miserable, and avoid getting sent to a workhouse or poorhouse.

Applause from the teleconference participants.

Warren Buffer: This kind of inhumane treatment must give rise to some of the explosive riots and demonstrations we are seeing today.

Guardian of Incarceration: Our security systems are very developed and use the latest incarceration techniques. But it's true that the current conditions can breed problems among troublemakers, who have found ingenious ways to escape. If necessary, we will use our domestic drones, on loan from the military, to shoot these surplus rabble from the sky. [*Donal Trumpcard waves his pistol and fires a couple of rounds.*]

Worthy Surper: Thank you, Guardian of Incarceration. Incarceration will always be the last resource of our control system in the Surplus People Retention Centers. Now let me introduce the Guardian of Emigration.

Guardian of Emigration: Ladies and gentlemen, it's a pleasure to update you on our Emigration Initiative. As you know, in 2018, the president announced formally our transition from an immigration to an emigration society. This reflected the trends of almost a decade, which led more and more surplus Americans to look for jobs in China, India, Brazil, or other foreign countries. This was especially true of educated young people, who couldn't get jobs here and desperately needed to pay back student loans. Once they realized their degrees meant a big zero in the US, they may have felt betrayed, but young people see the world as their big stage, and they always feel hopeful.

Sendu Packing: I know the president has explained the new Emigration Initiative to the nation, indicating the way the US is prepared to help those with the boldness and entrepreneurial spirit to find jobs in other societies. He knows that these workers may end up working for US companies operating in other countries, of course, at far lower wages than they would pay in the US itself. It's a win-win as far as the young people are concerned. They finally get a job, while also getting to see the world.

Bill Gateskeeper: This is a global initiative I can support. It helps build the sense of global community that our corporations and our nation must foster.

Goldman Sacker: More to the point, it's a brilliant way of dealing with the surplus people crisis. When millions of them emigrate, we ease the pressures at home. Fewer people to hire; less overflow problems in the military, prisons, schools, and other surplus-absorption institutions. Getting them out of the US in large numbers, as fast as possible, will stabilize the nation and tamp down the conditions giving rise to the mobs out there.

Donal Trumpcard: This seems a fitting punishment for the surplus rabble. If it were up to me, I'd load these folks up in spaceships and send them off to Pluto.

Loud laughter from the elites.

Guardian of Emigration: Actually, we are coordinating with NASA to discover whether there are cost-efficient ways to send significant numbers of surplus people off the earth into space, Mr. Trumpcard. Space travel is becoming more commercially viable, and the population and surplus crises are becoming too intractable. If not Pluto, Mars might be a fitting destination.

Larry Summit: Just as the British sent their surplus to Australia, some distant planet could serve the same purpose for us. If we can export our pollution to the Third World, as I recommended and you may remember, why can't we send the surplus rabble to other planets?

Narrator: Look, here's the ghost of the great nineteenth-century social theorist, Karl Marx! [*Play Twilight Zone music and have lights flash on and off.*]

Karl Marx: Even Malthus would have found you all barbarians as you happily discuss this absurdity.

Sendu Packing: What is this strange apparition? A ghost playing Karl Marx, of all spooks?

Laughter from the elites.

Karl Marx: You may all laugh. But my spirit lives on—and will as long as capitalism continues to survive and brutalize the world's people. Those people out there on the street are the victims I predicted your ruthless system would produce. I am still a specter haunting your global system, which is doomed by its own successes and the mass of surplus people it has produced.

Sendu Packing: Marx, if you are really his spirit, you're irrelevant today. Nobody believes in you. You're living still in the nineteenth century. But let's pretend to take your absurd ideas seriously. As one of the world's great entrepreneurs, I've always been willing to entertain the unimaginable—which is how I see your presence as a ghost. But think, then, you foolish Ghost Marx. You, yourself, knew that capitalism had to expand everywhere—and now outer space is a possibility. Of course, most of the surplus population in the emigration programs, for now, will be recruited for emigration to other countries on Earth. I am happy to consider hiring the worthy surplus in my plants in China and India, as long as they accept the wages and hours I require there.

Goldman Sacker: I feel the same way. As we downsize on Wall Street, many of our laid-off workers are good candidates for jobs with us in Rio or Shanghai. We are increasingly downsizing our financial operations in the US and picking up some of these same brokers and other staff at lower wages in other countries.

Guardian of Emigration: This is precisely the priority for our emigration policies in the Surplus People Retention Centers. We carefully screen our residents to find who could be productive workers abroad for Goldman Sacker or Sendu Packing.

Sendu Packing: These are often young highly educated Americans who just haven't been able to find jobs here at home. We find they are desperate to use their skills and can be trained to actually desire emigration, to pursue new lives in other countries as part of a pioneering global exploration.

Warren Buffer: But what about those who refuse to emigrate and accept such low wages?

Guardian of Emigration: This distinguishes the worthy from the unworthy. Those refusing emigration are proving their unworthiness and lack of motivation. A sign of worthiness is recognizing your place and not challenging authority. We send many of these unworthy folk abroad, though many will not find work in other countries and will not survive.

Karl Marx: This is even worse than what I predicted 150 years ago. I knew capitalism would hurtle workers in advanced countries down into the sewers of the reserve army of the unemployed. I knew many of these lumpen proletariat would suffer and might die. But perhaps because I thought your brutal capitalism would collapse much earlier, I did not consider that you would develop such a systematic policy to expel your own population wholesale, to sink or swim in other nations. But now as I look at the protesters in the street, I think maybe my prophecies are finally becoming true. These ultimate refugees will create a world far better than the one you are destroying.

Warren Buffer: I am hardly a Marxist, and I despise his socialism, but I share his outrage. Your callous emigration policy violates the decency and common sense that I learned as a child in Omaha.

Guardian of Emigration: We are acting on the orders of the president and the nation. This is both a national security and an economic issue. The global markets are the best judges of how to organize the global labor force. Stability at home requires purging many of our surplus people. Expelling the unworthy surplus is economically efficient since it gives these unworthy folks the largest possible market to find a job. If they cannot make themselves attractive to employers anywhere on the planet, then they deserve their fate. Emigration is their best chance to get a life.

Donal Trumpcard: Life is a privilege and they haven't earned it!

Worthy Surper: We do, though, offer some jobs in this country as well, particularly the work that used to be done by illegal immigrants before we expelled them all. Let's turn now to our Guardian of Immigration-Expulsion and Work Opportunity.

Guardian of Immigration-Expulsion and Work Opportunity: It's my duty to tell you a little about the rehabilitation program at our retention center. In 2015, the president signed a law deporting all illegal immigrants in the country. Those parasites took jobs Americans wouldn't accept. Our Mexican Wall never did the job of keeping them out. They acted like Texas, Arizona, and California once was their country. Therefore, the military had to forcibly remove all undocumented aliens with drones and special forces.

Donal Trumpcard: Thank God we finally cleansed the country of these aliens.

Guardian of Immigration-Expulsion and Work Opportunity: The Expulsion Act of 2016 showed our commitment to our own citizens. And for the surplus population, it opened up jobs, helping us demonstrate that America was still the land of opportunity. These new jobs were ones that Americans could not get before, because they were too spoiled to accept the wages and hours that the lazy parasitical immigrants happily took.

Chamberpot Commerce: We had originally supported some undocumented workers because Americans were too spoiled to do what they called "slave labor." But we soon realized that the surplus crisis would get Americans to do just about anything. See, Marx, we capitalists know how to benefit from crisis!

Marx [*scoffing*]: Nuttensohn!

Donal Trumpcard: Damn it, I don't care if you're a ghost! In America, we speak American!

Worthy Surper: Exactly, Trumpcard, that's why we started our expulsion immigration program; it offered a new avenue for us not only to prove the opportunity remaining for true Americans but also to sort the worthy from the unworthy. We generously offer residents the opportunity to do work the aliens had done, such as lettuce-picking at minimum wages. Many refused, saying no American should be asked to work under such inhumane conditions, without any protections guaranteed by law or the Constitution, as if the Constitution was written to protect the lazy and unfit!

Goldman Sacker: But others accepted this work happily?

Guardian of Immigration-Expulsion and Work Opportunity: Yes, many did. Those willing to pick grapes and dig holes for 15 hours a day at virtually no wages and with minimal protections were showing a willingness to use whatever opportunities opened up, just like the undocumented immigrants. Unlike those aliens, worthy Americans deserved this opportunity. Nonetheless, many unworthy didn't stick with it. But others showed a willingness, even enthusiasm, to be able to do any work at all.

Sendu Packing: And what about the others?

Worthy Surper: Well, those who refused all work were incarcerated or expelled. But those who showed some initiative were given the chance to enter our large system of therapy programs. Successful management of surplus populations depends on shifts in their psychology and mindsets. Let me introduce you to our Guardian of Therapy, who oversees this vital work here.

Guardian of Therapy: How are we feeling today, ladies and gentlemen? As you can imagine, rehabilitation is an important part of surplus people treatment. Therapy plays a very big role.

Donal Trumpcard: Forget therapy! Drug them into oblivion. Drugs are cheaper. And make them too drowsy to rebel.

Guardian of Therapy: Actually, a model of therapy known as cognitive behavioral therapy has demonstrated great effectiveness in recent years. Developed originally to treat clinical depression, we have adapted it to shift the way of thinking of our surplus lunatics ... I mean residents. I should add, most surplus people experience depression after losing their jobs or realizing how difficult it will be for them ever to find jobs. An important part of treating depression is getting patients to realize it is just a subjective psychological state and there is no objective reason to be depressed.

Chamberpot Commerce: I have to agree with Trumpcard. Therapy sounds like coddling the rabble. It stinks! Lock 'em up, expel 'em, drug 'em!

C. Wright Mills appears. [Play Twilight Zone music and have lights flash on and off.]

Sendu Packing: Speaking of drugs, is that another ghost?

Karl Marx: It's C. Wright Mills, maybe the greatest American sociologist of the mid-twentieth century!

C. Wright Mills: You members of the "power elite" want to manipulate mass society to serve you. You fear that the surplus population will develop the "sociological imagination." The surplus knows they have many personal troubles: unemployment or underemployment, poverty, displacement, isolation, no meaningful purpose, competition both for position and possessions. You want them to see all their problems as their own doing. But these are not personal troubles; they are public issues that you have created.

Guardian of Therapy: This spook has just the kind of attitude that we see in our most rebellious and worthless surplus rabble. Give Mills electric shock therapy!

C. Wright Mills: Try therapizing me, you brainwasher. I studied your forms of manipulation for years. You don't want anyone to see that the power elites sacrifice the public good for their own private gain. You want everyone to see everything in psychological terms. You want your surplus victims to believe they are individuals condemned by fair, objective, invisible forces.

Chamberpot Commerce: If you mean the market, Ghost, there ain't anything more fair and objective.

C. Wright Mills: If the people had the sociological imagination they would recognize that their private troubles are really public issues created by you, the power elite, in your search for profit and control. The sociological imagination would tell them they must solve their problems collectively. It would cause them to bond together to end your system of oppression. But you failed. Look down in the street; you will see the sociological imagination in action as the people work together for their common good.

Guardian of Therapy: Let's ignore this absurd academic-sounding spook. But Trumpcard and Chamberpot, I understand your skepticism. Let me show you an ongoing session to demonstrate our therapeutic approach.

All teleconference members leave stage. Stage lights show a room in which a therapist and surplus resident—played by the earlier inmate who got maced—are facing each other in chairs, engaging in a session. Around the room are signs saying "Have the Courage to Blame Yourself," "Think Positively about Your Jobless Future," and "There Is No System."

Surplus Resident [*wearing a straightjacket*]: I still feel that it's not my fault. I studied hard and I always worked hard. I want a job, but they're just not there!

Therapist: So you're still blaming somebody else? This is exactly the problem.

Surplus Resident: I know that it's partly my fault, but *ALL* of us? So many people don't have jobs. There must be a problem with the system and the people who run it.

Therapist: There you go again. Blaming "the system" [*makes quotes with hand gesture—two fingers held up in each hand*]. There is only the freedom of the markets; there are no people running this "system" as you call it. The markets are ingrained in the laws of nature. They are self-regulating and don't require any direction from leaders. Questioning this proves that you need more therapy. You must not challenge the good intentions of the authorities, who have been chosen by the market for their wisdom, efficiency, and skill. If you think we are trying to persecute you and lock you up, you are only being paranoid. We shall have to lock you up for your own benefit.

Surplus Resident: OK, maybe nobody controls those markets, but please don't lock me up. There is no need for it. I realize you are only concerned about my welfare. But I don't see how you can blame me when I have studied and worked so hard [*starts to cry*].

Therapist [*hands resident a tissue*]: There, there. You are making progress. You understand there really is nobody at the top capable of redirecting the markets. The system, if you want to call it that, runs itself, offering maximum freedom and prosperity around the world. It is really part of nature, part of God's beautiful handiwork for human liberty. But it requires that everyone take personal responsibility.

Surplus Resident [*still crying*]: But what else could I have done? What else can I do?

Therapist: Oh, there are many options for you to consider. There are jobs abroad. If you stay here you could join the military or work in the prisons, but there is intense competition for the other remaining jobs in the United States. The market, on its own, selects the very best. You just didn't make the cut. You may think you were qualified and industrious, but there were others who surpassed you.

Surplus Resident: Is there any hope for me?

Therapist: It all depends on you. I feel you are beginning to assume responsibility for your own failures. Just forget this nonsense of a system or leaders who don't have your best interests at heart.

Surplus Resident: Yes, it doesn't make sense to blame others— I'm the failure! Perhaps I just haven't been strong enough to take responsibility for myself.

Therapist [*handing another tissue*]: Very good. I see signs of progress. This is the beginning of your recovery and redemption.

Surplus Resident [*still crying*]: Oh, therapist, thank you so much for your guidance. I will try harder.

Lights go back to the Guardian Therapist, talking to elites.

Guardian Therapist: Ladies and gentlemen, the rehabilitation process [*points toward Surplus Resident while addressing the audience*].

Loud applause from the elites; return to stage.

Chamberpot Commerce: Now I see the merits of your approach!

Donal Trumpcard: I have to agree. This is the kind of mind-shift we need in the whole surplus population. When they blame themselves and see there is no "system" to blame they are easier to fire. I've been doing this for years! Do you see the way they kiss my ass on my TV show?

Applause from the teleconference participants.

Michel Foucault appears.

Sendu Packing: Not another ghost!

Karl Marx: It's French philosopher and social theorist Michel Foucault. He has a lot to say about mental illness, crime, and rehabilitation.

Michel Foucault: Marx says control of the "means of production," economic institutions, makes you a ruling class. I agree with him. It also gives you control over the "means of reality" or the "terms of discourse." This includes control over how people understand and interpret the world, the very categories through which we interpret time and space, including control over how an act or even a thought gets labeled "insane" or "criminal." You, the ruling class, decide what is normal or healthy. A challenge to your authority becomes a disease or a crime. You use what another theorist, sociologist Erving Goffman, called "total institutions" to lock people up "for their good." Indeed, you can decide what is someone else's "own good." Their good is the good of "society," not what would make them happy, comfortable, and fulfilled. The people in the street, who you want to call mentally ill or criminals, are the really healthy ones. They understand the truth and are not letting you control how they think.

Donal Trumpcard: Who let these psychobabble spooks in? Lock the doors and call the ghost-busters!

Michel Foucault: No ghost-buster can bust me. I'll tell you what your therapy is all about. You use the word "society" to get the masses to identify your interests with their interests. You have the means of hard control: prisons, torture chambers, gallows, guillotines, and gurneys. But these brutal tools make your power too blatant and likely to provoke rebellion. So you prefer to use softer means, when possible, when the victim is cooperative enough to permit it. The most common soft method is what you call "rehabilitation," where you help the victim to "adjust" to society. They must never ask where does society come from or is this a society to which they should adjust. They must become therapists, learning to internalize social norms without ever questioning them. Each becomes her own disciplinarian, essentially surveilling herself so that she acts the way you would want her to.

Chamberpot Commerce: Thank God this is a spook we don't have to worry about. The French intellectuals are bigger crackpots than ours! After hearing this nonsense, I'm glad I eat my "freedom fries," not French fries.

Yourall Fired: Ladies and gentlemen, we need to interrupt our meeting. We are getting more reports of huge mob uprisings around the country.

General Beatem: I wouldn't be too concerned. The military will crush this revolt if the police and Retention Center Guardians don't get this nonsense under control.

Yourall Fired: I'm sure you're right, General. But listen to the shouts and some of the outrageous disruption right here on Wall Street. These hooligans don't even have the manners to wait for us to digest our lunch and finish our meeting.

Yells from outside:

JOBS NOW! DEMOCRACY NOW! JOBS NOW!

Yourall Fired: Can you hear the banging on some of our buildings? The rabble out there are breaking through the police barrier and trying to enter the Towers of Power. Why don't we wrap up the meeting today and convene again tomorrow. By then, we will have the latest security reports and these ingrates should be securely locked down. Please return to your pleasure domes and enjoy the rest of the evening.

Lights dim as the yells from the rabble get louder. Glass shatters from building windows on the ground floor, and the camera hones in on trash cans pushed over, with fire smoking out of them. Teleconference participants are seen hastily leaving their offices, looking worried.

ACT II
THE MELTDOWN (TEN YEARS EARLIER)

Scene 1: Back to the Great Recession, 2010

Ghost appears in Packing's plush bedroom; cue Twilight Zone music and flashing lights.

Ghost [*motioning toward Packing*]: Packing, come over here, I'd like to have a word with you.

Packing gets out of his bed and ambivalently moves toward Ghost.

Ghost: Packing, I am the Ghost of Surplus People Past. Several years ago you fired me when you relocated a Hacker-Packer Computer plant in Singapore. I never did find another job, and I keeled over a few months ago from a heart attack.

Sendu Packing [*his voice shaking*]: Don't hurt me, don't hurt me!

Ghost: You and your corporate posse are monsters.

Sendu Packing: What do you want from me?

Ghost: Packing, I am here to educate you, not hurt you. To understand how you got to this frightening place, we are going to begin your first history lesson. For hundreds of years, my people have suffered at the hands of people like you, the surplus-makers. You have been around since the beginning of capitalism. Your capitalist ancestors always used job-cutting as a central tool. But never at the scale you have created today.

Sendu Packing: OK, maybe I need to hear a little of your history to save my head.

Ghost: Mr. Packing, let's go back to a pivotal moment only a decade ago. Welcome to the world of the Great Recession that began in 2008.

Lights turn on in the upper story of one of Wall Street's biggest firms, where bankers and corporate CEOS are discussing the financial and economic meltdown in a luxurious suite. They are drinking whiskey, smoking cigars, and eating caviar as they talk. There are faint echoes of protests down on the street way below them, where a group of angry workers, students, and the unemployed is gathering.

Narrator: Ladies and gentlemen, I give you the Wall Street elites in a suite and the Occupy Wall Street protestors in the street.

Occupy Wall Street Participants: WE ARE THE 99 PERCENT! YOU ARE THE 1 PERCENT! Your name is CORPORATE GREED!

Protester 1: Show me what democracy looks like!

General Assembly: THIS is what democracy looks like!

Protestor 2: How do we fix the deficit?

General Assembly: End the war and tax the rich!

Protester 3: WE ARE SICK OF SUFFERING WITHOUT HOMES AND JOBS WHILE YOU EAT YOUR CAVIAR AND SMOKE YOUR CIGARS!

Protester 4: Mike check.

General Assembly: Mike check.

Protestor 4: People before profit. Regime change begins at home!

General Assembly: People before profit. Regime change begins at home.

Protester 4: Compassion for all, even the 1 Percent!

General Assembly [*waving their fingers, in sign of agreement*]: Compassion for all, even the 1 percent!

Yourall Fired: You can see the kind of nonsense we are hearing from the streets. They seem like a cult, don't they? But don't be concerned. They will fade away as it gets colder out there.

Warren Buffer: Let's admit that we are the 1 percent and we've done pretty well. The rest haven't.

Donal Trumpcard: Spare me, Buffer. Let them try to Occupy Trumpcard Tower. Then I'll teach them a little about how real democracy works.

Chamberpot Commerce: These idiots think they know more than we do, but really they know nothing about the way the economy works. But that doesn't stop them from forming their mobs. It's disgusting.

Goldman Sacker: Let us not get distracted by this nonsense from the wretches on the streets. Damn right we've been making out well in this "Great Recession." I got bailed out by our boys in Washington, including both Bush and Obama. So did most of you. Those lazy incompetent bums on the street aren't doing so well. Of course, it's their own fault. The economy is weeding out these unworthy folk as we go global. We don't need most Americans, especially THESE SCUM [*pointing to protestors below*].

Chamberpot Commerce: Our companies are far more profitable if we downsize at home, replace our workers with robots, and outsource to all those cheap labor sites in Asia and Latin America. I mean, look at this [*pulls out ridiculously fat wallet and shakes it*].

Maura Lee Bankrupt: You think that's impressive? [*pulls out even bigger purse*] Size *does* matter, boys. Bank of America. Land of the Fee ... I mean Free. As the only woman here, let me agree strongly with Sacker. Our responsibility is to our global shareholders, not US workers. We are Bank of America, and that means we don't need American workers. Only American profits. Don't call us cutters. Call us creatives!

Sendu Packing: Yeah, we just don't need Americans anymore. I like my workers MADE IN CHINA [*using stamping hand motion*].

Mutt Banecapital: Let's be honest. I just like firing people. Period.

Bill Gateskeeper: Not only that but we are helping the world's poor in this Great Transition. True, American workers are paying the price. But in shifting the American economic infrastructure and American jobs to poor countries such as China, India, and Vietnam, we are helping the rest of the world develop. It makes our companies rich, and it has made me the world's richest man. But it also set the table to finally bring the rest of the world out of the desperate poverty so many suffer in Asia, Africa, and Latin America.

Chamberpot Commerce: Gateskeeper, you're a dreamer and sentimentalist. It really comes down to basic economics. There's no comparative advantage for business in America any more. The only legitimate goal of our companies is to make money for our shareholders. We can only do that by investing where labor is cheap, regulations are low, taxes are nonexistent, and governments are too weak to stop us. So it's not rocket science and it's not Gateskeeper's idealism. We are simply doing what good capitalist business people have always done. Go where the profit is.

Enthusiastic applause from the CEOS drinking their whisky, smoking their cigars, and eating their caviar. Protest echoes from the street below:
WE WANT JOBS! WE WANT JOBS! WE WANT JOBS! DEMOCRACY NOW! DEMOCRACY NOW!

Protester 1: We will, *we will* occupy Wall Street!

General Assembly: We will, *we will* occupy Wall Street!

Protester 3: We are the 99! You are the 1!

General Assembly: We are the 99! You are the 1!

Protester 4: It's simple. STOP CORPORATE GREED! Create jobs for all! Even for the 1 Percent!

General Assembly [*waving fingers in agreement*]: It's simple. Stop corporate greed! Create jobs for all! Even for the 1 Percent!

Chamberpot Commerce: Listen to these smelly, pathetic mobs. They don't want to work—they'd rather smoke dope and chant together. When was the last time they took a shower? If we gave into these parasites—who just want to be coddled on welfare and Obamacare—the whole global economy would eventually crash. OCCUPY MY ASS!

CEOs in unison start chanting: We are the 1 percent! We are the 1 percent!

Donal Trumpcard: Get soooooome!

Mutt Banecapital [*throws pink slips out of the window*]: Here, take some of these, free of charge.

Buffer and Gateskeeper look somber.

Robber Rubiner: My name may be Robber, but don't call me a thief. This shift of production outside the US will ultimately help America too, even those misguided mobs down there. Our outsourcing will discipline workers and the unemployed to educate themselves and work harder, and restrain them from joining unions and making unreasonable demands. And our free trade agreements will bring new export markets, allowing eventually for more workers to be hired at home. When most work goes abroad, billions of Asian, Latin, and African workers will demand the high-quality goods that newly motivated American workers can provide.

Sendu Packing: Yes, I've always said that cutting jobs is the only sensible strategy for long-term job building. That's why I call myself a jobs-builder.

Mutt Banecapital: You have to cut some jobs to save others. Especially to save ours.

Warren Buffer: Packing and Banecapital, there you go again. The truth is, you're destroying the very economic infrastructure that made America great. The official unemployment rate is

hovering around 10 percent, but the real rate is 20 percent. You call that creative destruction? I call it massacre. And when you massacre, you're going to get protests like those people gathering beneath us on the streets. Listen to them:
Shouts from the street of JOBS NOW! JUSTICE NOW! JOBS NOW! JUSTICE NOW!

Chamberpot Commerce: Buffer, you're a bleeding heart billionaire. Chill out! Leave it to us and our friends in Washington to deal with the mobs.

Goldman Sacker: I'm with you, Chamberpot and Packing. All of us here are just involved in creative destruction.

Maura Lee Bankrupt: Here, here, Sacker! We American bankers will be the engine of the global economy. That is now our sacred mission because it will pay the highest return to our one true constituency: our shareholders. And of course, ourselves [*nods head toward huge purse again and winks*].
Smiles and nods all around, even as the noise on the street gets louder. They ignore the chants getting louder: JOBS NOW! JOBS NOW! JOBS NOW!

Warren Buffer: It doesn't add up, Sacker. Everyone knows this is the "Great Jobless Recession." There are now millions of Americans who don't feel needed and struggle to survive, even though they have much to offer. I wouldn't call that efficiency. It stinks!

Bill Gatekeeper: And Buffer is not even counting all the other surplus people besides the officially employed. What about the people warehoused in prisons, put in the military, admitted into higher education because they couldn't find jobs? Our Great Recession has made it clear to everyone that we have a massive crisis. It's unacceptable.

Ghost of Surplus People [*as if murmuring to himself*]: Yes, unacceptable, unacceptable, unacceptable. . .

Chamberpot Commerce [*ignoring the ghost*]: Come off it, Buffer and Gatekeeper. You're the richest men in the world. Both Bush and Obama bailed us all out. The public sees us as job-creators, or, as our Republican flunkies—uh, I mean allies—call us, "the jobs-makers." And all these surplus rabble down on the street are evidence that capitalism is doing its job, weeding out the parasites, making room for the more ambitious and talented workers all over the world.

Mutt Banecapital: Forget the Bush/Obama bailouts. Who needs the government? It only stands in our way. We private creative innovators once built the Interstate Highway System and the

Hoover Dam. Today, there's so much government interference, we can't even drill for oil in Manhattan.

Bill Gateskeeper: Wait a minute. Didn't the federal government build the highway system and the Hoover Dam?

Warren Buffer: Of course it did. And much of the Internet too, not to mention the transistor and computer developed in the Pentagon.

Mutt Banecapital: Well, OK, let the government do the developing and we'll make the profit. But don't tell anybody [*winks*].

Robber Rubiner: Gentlemen, of course we need the government to bail us out. We are responsible for a global system now, not just the United States. We on Wall Street are financing development everywhere in the world with the help of Uncle Sam. But we can't favor American workers over less expensive and harder working people abroad.

Larry Summit: Speaking as an economist, I can assure all you gentlemen that Rubiner is right on the mark. Globalization— and the technological revolution that made it possible—makes millions of American workers redundant. But we can't coddle them or we undermine the entire global capitalist economy.

Ghost of Surplus Past: Summit, your idiocy is killing me. Again. Those crowds on the street are going to grow, as you fire millions of more American workers in the next ten years. Most working Americans are beginning to realize that the people in this room have no need at all for them. They feel like permanent surplus people—and they're going to come after you. As they say in Texas, it's going to get "pretty ugly" for a lot of you.

Bill Gateskeeper: Summit, as the richest man in the world, I hardly need your lectures about how capitalism demands a hard-headed approach. I've been ruthless in my business career, and I'm all for globalization and technology. When I founded the personal computer, I was being a capitalist revolutionary, making the information-age technology possible and bringing new possibilities to billions of people. But I never believed that my PC would bring down the American worker. In fact, I still don't see it that way. We just have to educate the American worker to compete in a global information age. America doesn't have to have a huge pool of surplus people. Those poor people down on the street can be reintegrated into society, if we train them in the technologies of the future. We need new technical training institutes, vocational schools. I'm not talking about more liberal arts schools, where the troublemakers tend to come from.

Chamberpot Commerce: Gateskeeper, I guess only the richest men in the world can afford to have your kind of idealism. Most of those parasites down there want something for nothing. They want fat welfare checks and big unemployment checks. But we have a world of workers dying to work for us. American workers are too spoiled. Let those parasites [*pointing to people on street*] emigrate and see how workers in China and Vietnam are busting their butts for us.

Bill Gateskeeper: I care about people, but I'm making a business case to help our capitalist system. If the majority of Americans become surplus people, they will become dangerously angry and uncontrollable. Chamberpot, you dunce, I'm trying to save you from yourself. Disposing of the mass of Americans is suicide for you and the capitalist system that we both believe in. We need Americans to believe that we truly care about them. They must trust us, thinking that we want their creative contribution and consumption of our products. God save us, if they lose that faith in us.

Sendu Packing: Gateskeeper, the simple truth is that the new globalization means people all over the US are not going to be needed. Even if they are educated, there are hundreds of millions of well-educated Chinese and Indians who will work as skillfully as Americans, but at one-fourth their wages. There's no way around that simple truth—and education won't solve it. A few may lose faith in us, but we will convince most of them that we are still looking out for them.

Chamberpot Commerce: You're right, Packing. But you know we have more subtle ways of dealing with the unworthy. Most of them are not down on the streets. They are home, depressed. Our job is just to make sure they fret at home and feel their own personal responsibility and inadequacy. The system gave them every opportunity.

Maura Lee Bankrupt: Yeah, and the cream still will always rise to the top. Just look at me. I'm a woman, and where else in the world can a woman make it in high finance? I'm living proof of the marvels of our opportunistic society.

Loud applause and big smiles from all the assembled CEOs.

Goldman Sacker: Drink up and eat more caviar. There are a few trouble makers down there, but most surplus people don't see us as their enemy. They see us as the only ones who can save them by hiring them. We've perfected our national rhetoric about the land of opportunity. The surplus people are true believers, just like most of the rest of Americans. They believe everyone is responsible for himself and that the outsourced and downsized just don't have the drive or talent to make it. They want to be us because we ARE the American Dream.

Donal Trumpcard: Who wouldn't want to be me? They all do!!!

Chamberpot Commerce: Yeah, they understand everyone is responsible for themselves. They realize that us big money people on Wall Street work twenty hours a day and deserve every freakin' dollar we make.

Warren Buffer: I can't buy into this happy crap. A jobless America is just greed and arrogance, and, I must say, a bit of lack of patriotism, as we see it from Nebraska.

Larry Summit: This isn't about patriotism. It's about the laws of global supply and demand. Let me explain.

The room becomes quiet, all heads turned toward Summit.

Larry Summit: Globalization today is different, built around outsourcing rather than insourcing.

Donal Trumpcard: What the hell does that mean? These fuzzy-headed academics make me nuts.

Larry Summit: In earlier centuries, when powerful countries such as England created their own global economy (which they called the British Empire), it brought jobs into England rather than outsourcing them to the British colonies. For example, take India, the crown jewel of the British Empire. Before the Brits took over India, the Indians had developed quite a strong domestic textile industry. But to build their own textile industry, the Brits took over India, made it a colony, and shut down the Indian local industry. They built up their own British textile plants in England and "insourced" the Indian jobs into Britain. That is the exact opposite of what US globalization is doing today. It is shutting down industries in the US and relocating them in India and other poorer countries.

Chamberpot Commerce: Sounds nuts to me. Why didn't the Brits outsource?

Larry Summit: The Brits needed to build up their industrial infrastructure. One way to do it was shut down all competitors abroad and create a monopoly at home. Also, the Indians were seen as primitives who could not be utilized as productive workers. All in all, the task of globalization at the beginning of industrial capitalism was very different than now. It was to build the infrastructure of a modern capitalist economy in the first country where it could succeed, in the country which had the best prospects of being a showcase: one showing that capitalism can create prosperity beyond anyone's dreams.

Warren Buffer: Well, Summit, you may be right about the Brits, but that doesn't justify outsourcing our entire industrial infrastructure today. We still ought to be focused on how we can sustain our economy at home.

Larry Summit: About a century ago, American business created the world's most efficient industrial infrastructure. But now the global economy is the priority, as Robber Rubiner said. The only US corporations that will survive are those that move their operations abroad or replace their workers at home with robots. Going abroad is mainly for cheaper labor but also because regulations and taxes are less burdensome abroad and the workers over there are far more desperate and obedient. Moreover, the world economy will thrive only when a new balance is achieved. The economic infrastructure of the rest of the world will grow and become more competitive with American infrastructure, spurring more competition and efficiency. Brilliant Americans will do just fine. Did I mention that I won the prize for America's most brilliant economist?

Ghost of Surplus People Past: You are devils, destroying America! Can't you hear those yells of pain out in the street?

Sendu Packing: Ignore that spook [*dismissing him with his hand*]. Human pain is tragic, but it diverts us from seeing the magic of the global market.

Warren Buffer: Summit, I'm afraid you've got your head stuck in the ivy academic clouds. There's a tipping point where the hollowing out of the US infrastructure goes too far. Then, the US will never compete, especially with the new dynamic infrastructures and companies in India, China, and Brazil. You're risking the permanent decline, even collapse, of the US middle classes, since there will be nothing to support them here. We'll all just be saddled with huge expenses for crime, prisons to hold these people, or a huge welfare budget, even if we shrink welfare payments just to barely keep them alive.

Bill Gateskeeper: Summit, the information revolution that I began is going to empower everyone eventually. Everyone with a computer can become a global entrepreneur. Everyone can connect with jobs or customers all over the world. American workers are no exception. If our government invests in education and jobs, which you guys except Buffer are abandoning, we can employ nearly all Americans again.

Larry Summit: Yes, Gateskeeper, government and technology can create jobs, but they also destroy jobs. The effects of your information revolution on jobs is different than what happened during the industrial revolution. The industrial revolution created manufacturing jobs and infrastructure in the developed world. But the information revolution is helping dismantle that

Western industrial structure and making it possible to rebuild it more efficiently in Asia and elsewhere.

Bill Gateskeeper: But my technology is the foundation of a new postindustrial high-skill high-tech infrastructure in the US. That is where American surplus people can find jobs, if we have the political will to train them.

Chamberpot Commerce: Gateskeeper, you're a genius, but your philanthropic mission is clouding your business savvy. Software engineers from developing nations are happy to take the jobs of our most talented people for very low wages. And we are more than happy to hire them.

Ghost of Surplus People Past: Chamberpot is cruel and greedy, but he is honest enough to tell the truth. Surplus people in the US know that it is not just factory jobs but office and high-tech jobs that are being outsourced. We know that getting an education in America can win you a diploma that isn't worth as much as the piece of paper it's printed on. Sure, educated people are currently finding more jobs in the US than school dropouts. But the handwriting is on the wall. Having a degree in the future won't mean squat.

Larry Summit: The truth is hard to sort out. Yes, the information age technology is a huge threat to millions of jobs in the US. But it also creates new jobs for the most educated and entrepreneurial American workers of the future. America still has the best universities and the best high-tech companies in the world. These could be the foundation of a new postindustrial economic infrastructure in the US. So, Gateskeeper is right that technology will not wipe out all American jobs, although it will certainly make finding jobs very difficult for people who don't have a lot of digital-age education and a lot of high motivation.

Ghost of Surplus People Past: You're all in denial. Ask those people down in the streets. A lot of them have computer degrees or MBAs. A lot of them are college graduates in the humanities and social sciences. They paid $50,000 a year for their degree, and then they can't find jobs with high enough wages to pay back their student loans. In fact, many can't find any jobs at all.

Young People Shouting from the Streets: WE STUDIED HARD. WHERE ARE OUR JOBS? WHERE IS OUR AMERICAN DREAM?

Donal Trumpcard [*opens window and yells out*]: Didn't I fire half of you on season one?

Larry Summit: Yeah, I recognize some of you. You didn't do a day's work in college.

Chamberpot Commerce [*yelling out the window*]: You over-educated kids are spoiled brats. My grandma works harder than you and she's dead! [*turning back to the others*] Let these bleeding-heart liberals learn something about the real world. If they are entrepreneurial, a lot of them will take jobs in Asia and Latin America, places that can use some of their skills. And there are still service jobs in this country that can't be outsourced, like aides in hospitals or nursing homes. That's a good way for them to show they really believe in their bleeding-heart liberal values.

Goldman Sacker: Yeah, and If I dangle enough money in front of them, we'll see how committed they are to that bleeding-heart mush.

Donal Trumpcard: Right, Sacker. The mobs below should go home, take a shower, and get a job, any job. There's a reason they're called the slacker generation.

Bill Gateskeeper: Trumpcard, you're writing off a whole generation of US kids. If we don't put their real skills to work in my information-age economy, the US will go into permanent decline.

Chamberpot Commerce: Gateskeeper, stop talking that philanthropy dribble and be a businessman. Our responsibility is not to America or any other country. It is to our global shareholders. Our only mission is to maximize profits for them and, of course, for ourselves. We can only discharge that responsibility if we shift production abroad and take advantage of all the job-savings technology that you and Packing have pioneered.

Bill Gateskeeper: I don't think I need your advice, Chamberpot. Philanthropy is good business. We need a prosperous, secure, stable society to invest in. My foundations are intended to guarantee that.

Goldman Sacker: Chamberpot is right. Our banks don't fly any national flag. We are global players. Of course, because we are very advanced in financial services here in the US, world banking will still have a place in America. We continue to invent the new most creative financial instruments in the world. That's why 40 percent of our economy is now based on financial services. We are number one. We bankroll the world.

Shouts from the street: You bastard bankers! We trusted you, and you gambled away our national wealth and played Russian roulette with our loans and credit. You destroyed our future!

Donal Trumpcard [*yelling out window*]: Show me your birth certificates!

Goldman Sacker: Of course, when you hear those idiots in the streets, you realize we do depend on the US government to control these malcontents and parasites down there. We must have law and order in the US and in the world. That is the most important function of the US government, and we give a lot of money to American politicians to carry out that role. We can't have mob rule.

Maura Lee Bankrupt: Lock 'em up. Lock 'em up.

Applause from the CEOs around the room. They refill their glasses and get more caviar.

Bill Gateskeeper: It is cheaper and more effective to placate them and win their support than beat them.

Robber Rubiner: Gateskeeper, I think Sacker raises an important point. While our responsibility is to our global shareholders, we still need the US government. Not just for law and order. It also provides the favorable regulatory environment for us to continue our financial innovations. And it provides us with bailouts when we need them. We needed the Fed to keep the global economy from crashing over the last few years.

Chamberpot Commerce [*laughing*]: Let's not go too far with this government socialism, Rubiner. Sure, we rely on the government for lots of things; we know we couldn't survive without it. But we can't let that dirty little secret out of this room. Imagine if the Tea Partiers supporting us heard.

Laughter breaks out from the CEOs all over the room.

Larry Summit: There's another serious problem. If we want to keep making our huge profits, we need people to buy. We have built a consumer capitalism. Our workers take low wages and even periods of unemployment because their identity is based on their consumption, not their work. But they need to be able to continue to consume at high levels for us to get big profits. That lavish consumption is very difficult for surplus people.

Goldman Sacker: That is why we created credit cards. Easy money, easy debt. The American way [*peering out the window*]. OK, maybe we took it a little too far, perhaps as our current crisis showed. But our economy needs consumers. And as surplus people fall in and out of the labor force in the US, they will continue to rely on easy credit. We will have to provide that, and only the US government can back up our loans and credit schemes.

Shouts from the street: You loaned us money, told us to go shopping, but took our jobs away. We can't pay our credit card debt. Now we're bankrupt, you bastards!

Donal Trumpcard [*yelling out window*]: And my casinos took your money too!

Robber Rubiner: The mob down there must be policed and silenced, that is for sure. But the problem of surplus people does threaten our consumer capitalism. Seventy percent of our economy depends on domestic demand for goods by our consumers. We are going to have to continue to find ways to get surplus people to consume, until we slowly build up our exports to the point that consumers in other countries will buy our goods. Then, we won't depend on American consumers, as we do now.

Chamberpot Commerce: I agree with you there, Rubiner. As we outsource, we will build the purchasing power of people abroad. They will buy from our companies and keep our profits high. And as our export economy grows, we won't have to listen to the silly arguments of those liberal economists such as Paul Krupman, who spout the outdated economic theory of John Maynard Keynes and say we need the government to invest in American social welfare and surplus people, to stimulate our economy. How many times do I have to say it? The welfare of the American people is not our responsibility. As our country's second-greatest president, Calvin Coolidge, said, "the business of America is business."

Goldman Sacker: And those profits are going to come from both production and consumption where most of the world is: in China, India, and other parts of Asia and Latin America. As their people become more prosperous, we will need Americans less and less.

Larry Summit: Yes, that is the future, but don't be too hard on the Keynesians. There is a long period in which we will continue to need the US government to keep the US economy alive. You can't have a complete collapse of the American economy or you'll get a revolution. So you need the government to spend just enough to keep the surplus people feeling some hope.

Chamberpot Commerce: There's truth to that, Summit. We talk about jobs, jobs, jobs, but we can't tell the truth to the US public. We need to pretend that we have some continuing interest in US jobs or the hypocrisy will look obvious.

Warren Buffer: You gentlemen ought to be ashamed of yourselves. You're admitting the hypocrisy of your PR. You swear your religion is to create jobs. But you're really just interested in money. You really don't give a damn about jobs. You just want to keep fooling the public. It's dangerously wrong. Unless we provide for the American people, we can't have a stable investment climate.

Robber Rubiner: Buffer, Buffer, you're being unfair to Chamberpot. He'll support some government infrastructure investment because he really does need some US workers to keep their jobs. Otherwise, the American economy will collapse, with no consumption and open rebellion by the surplus mass.

Larry Summit: Right again, Rubiner. The action is going to be in Asia, but America has to be propped up for now. Asia isn't ready yet. Technologically, the US is still the leader in innovation. Militarily, only the US can police the world. Politically, only the US can create the stability the global economy needs.

Chamberpot Commerce: There you go again, Summit. Yeah, throw a few bones, like Obama has done, to the surplus rabble. We do need government to subsidize us with the billions in tax breaks, contracts, and depreciation they give us. But we want Americans to be Tea Partiers, not Occupiers. What can be better for us than to have people who can never be rich identify with us and blame all their troubles on government, the very institution that can save them?

Ghost of Surplus People Past: There's another problem with brainiac Summit's Keynesianism. As the US has dismantled its infrastructure, and rebuilt it abroad, it has undermined the ability of government spending to do much. Especially given the ridiculously small amount of government infrastructure and job spending that the rich people in this room will permit. We know, as surplus people, that Obama has been throwing bones at us, as if they were red meat. But we need the government to get serious about job creation at home. That means direct creation of massive numbers of jobs, yes, by the government. That's the real function of government in a nation of surplus people.

Chamberpot Commerce: This ghost sounds like a Marxist, a communist. No wonder he's dead!
Appreciative laughter from the CEOs all around the room.
From the streets, louder voices that sound closer to the Tower:
WE WANT JOBS NOW! WE WANT JOBS NOW!
CEOs around the room put down their glasses. Some look worried.

Warren Buffer: Maybe we should be listening to the ghost, even if he sounds a bit Marxist. Americans know government is coddling everyone in this room. And they know we are undermining this country by letting our infrastructure rot while we build our new gleaming infrastructure in China and Brazil and even Vietnam. If there is no infrastructure, the United States will not have the collateral needed to be a good credit risk. If we don't fix the problem, a little revolutionary fever could spread among the surplus masses.

Chamberpot Commerce: Come off it, Buffer. The government hasn't been coddling us. It's been regulating us to death. And as for the surplus rabble, don't worry. Our country knows how to control revolutions. We've been doing it for years around the world with our military, and, believe me, we know how to police the unruly surplus rabble at home.

Donal Trumpcard [*waving a huge American flag*]: We are the world's policemen. Thank God!

Chamberpot Commerce: We've got plenty of prisons. More important, we've convinced even most of the surplus Americans that capitalism and globalization are the only solutions to their problems. The revolutionary fever is mostly among the Far Right Tea Partiers, not among the Leftist Occupiers organizing those protests below us. The Tea Partiers want the government to do even less to help them economically and want to give us billionaires an even freer hand to run things as we see fit.

Bill Gateskeeper: Part of the solution may be to encourage our surplus Americans to work abroad. Young people are idealists. They will work in the Peace Corps or the Marine Corps.

Chamberpot Commerce: Notice this, they see joining the marines, fighting, killing, and dying to build the empire, to make globalization and outsourcing possible, to secure our investments, as being idealist.

Ghost of Surplus People Past: You have created an Emigration Nation. You're fighting off immigration even when emigration is becoming the real danger—so many of our best people in ten or twenty years will leave America, a reverse brain drain.

Chamberpot Commerce: It's one world now. We'll keep the best and most ambitious workers here, and emigration will weed out the surplus. Forget Marx, Ghost. We're living by the laws of Mr. Darwin and Mr. Malthus. Survival of the fittest is the rule now.

Warren Buffer: Nonsense, Chamberpot. Of course, we're going to invest and manufacture globally. But there's plenty of work to reconstruct our infrastructure at home. The ghost is right that his people on the street can be put to work rebuilding our energy infrastructure, saving our rotting roads, bridges, and sewers, and renovating our schools. Green jobs may be the most important solution to the problem of a mass surplus workforce in the US. I just hope it is not too late, that infrastructure is not already too far gone to repair.

Chamberpot Commerce: Now you sound like Obama, Buffer. Are you saying we should be bringing Al Gore, with all his scare tactics about global warming, into this room? Climate change is just code for big government and jobs-killing regulation. Thank God the American people have been smart enough not to fall for this green quackery. They just want cheap gas at the pump and real jobs. They know the laws of supply and demand and they know socialists in green uniforms when they see them. Even the surplus folks want to work in the private sector, not in some short-term government make-work.

Groans from the room. From the street:
DOWN WITH WALL STREET! DOWN WITH GLOBALIZATION! DOWN WITH JOBLESS CAPITALISM!
There is banging on the doors of the Tower. The crowd has closed in. Some are throwing rocks and breaking windows. Suddenly the lights flicker.

Goldman Sacker: Gentlemen, excuse me while I call security and the mayor. Remember, Mayor Bloombug recently warned us that the educated unemployed young people were getting restless and some might take to the streets because they can't find jobs. He compared them to the young protesters in Cairo, Egypt. He sympathized with them, but he's on our side and knows when it's time to get the mob under control. It'll only take a minute. Please have another drink and eat up!

Scene 2: Five Years Earlier than Scene 1

Ghost of Surplus People Past [*in Packing's bedroom*]: Packing, I have to interrupt this little dream you've been having.
Sendu Packing: You again? Get lost.
Ghost of Surplus People Past: Look at you. You're too agitated to sleep anyway. You're thrashing around so much that you have knocked your silk pillow cases onto your beautiful marble bedroom floor.
Sendu Packing: That's because there's a ghost in my room that won't shut up. Don't you have anything better to do? Leave me alone!
Ghost of Surplus People Past: Have you no soul? Don't you wonder why there are mobs of people begging for your head? If you really want to understand why the people below are coming after you, you have to go back to President Reagan's regime change in America. Packing, welcome to the Reagan revolution and a dinner in 2005 that you've conveniently forgotten.
Bright stage lights. We see a plush dining room on the 45th floor of the Tower of Power. Sitting around the table are CEOs who dominated the Bush and Reagan years, while presidents and other political leaders, and also a few labor leaders and columnists, make an appearance. The champagne is flowing freely, and filet mignon, roast duck, and scalloped potatoes grace a massive and lavish circular dining table.

Sendu Packing: I think I remember this dinner. It was September 2005. There are all my old friends and some people I wish I had never met! But, Ghost, I've seen enough. Is this real? Am I dreaming again?

Ghost of Surplus People Past: Patience, fool. It's not me that is really haunting you. It's the homeless and hungry on the street. You already knew at this dinner that your outsourcing of your computer factories was robbing millions of Americans of jobs. You knew that your manufacturing CEO buddies were creating industrial ghost towns in the Rust Belt from Detroit to Toledo. The surplus industrial workers were living in shuttered warehouses and locked-up factories, with no other place to go. And even your high-tech workers in Silicon Valley and around Boston were getting nervous, as they saw you outsource programming jobs to software engineers in China and India. Americans were getting anxious, feeling in their bones that America was in decline. That made you nervous too.

Sendu Packing: Not at all. I thought my technological revolution was making everybody better off. Since 1980, I have been grateful to Ronald Reagan for his appreciation of the creative American entrepreneur, such as myself [*picking up a mirror and admiring himself*]. He knew our potential.

Ghost of Surplus People Past: Speak of the devil!
Ronald Reagan appears on stage, riding a horse and wearing a cowboy hat. Cue angelic music.

Maura Lee Bankrupt [*primping for Reagan*]: Oh my god!

Donal Trumpcard [*mumbling, jealous of Reagan*]: My hair's still better.

Ronald Reagan: Now, what was I saying? Oh yeah! It is morning in America. What's all this talk about gloom and doom? America's best days are ahead of us as long as we have the will to prevail. We have the most creative corporations and bankers in the world, without a lot of unions and regulations to hold them back. I made sure of that, by talking about the evil of big government, both in the Soviet Union and the US. Now almost every American realizes big government is bad and that all those New Deal social welfare programs led the nation to oblivion or communism. We have a military arsenal that nobody would mess with, and we let the world know America is free to go anywhere it wants, anytime it wants. The only thing that can defeat the United States is the United States: I'm talking about those liberal elites from within who hold our values in contempt. They're all over the government, the university, and the mass media. I say this as someone who knows, who comes from Hollywood. The liberal elites are parasites who never ran a business or engaged in productive work. All they do is critique, belittle, and undermine the spirit of our county. They breed doubt in America's free market capitalism and its inherent goodness.

Chamberpot Commerce: Mr. Reagan, I think I can speak for all of us when I say thank you. For this, we all tip our hats to you.

Assembled group stands up to honor Reagan:

Hip, hip hurrah for Reagan! Hip, hip hurrah for Reagan!

Everybody clangs their champagne glasses.

Chamberpot Commerce: Let's remember that before Reagan, the US truly was in decline. To fully appreciate what Reagan did, we at the Chamberpot of Commerce prepared a PowerPoint presentation:

Slide One [*image of hippy smoking pot in VW bug*]

Chamberpot Commerce: The crazy young radicals of the 1960s almost undermined the American free market system and belief in the American way.

Slide Two [*extreme chart depicting economic growth in Germany and Japan in comparison to US*]

Chamberpot Commerce: And in the 1970s, the Japanese and Europeans were moving rapidly to exploit American weakness and generosity. While the US was spending on the military to protect the whole free world from communism, the Japanese and Europeans were building VWs and fancy electronic gadgets. They were free-riding on us and trying to get a competitive edge, and without Reagan it might have worked.

Slide Three [*image of Reagan on a horse with a billy club, striking an air traffic control tower*]

Chamberpot Commerce: He turned back the wave of the 1960s. He made clear that Americans would have to work for a living in the new global economy. No more union bosses or welfare queens or free riders. His first act as president was to fire all the air traffic controllers and bust their greedy union. Reagan stood up for the creatives and the productives, and he showed that these 1960s hippies and crony union bosses were just lazy and self-centered, looking for a handout from government, the same way they got handouts from their permissive parents who had read the child-rearing liberal books of Dr. Benjamin Spock, who actually led them to resist the draft.

Sendu Packing: Mr. Reagan, you were a patriot but also the best kind of free marketer. You broke down the trade barriers, ended silly notions about loyalty to coddled and unionized American workers, and used the US military to open the world to the creatives in this room.

Ronald Reagan: Well, I'm not one to boast, but I am pretty great!

Donal Trumpcard: Well, I still have a better looking wife!

Warren Buffer: Which one?

Chamberpot Commerce: Mr. Reagan, you gave us tax breaks when we shifted production abroad; you made the world our oyster.

Maura Lee Bankrupt: And I loooovvveee oysters! [*loudly eats an oyster*]

Larry Summit: As the world's smartest economist—that's got a nice ring to it—let me speak for all of us. We understood the value of globalization and international free trade. That's why we helped both the Democrats and Republicans encourage corporations to go global. We know the laws of comparative advantage and the necessity of free trade and a fully globalized economy. This was just Economics 101. Mr. Reagan, you may not have my PhD, but you knew what you were doing.

Ronald Reagan: All this flattery is making me hungry. I'm gonna go grab a bite with Newt.

Ronald Reagan exits stage.

Chamberpot Commerce: What a president!

Sendu Packing: What a guy!

Maura Lee Bankrupt: What a stallion....the horse, I mean.

Nelson Rockefeller appears, grabbing oysters off of Maura Lee Bankrupt's tray.

Nelson Rockefeller: Let me add something since I am older than most of you. Forgive me; I'm going to give you a history lesson.

Maura Lee Bankrupt [*poofs her hair*]: Well, he is the .00001 percent....

Nelson Rockefeller: I ask you to remember my era, in the 1970s, before Mr. Reagan became president. The truth is that the United States went into economic decline, after the costs of the Vietnam War and the rise of Europe and Japan. We must now recognize and accept that fact. We cannot build globalization on our own—here I differ from some of you. We must work with the Europeans and the Japanese (and now the Chinese) to jointly reorganize world management. My family helped form a Trilateral Commission—America, Europe, and Japan—to deal with the problem. Clearly, a major source of the trouble in America is that workers, especially educated and unionized workers infected by the 1960s revolts, feel too entitled. They are ungrateful and biting the hand that feeds them. They are trying to interfere with our prerogative to run our corporations and to run the world, which we have created, as we see fit. There is excessive democracy, a democratic distemper, that must be contained. The problem is worldwide. Ever since the Vietnam debacle, respect for the United States has been declining. You see, Mr. Reagan is right, we do need a military, second to none, and must spend all that is necessary to maintain it. But this requires restoring deference to authority and reawakening patriotism. We must get the American people to agree that we have to spend more on armaments as they accept a declining standard of living, while corporate profits soar. For this, we needed a communicator, an advertiser, maybe even someone who was once an actor. That is the role Mr. Reagan so brilliantly played, even though he sometimes overplayed the John Wayne part and didn't realize the need to work closely with our European, Japanese, and even Chinese partners.

Kochaine Brothers [*dressed like Tweedle Dee and Tweedle Dum, speaking in unison*]: Listen to what Reagan proposed, Rocky: More money for us billionaires, lower taxes, fewer regulations, with no conditions. You old East Coast Establishment elites never truly appreciated what Reagan has done for you and all of us. He opened the world to us by crushing the unions and creating the trade agreements and organizations that ensure us huge global profits. He subsidized our shift to production abroad. He won the support of the lower classes by making America the Great Superpower again and telling them that money given to us will trickle down to them, but hasn't done anything that forces us to share with them.

Ronald Reagan returns from lunch.

Ronald Reagan: Man, that Newt can eat!

Kochaine Brothers [*still in unison*]: Welcome back, Mr. President, thank God. Actually, the hard truth is that maintaining factories in America has gotten too expensive. Now we must use Reagan's free trade and tax policies as the incentive to close the remaining American steel mills and move production to where labor is cheap, where we don't have to worry about environment or occupational health and safety standards, where the people will be grateful for the opportunity we are giving them.

Warren Buffer: In America, factories are closing, inner cities are being abandoned. The jobs that gave blue-collar workers access to a middle-class life style are disappearing. The American dream is becoming an illusion. Rather than wealth trickling down, the gap between rich and non-rich is growing. This, my friends, is the real legacy of Regan. Wake up!

Ronald Reagan: Buffer, my friend, it's always morning in America! My real legacy is more prosperity and more billionaires like you. The streets of the global economy are paved with gold.

Warren Buffer: Yes, there are more billionaires. And I like being one of them. But will I be able to keep my money if salaries are not enough to meet the mortgage or even raise a down payment?
Paul Krupman appears on stage.

Paul Krupman: My invitation to this party must've gotten lost in the mail. As a Nobel Prize–winning economist I have to add my voice to Buffer's and Gateskeeper's. I know many of you don't appreciate me, but you better listen. The country is in grave economic crisis. Consumer debt is rising along with government debt. As Buffer just said, that is very dangerous not just for the US but for the world economy. Deficits are not a problem as long as they stimulate productivity. But Reagan-era policies created the wrong deficits and ran them up to the sky. Just like FDR did in the Depression, we must use the government immediately to reinvest in the US and rebuild America itself. If we don't see the positive functions of government intervention and invest billions of government stimulus in America, in jobs for the US surplus population to rebuild our nation, both the US economy and the global economy are doomed. The protesters in the street know this.

Kochaine Brothers [*in unison*]: Who let this coke head in? He's a communist, even though he calls himself a Keynesian.

Reagan's Horse: I know what it's like to have the 1 percent on my back.

Ronald Reagan: Hey, who feeds you? Stop talking. Krupman, you big-government liberals and New Dealers are really the selfish ones. You are only trying to soothe your conscience. You call yourself compassionate, but you really can't stand looking at the poor. You give them a bone and deny them the spark they need to uplift themselves. Let them feel the cost of laziness and they will have the motive to seek a better life. For some, homeless may be a transition they will have to endure on the way to independence. Government programs just breed dependency. Roosevelt may have had his fireside chats, but I will show you soon why I am called the Great Communicator.

Paul Krupman: With all due respect, Mr. President, you are a big government man yourself. You massively increased the deficits with huge government spending on the military and huge subsidies for the big corporations. You're not against big government—you created larger deficits than almost any president before you. You're just against big government spending for ordinary people. You're a champion of big government for corporations and the military.

Ronald Reagan: I'm so tired of the communist rhetoric that I feel sleepy again.

Lyndon Johnson appears on stage.

Lyndon Johnson: Nice pony, Reagan [*motioning to Reagan's horse*]. I guess everything *is* truly bigger in Texas. I know you all see me as a historical relic, but I too must speak. Reagan, you are not telling the truth. Krupman is right. When you say cut government, what you mean is cut the social safety net, not the huge corporate welfare safety net. You talk about prosperity, but for much of the population, it's the Great Depression all over again. You cut the welfare rolls, closed public housing, and brought back homelessness. As the number of boarded-up houses and business grows, those who can find someplace else to go, move. You need to listen to Krupman and follow my example. Create the Great Society! Save Social Security and my great creation, Medicare. If you are going to create all these surplus people, at least have the humanity to keep them alive in their old age.

Ronald Reagan [*waking up a bit*]: Krupman and Johnson, let me show you what the American people really want. I'm going to show you the true American spirit, what the real Americans believe.

The room becomes quiet and fades as the CEOS watch on television a view of Reagan on his horse, microphone in hand, on the streets. There are huge loud speakers all over a public plaza, with a big crowd on hand.

Ronald Reagan: Hard-working Americans, parasitical elitists have told us to trust in government more than in ourselves. They have tried to sap our strength. They have anointed themselves "social planners" and think they know how to manage our money better we can ourselves. The trouble we are in today comes from their misguided schemes. They have destroyed our faith in ourselves, made us afraid to act, and allowed the world to laugh at us. They have used the government to take wealth away from the very people who create it and give it to parasites like themselves. Their idea is to spread the wealth. In America, they call that idea "the welfare state"; in the Soviet Union, they call it "communism." They give your hard-earned money to people who don't work, who spend it on drugs, booze, and having babies they can't support. We all know welfare fraud is everywhere. Lazy people collect their welfare checks and then make more money, working under the table. Many even make more than you do. They have televisions, DVDs, lots of beer, and some ride around in Cadillacs. They are lazy and they want your jobs. They want affirmative action; they want to be hired before you, even though you are more qualified. They prey on America's conscience, especially white guilt. They tell us we owe them because their ancestors were slaves or were driven from this land where their ancestors lived before we did. They want the opportunities America offers without earning them and freely, illegally cross into California, Arizona, and Texas, as if they were once part of Mexico. Let's let the people who earn America's money use it, expunge the elitists, not coddle parasites and make America great again!

Protestors in the crowd replace their picket signs with American flags.

Protestors: USA! USA! Fight poverty! Work! Cut the government! Cut the parasites! America for Americans! Send the Native Americans back where they came from!

Donal Trumpcard appears in front of the crowd. He rips his shirt off to reveal his "muscles." Lights go back on in the dining room of the Tower of Power, where the conversation now continues as the TV image is turned off and Reagan rejoins the CEO in the conference room.

Chamberpot Commerce: Impressive, Reagan. You promised them nothing and brought them on our side. They identify with us, and our interest becomes their interest. They will see themselves as part of a great American nation. To protect what they have, they must fight the unappreciative, the lazy, the dark, the impure, the alien.

Kochaine Brothers [*in unison*]: Many immigrants today don't want to create; they want to take, use our services, our welfare, our medical care, our schools. Take take take.

Donal Trumpcard: Right. And these moochers are taking our jobs.

Chamberpot Commerce: Yes, Kochaine brothers, America for Americans. Let's appeal to the reawakened patriotic spirit and renew the "buy American" campaign. Of course, almost all Ford plants have moved to Canada, Mexico, and more exotic countries, but they are still American owned. Toyota and Honda have taken advantage of American workers, desperate for jobs, and built plants in Alabama, Mississippi, Indiana, Texas, and Ohio. Some subversives who want to build division among our people have said, "If you want to buy American, buy a Toyota." They neglect to point out that if you want the profit to go to Americans, buy Fords or Chryslers.

Paul Krupman: How effective do you think the "buy American" campaign will be when so little is actually made by American workers? Since the 1950s, the main thing made in America has been weapons. We have accelerated the production of nuclear weapons and missiles and stopped manufacturing cars, steel, and consumer electronics. True, Reagan provided a short-term boom for billionaires, but he undermined our long-term competitive advantage by demonizing government, unraveling our industrial infrastructure, and romanticizing the military. How many more CD or DVD players can you sell than MX missiles? How many more surplus Americans can we employ if we rebuild America instead of building our armaments to infinity?

Sound is heard: THUD!

Ronald Reagan [*waking up after falling asleep*]: That's the sound of the Soviet Union collapsing. See, my strategy worked. I accelerated the arms race, made them spend more on weapons than they could afford, drained their economy, and caused the evil empire to fall. The Soviet collapse—my great accomplishment—made globalization, a unified world market including the whole former Soviet bloc, part of the great American Empire, I mean, global economy.

Paul Krupman: It was more complex than that. The Soviet Union fell mostly because of its own internal corruption and authoritarianism.

Nelson Rockefeller: The fall of the Soviet Union leaves the United States as the world's only superpower. We won the cold war. We could use this opportunity to have a peace dividend, vastly reduce military spending, and use the savings to lower the deficits, rebuild civilian infrastructure, restore domestic industries, and shrink the gap between billionaires and ordinary American citizens. But that would require retooling and shifting resources. It may be the wisest policy, but it would mean sacrificing the short term for the long term. It would cost us billionaires. Why bother? Instead, let's find a new enemy who will provide a new excuse for a full war-scale economy.

Donal Trumpcard: Right on, Rocky. And now the Arabs have gotten pretty uppity. They are acting as if it is their oil and demanding too much tribute from Exxon, Mobil, and other Western petroleum companies. That's let us use that scary word "terrorist" to label Arab nationalists and revolutionaries, who dare to claim the same right as the United States to use military operations to intimidate other peoples. We can declare a war on terrorism: terrorism, a tactic, not a country or even an ideology, something desperate people do when they don't have the resources to fight like a world power. There are no defined borders for terrorism; it will truly be a world war. Terrorism will never go away. Since the enemy can appear anywhere, we can instill fear in the surplus population, rally them to do their patriotic duty and enlist to go off and fight a Satan who can never be eliminated.

General Beatem: Hoo Rah! [*high-fiving Trumpcard*]

Kochaine Brothers [*in unison*]: You guys have finally got it! We oil men know there is nothing better than a good endless war on terrorism.

Left-wing author Howard Zinn appears on stage.

Howard Zinn: Who are the terrorists? I am looking at a room full of them. As long as there are Reagans, Rockefellers, Maura Lee Bankrupts, and Kochaines, you are right, terrorism will never go away. Meanwhile, your lies seem to have mesmerized the people.

Chamberpot Commerce: Who let in all these communists?

Paul Krupman: You don't want to listen, but let me speak about the true legacy of the Reagan revolution, which all you surplus-makers are now carrying forward.

Donal Trumpcard: Oh God. Not another lecture.

Podium is brought out for Krupman. Reagan puts head down and falls asleep, snoring.

Paul Krupman [*speaking loudly over Reagan's snores*]: Reagan, when you entered the White House, the United States was the world's largest creditor; when you left, it was the world's largest debtor. Reagan, you attacked New Deal and Great Society liberals for financing the government through deficits, but you doubled the deficit. The United States had been the world's largest debtor before, in 1914. That was a sign of a dynamic booming productive economy, attractive to foreign investment. It was becoming the leader in steel, railroads, chemicals, petroleum, automobiles, and other industries. During the world wars, the United States paid off its debts and became the world's largest creditors, as its allies turned to America to finance their militaries. As the world's unqualified dominant economic power, it retained its creditor status through the 1970s, but it sacrificed its civilian infrastructure for weapons, as it exported jobs and industry.

Reagan snores even louder.

Paul Krupman: Reagan, you cut taxes for the rich, increased military spending all the more—despite the fact that it had become an economic liability—and encouraged dismantling civilian industries. To be blunt, you locked in the transformation of America into a surplus nation filled with surplus people. To maintain support for your policies, you had to create the illusion of continual prosperity, without a declining standard of living, at least for the so-called middle class, now a surplus class. With real productivity falling, the way to do this was through borrowing, on the part of both the government and the private consumer. With an economy in real decline, the country was borrowing to keep a lifestyle that its surplus people could no longer afford. Its greatest creditor is China, an official communist country, which until recently was considered poor and Third World, where the average citizen has a standard of living way below that of Americans. Chinese manufacturing expands as America's contracts. China's industries are so profitable that it can support a lifestyle for Americans that it denies its own people. Our surplus population are now really dependent on the Chinese economy. What a legacy, Mr. Reagan.

Loudest snore of all.

Howard Zinn: Reagan, your legacy is even worse. Krupman thinks you can still save capitalism. But your policies have dismantled and exported the American infrastructure. Not even Krupman's huge government spending policies can revive an economy without a social and economic infrastructure. And the people in this room have made it their priority to starve the social welfare state and prevent spending on rebuilding America. You call it communism. The people in the street call it justice and democracy.

Chamberpot Commerce nudges Reagan to awaken him.

Ronald Reagan [*blurting out from his sleep*]: Fight Communists! Fight Terrorists! Fight Darth Vader! [*Star Wars theme song plays*]

Ronald Reagan: Stir up the patriotism of the surplus Americans and they will follow you forever.

Ordinary people in the streets who are not part of the demonstrations: How dare they ride their camels over our oil! Support OUR troops!

Maura Lee Bankrupt: Support OUR Troops. I like that. Support the cannon fodder because of the sacrifices they are making. That way of thinking will give us a mass that will blindly follow. And of course, the word "our." It eliminates any concept of class conflict, even in an America divided between billionaires and surplus people. The masses and the ruling class are part of a single unified whole. Everyone is in it together.

Bill Benedict, drug war czar and education guru, appears on stage.

Bill Benedict: Yes, we need a compliant population, but militarism is only one of our tools. Education is another. We need an education system that develops a modicum of critical thinking, at least within a selected population. Perhaps what we need is two school systems: one to create innovators and managers, and one to breed docility among cannon fodder, workers, and, especially, surplus people. Essentially, we already have that, but there has been a progressive education movement, which served as a womb for much of the 1960s radicalism.

Howard Zinn: Thank god for the 1960s. Its motto was Question Authority. For the first time in a long time, Americans learned that patriotism was not obedience. It is, in fact, challenging authority—that is the true American revolutionary spirit. If you look in the streets, you will see the legacy of the 1960s being carried on today.

Bill Benedict [*ignoring Zinn*]: Zinn, shut up! I was the secretary of education, not YOU! Indeed, many veterans of the 1960s left and counterculture have gone into schools and fostered what they call "child-centered" learning, where students are encouraged to explore on their own and not necessarily conform to a preset structured curriculum and pedagogy. No longer are the desks in many classrooms arranged in rows, all focused on the teacher as the clear authority. We need a "back to basics" movement in an America of surplus people. Sound the alarm that America is a "nation at risk." Let's have more rote memorization, use workbooks with specific short answers, make it clear, teachers are to teach and students are to learn, demand respect, establish that there are unquestionable authorities and experts and everyone else is to conform to their expectations. Teachers should convey an air of authority over students, but they should be stripped of control over content or pedagogy and simply carry out expectations dictated from above. There should be regular standardized testing of students to make sure they have mastered the prescribed curriculum. A school will be deemed just as successful if it sends a sufficient percentage of its graduates to the military as well as to college. The surplus population can be sent off to fight our wars.

Whole group of CEOs and politicians stands and salutes the flag. Trumpcard removes his wig to salute.

CEOs and others: God bless America! Home of the Free! Land of the Brave!

Maura Lee Bankrupt: Just as we corporate creatives need a limited number of critical thinkers, who are not so critical that they turn against us, we also need a surplus population ready to carry out violence in our defense. To encourage violence, you need to provoke anger. We want a disciplined surplus population that follows orders and directs its anger against whomever we label the enemy, but what if that anger becomes focused on us? People, acclimated to violence, especially surplus people without the necessary analytical or social skills to maintain a good job, may find themselves on the street, aimless, if they do not end up in the army. They must redirect their aggression somewhere, and that must not be against us in this room but against the terrorists abroad.

Goldman Sacker: Let's remember Timothy McVeigh in 1995.
The group collectively remembers April 19, 1995, when the Oklahoma City Federal Building blew up.
Boom!

Chamberpot Commerce: This speaks to Maura Lee Bankrupt's point. Look at Timothy McVeigh. He was part of the surplus population that was temporarily absorbed by the military. We turned him to violence, but he felt betrayed. Yes, a militaristic society—which we desperately need to control our surplus population—is a violent society, and that is something dangerous that we have yet to find an effective way to control. To control them we need an external enemy.

Goldman Sacker: Let's all remember 9/11.
All in the boardroom collectively remember 9/11.
Boom!

Kochaine Brothers [*in unison*]: When the Oklahoma City bombing first occurred, most everyone was convinced it was Arab terrorists. When Muslim fanatics really did attack on 9/11, we should maximize the hysteria; make people—and especially all the surplus people—believe that Arabs are a permanent existential enemy who can only be met through endless war. Emphasize that they are an "other" unlike right-wing survivalists, against whom the only response is a life-or-death "clash of civilizations." For the sake of security, have people expect—no, demand—an assault on their civil liberties; bring them to accept centralized control. Say they must give up their freedom to save their freedom. Make scrutinizing bags at airports routine. Replace the Bill of Rights with a Patriot Act. Don't you love that name? Only a traitor, a terrorist, can argue with it. In fact, declare "You are either with us or with the terrorists." The Patriot Act will authorize holding people in concentration camps without trial or even cause, the ultimate way to control the surplus population. It will permit wiretapping civilians and even allow the state to scrutinize the books people take from libraries. Of course, not all of the surplus population will go to concentration camps. Some will cheerfully go into the army, if that is all that different, convinced they are doing their duty, protecting their frail country, will a military arsenal equal to the next 20 countries combined. They will kill and die for us, secure our petroleum fields in Iraq and the rest of the Middle East, believing they are fighting to protect their country, not oil companies. Above all, we must make sure they never realize that the so-called national interests are the interests of the corporations, the military, and the state and have little to do with interest of the ordinary citizen, surplus or otherwise.

Ghost of Surplus People Past appears on stage.

Ghost of Surplus People Past: You have no idea how many are going to come after you. Your time is over, bring on the new, bring on regime change at home.

Laughter from the participants.

Yourall Fired: Let's not get spooked by ghosts. Enjoy your desserts, and I mean your just desserts. We're all millionaires and billionaires, and we're not going to let a few spooks or protesters spoil our party.

Cheers from all participants as they leave.

ACT III

Sendu Packing is haunted in his bedroom, located next to his office in his Tower of Power, by ghosts from different historical periods, who all comment on their own eras while also speaking eloquently about events in modern times. The effect is a cacophony of ghosts from different time periods, reflecting the ability of ghosts to time travel and bring a broad time perspective that humans such as Packing lack.

Scene 1: The Duke

Narrator: The next day. Sendu Packing has gone to bed early. He is even more agitated than the night before. He fears the crowd even more. And before he can fall asleep, the Ghost of Surplus People Past reappears, scaring Packing almost as much as the night before.

Sendu Packing: I thought I was rid of you, Ghost. I've already had my history lesson.

Ghost of Surplus People Past: No, Packing, you've just heard the most recent history. If you want to deal with the demonstrators, and understand their rage, you better know all the horrors my people, the surplus people, have endured at the hands of people like you, for centuries.

Sendu Packing [*holding his head in his hands*]: No, No, I'm too tired. I've learned enough.

Ghost of Surplus People Past: To understand why they want your head, we must go back hundreds of years. Welcome to the world of the aristocracy, the world of lords and serfs, monarchs and dukes. Welcome to the world of feudalism. And here is the Duc de Loisirs from that world.

Le Duc de Loisirs (the Duke of Leisure), a tall, imposing aristocrat wearing a blue waistcoat, a big gold chain around his neck, and his family coat of arms on his waistpocket, appears before Sendu Packing. The Duke has been decapitated and is carrying his head, still topped by his powdered wig and tri-cornered hat.

Sendu Packing [*looking startled*]: Am I dreaming? Who are you? What are you? And what is *that*? [*points to head*]

Duke of Leisure: You have a lot to be afraid of, Mr. Packing; this could be you [*holding up his head*].

Sendu Packing: Look, I don't know who you are, you pompous dandy.

Duke of Leisure: I come from France, where I lived before the French Revolution of 1789. I am a duke, a lord in the great system that you now call feudalism. And while it lasted nearly 1,000 years, it gave everyone a secure place in the social order. Unlike you, we wanted to prevent a surplus population. Our serfs had the right to stay and farm their land their whole lives. They had to work very hard, but we gave them the security you never offered the mobs outside your Tower of Power. I was never a jobs cutter like you, you greedy money grubber.

Sendu Packing: Well, you pompous duke, I'm no historian but I know enough that the "secure" serfs or peasants who farmed your land decided to cut your head off with the guillotine in the French Revolution.

Duke of Leisure: Oooh! Touché! That guillotine, 220 years and it still hurts. All I did for my people, and look at what they did to me! Yes, they turned on me, but only after 1,000 years, when our feudal system broke down.

Sendu Packing: So feudalism didn't work in the end, even though you tried to prevent creating surplus populations.

Duke of Leisure: The mobs in the French Revolution who cut my head off were surplus people themselves. We dukes got into debt. We actually became early surplus-makers, violating our commitments and throwing many peasants off their land. The main reason was we were in debt to you capitalist filthy money lenders. Many of these surplus serfs turned into vagabonds—and by the time of the French Revolution there were huge numbers of these surplus people who stormed the Bastille. They are the types outside your Tower of Power who could guillotine you today, the same sort of parasitic mobs.

Sendu Packing: So YOU are a jobs cutter, Duke!

Duke of Leisure: But for centuries, everybody had a secure place for their whole life. And nobody, except the growing number of vagabonds, had to worry about being displaced or outsourced.

Sendu Packing: Your serfs lived in poverty while you, Duke, were fabulously wealthy and lived the life of leisure in your powdered wigs.

Duke of Leisure: The commoners love to see us live well. Look how fascinated they were with the British royal wedding in 2011. People still flock to Versailles to see the refined life that we nobles had there. To pay my debts for that lifestyle, I hired an efficient manager like you, Mr. Packing. He ran the manor like a business, not a community. As he improved my yield, I needed fewer peasants. I was forced to expel the least skilled, and they became vagabonds, part of the Paris rabble who rioted against their protectors. Parasites ruled. Propriety, sanctioned by God, was lost along with my head.

Ghostly Voices of Peasants: You let us starve!

Sendu Packing: We are a society of opportunity. Our serfs, oops, I mean people, are not cutting off our heads.

Duke of Leisure: Look at your serfs on the street. They may cut off your head soon. They have good reason to hate you, Packing. A brutal fate awaits you, especially you, since you are just a commoner like them, with no right to your status. All you care about is money; you capitalists have no sense of duty, of purpose. As far as you are concerned, your employees are just part of the cost of production. When you don't need them, get rid of them. Your stockholders love it when you, what is it? "down-size." You are an upstart; you weaseled your way to wealth. You are a leech; you profit from other people's misery. Don't you know avarice and gluttony are among the deadly sins? You make changes that make you money—you call them innovations—without thinking about what they will do to social order. Unlike you, I was chosen by God as the guardian, the protector of my people, peasants, who are far too simple to take of themselves. For this reason, I never disposed of them or made them surplus; I tried to take care of them until they died.

Sendu Packing: Feudalism never created wealth or prosperity; all it did was chain people to the land. You claimed to take care of your impoverished serfs, to never make them surplus people. But the freedom to fire people, especially the lazy and unproductive, was the crucial ingredient for making a prosperous economy. I disposed of people, but it was all for the greater good.

Scene 2: The Workhouse

Ghost of Surplus People Past: Don't be so cocky, Packing. Soon after the French Revolution, England was developing into the first truly modern industrial capitalist society. At the very start, capitalism created a big population of surplus people—surplus peoples and capitalism have been intertwined from their birth. Most of them were peasants thrown off the land by big capitalist farmers, merchants, and early industrialists. Their land was needed to build factories and create a more efficient agriculture. These displaced people—the first road kill of modern capitalism—were told they were free, but they were forced to live and work in something resembling slave labor camps, called workhouses, built to house the poor and other surplus people. Meet Sir Edwin Chadwick, the nineteenth-century Londoner who founded the workhouse system.

Sir Edwin Chadwick: Enchanté, Packing. I admire your creativity and brilliance. You are everything we dreamed about when we founded modern capitalism.

Sendu Packing: Thank you, Chadwick. I didn't know that you founded the workhouses. I could use something like that. Maybe I'll call it the Surplus People Retention Centers.

Sir Edwin Chadwick [*nods agreeably*]: Brilliant idea, Packing! We had plenty of surplus people in Britain from the beginning: vagabonds, lazy peasants, undisciplined and rebellious workers, criminals, and other rabble.

Sendu Packing [*smiling*]: We capitalists have always been realists. There will always be parasites, troublemakers, and others who stand in the way of our plans and progress. If we don't dispose of them, they will bring down our whole system.

Sir Edwin Chadwick [*nods again*]: I do say! We capitalists could never afford to be sentimental. We had the courage to kick these primitive people off the "commons"—to "enclose the commons" as your historians call it, and take the land for our own purposes. We made being poor, being in debt, a crime. Idleness is the devil's workshop.

Sendu Packing: You can't go easy on surplus people. They will clamor for more rights and more food. They'll turn to sin, lust, and debauchery. They want to live the life of well-fed parasites.

How do you organize the lives of the surplus rabble in the workhouses?

Sir Edwin Chadwick: The workhouse residents are given a minimum subsistence, just enough to survive. If they were overfed, especially if they were served meat, they might develop a false sense of entitlement, forget their station, and try to challenge their protectors. The workhouse sorts. The unfit die, but that helps eliminate the surplus population. The worthy uplift themselves; sometimes we allow them to help run the workhouses and control the unworthy. There is a more extreme level of unworthiness. They are an ungrateful uncooperative criminal element, who never accept workhouse discipline. They must be either hung or sent to Australia.

Sendu Packing: Well, I'm glad to see that my capitalist ancestors knew that it took tough love.

Scene 3: The Builders: Carnegie, Rockefeller, Morgan, and More

Ghost of Surplus People Past: Packing, we are now moving forward in history. You, Packing, have turned most Americans into surplus. But the robber barons who built modern American capitalism after the Civil War were another species from you. They built an industrial infrastructure of railroads, steel mills, and oil refineries that not only employed millions of Americans but drew hungry, enterprising immigrants from all over the world. At one time America was the jobs-creator of the world.

Here are George Pullman and Andrew Carnegie. They both made their fortunes after the Civil War, through creating service industries for the railroads, which were built through state subsidies. Railroads provided the markets for Carnegie's steel and Pullman's cars. They were two of the earliest great American jobs-creators.

Train whistle blows, and Pullman arrives in a railroad car.

George Pullman: Yes, we are the builders. We made America great. We created more jobs than any other society, and we did it fast. We were driven, ambitious, efficient, and enterprising. After the Civil War, we knew that agrarian America had to be transformed. The feudal spirit of the slave South was finished. We knew the future was industrial capitalism, and we would build it from the ground up. I built the railroad cars, and Carnegie, here, produced the steel. The railroads used our cars to connect the Atlantic and Pacific in a great unified American capitalist nation. We employed so many Americans and immigrants that we proved not just to Americans but to the world that capitalism means jobs and prosperity for all who are willing to work.

Sendu Packing: I've always admired you. You showed that America is the land of opportunity.

George Pullman: Yes, we are the builders of faith as well as railroads. We truly created the religion of American capitalism as opportunity, growth, and prosperity. We proved the American Dream is real, and we made it possible for all with drive, talent, and entrepreneurship.

Ghost of Surplus People Past: Before you boast too much, remember that millions of American workers were poor because you paid them such horribly low wages, and there were still plenty who you fired, who could not find work, or even were beaten to death by your thugs when they struck for higher wages and more jobs.

George Pullman: Tough love!

Andrew Carnegie: Even we builders could not create enough work to profitably employ everyone, and many were just unworthy, too lazy, or incompetent to do even minimal factory jobs. And we paid market wages for unskilled workers who often could not read or speak English. But everyone had their chance, and if they couldn't make it, they had no one to blame for their fate as surplus people but themselves. Unlike the feudal aristocrats and Southern planters, whose peasants and slaves lived with little change for generations, I used my workers to create a world never before seen. I may have made millions for myself, but my personal fortune is vastly outweighed by the wealth I gave to the nation. My steel made railroads, factories, and city skyscrapers possible.

George Pullman: Railroads cover distances in days, which previously would take months. My factory built luxurious lounging, sleeping, and dining cars, so railroad passengers could travel in style.

Ghost of Surplus People Past: Look who is here now, Karl Marx, the great critic of capitalism.

Karl Marx appears on stage.

Karl Marx: Pullman, You didn't pay your workers enough to even ride in the very cars they built. And plenty of unemployed workers and hungry surplus people hitched rides in your freight cars. Millions lived in tattered rags and had no place in society.

Andrew Carnegie: My workers were well provided for, and they would've appreciated what I did for them if it weren't for crazy communists like you, Marx. If you did not lie to them, they would know who gave them a job, a job that provided a life far better than they could achieve on their own. The most talented among my workers realized that they too could rise and lift themselves by their bootstraps if union and government regulations did not force them to share with the mediocre and lazy among them. Industry boomed during the Civil War. Everyone was put to work either in the factory or the battlefield. Then peace came and the veterans came home. Some went into the factories; some moved to new Western lands to farm or ranch, freed of savages, now accessible to railroads, and were provided free land out West. Our new economy absorbed almost all the surplus Americans.

Ghostly Voices of Farmers: Yes, but you put us farmers so heavily in debt that we were being crucified on a cross of gold.

Sir Edwin Chadwick: Sending Civil War veterans out West was not that different from sending surplus population to Australia. Whether or not their farms produced anything on minimally fertile soil, the farmers would buy seeds, fertilizers, machinery, and cloth. They identified themselves as independent yeomen, petty capitalists, and property owners, and made money for the banks and railroads upon whom they depended for loans. Away from the city, they were outside the labor market, a type of surplus people settling the Wild West, who would not be recruited into union uprisings. While some joined the populist rebellion, most never saw themselves as displaced workers or surplus people.

Andrew Carnegie: Wise workers know they don't need populists or unions. My company is a community. If it prospers, everyone keeps a job and profits—no surplus Americans in the Carnegie community.

Karl Marx: What do you mean by "community"? Underpaid workers had no secure place in your "community"—and you were happy to turn them into surplus people whenever it suited you. You made hundreds of millions of dollars, but when the price of steel fell, you cut wages and then threw workers out on the street—the very workers who built your factory. Adding insult to injury, you hired scabs, sent in the private Pinkerton army, and had the governor mobilize the national guard. You shed blood rather than let your employees have their rights. Laborers and bosses are class enemies, and when the workers rise up for their rights, you fire them or kill them.

George Pullman: We would not permit union organizers or government bureaucrats, who never built or managed a business, to tell us how to run our affairs. Only free entrepreneurs could create the jobs and wealth upon which everyone depended to avoid becoming surplus people. What native-born Americans did not appreciate, European and Asian immigrants did, as they flocked to the factories and the railroads. In gratitude, they were less demanding than native-born workers; they proved how grateful all should be for the jobs we capitalist builders created.

Karl Marx: You say you built this booming economy, with forever expanding employment as America became the world's jobs magnet. However, you admit you could not absorb the post–Civil War surplus population, and you used the West as a safety valve. The real reason you encouraged immigration is you thought immigrants would accept wages and working conditions that white native Americans would not. You thought if they had to face foreign competition, white American workers, up against the horrible prospect of becoming permanently surplus, would become too intimidated to demand their rights. You hoped to turn foreign and native workers against each other. That way, you could destroy class solidarity and break the unions, all by scaring workers that they would become permanently surplus people. And you did not build these industries! Your workers did!

Andrew Carnegie: We cared about more than profit; I virtually built the public school system myself. My money built schools, museums, and libraries across the country.

Karl Marx: Never underestimate how schools can be used to absorb surplus people and create the illusion they have a future. Packing, even in your twenty-first century you have built up schools to mask and absorb the huge number of your people, both native and immigrants, who will never find jobs and will fall into the sewers of surplus life. As I look on the street, I see the illusion you have taught them has failed. They see through you now.

Ghost of Surplus People Past: Let's hear what John D. Rockefeller and J.P. Morgan have to say. They were contemporaries of Carnegie.

John D. Rockefeller: Here's a dime, Packing [*hands Packing a dime*]. We created an American industrial infrastructure with endless jobs and opportunity for the rabble. You dismantled it and outsourced it to Asia.

Sendu Packing: Well, you made outsourcing possible by expanding into Asia and transforming America into a budding global corporate empire. If you had lived today, you surely would have done the same as I have. This early globalization you created led inevitably to the dismantling of American infrastructure and jobs. If you were around today, you would do it too.

John D. Rockefeller: War and globalization do not have to lead to surplus Americans. We took over countries, undersold their industries, and created new jobs for Americans at home.

J. P. Morgan: War itself makes money. Ramping up for World War I created millions of new jobs in America. War is a building project, and it absorbs surplus workers at home, creating the jobs that keep our workers employed rather than sinking into the surplus rabble.

Karl Marx: Such hypocrisy. Yes, wars make money. But in World War I, tens of thousands of American lives, millions worldwide, lost, billions of dollars wasted to keep the world safe for the House of Morgan, under the ruse of keeping the world safe for democracy. The war only created jobs temporarily; a decade later, millions of Americans lost their jobs and the "jobs engine" called America spawned the Great Depression. America became a surplus population, with one-fourth of the population officially out of work, and the real unemployment rate much higher.

Scene 4: The Crash

Ghost of Surplus People Past: Packing, listen closely to Marx because he is taking us to the next stage of the history of my people. The builders absorbed us in their great factories, but they set the stage for the next section of your history lesson. This is the era of the Roaring Twenties and the Great Crash. In 1929, Wall Street melted down and the economy crumbled like a house of cards. The illusions of the nineteenth-century builders—and of a new consumer and financial capitalism— were laid bare for all to see. A huge new population of surplus people was born.

Sendu Packing: You foolish commies, are you comparing me with the mad men advertisers who shifted America from production to consumption? Who destroyed America with feverish buying of luxuries and easy credit? And to the speculative financiers of the 1920s? Hogwash! I am more like the builders, except on a global scale. I create global work; don't blame me for the surplus people.

Karl Marx: Well, you built a great global computer empire but it created jobs mostly outside of America, where you can pay software engineers in India and China peanuts. And you resorted to a new generation of mad men advertisers and credit charlatans on Wall Street to keep your business afloat. You have the 1920s mentality that led to economic crashes and an explosion of surplus products and surplus Americans. Some of your computers are exciting and useful, but you're still a capitalist, willing to sacrifice people for profit.

Sendu Packing: You truly are a communist devil, Marx. I build jobs around the world to help everyone. Everyone knows this!

Karl Marx: Packing, you insidious surplus-maker, let me explain the history here. World War I, that senseless colonial war, which many American peace activists fought against, did create jobs for Americans. But when the war ended, there were far too few jobs for the returning veterans and the rapidly growing young population, all of whom could sink into a huge new surplus population.

Ghost of Surplus People Past: Here's Henry Ford, who was a builder but also a clever figure in the history of surplus. He employed this new surplus mass of Americans but in the process shifted America toward a consumer and credit-based society, destined ultimately to crash and turn the entire US into a nation of surplus people.

Henry Ford appears on stage.

Henry Ford: You can't resist progress. Yes, I solved the surplus crisis that loomed after World War I because I relied on the genius of "Fordist capitalism," if I may say so. Capitalism brings innovation as it casts the maladaptive aside. I realize that capitalism creates surplus people, as it engages in "creative destruction" and destroys whole industries. My automobiles rendered many of the railroads obsolete. Carnegie, I still needed your steel, but now there was less need for Pullman cars. People who can't adjust to progress must suffer the same fate as outmoded machines. They become surplus rabble. But too many surplus people can lead to mobs, like those outside your tower, Packing. So I figured a way to absorb and disguise surplus people, and to keep capitalism going, that might have worked if other capitalists and the bankers had followed my example.

Sendu Packing: Ford, you're a capitalist hero, but I don't understand why you are finger-pointing at me. You were the iconic industrial builder, and I am the fabled postindustrial builder.

Henry Ford: Yes, but I was a builder for the American worker. I created real jobs for real people in the US. My jobs kept them out of the surplus sewers flooding your society today. I saved the rabble from the hell of surplus, but I needed them to be compliant workers who obeyed me, not union agitators. I also needed to sell my cars. My assembly line was efficient, but its boredom and tedium bred anger among the workers. The assembly line allowed me to lower the price of Model Ts, but no matter how cheap I made them, while my workers could afford them, most workers couldn't. Packing, as of 1914, I paid my workers a minimum of $5 a day, about $115 in 2011 dollars. That was more than the value many of them produced for me. I paid them a kind of subsidy but it would quell discontent and sell cars. It also kept the economy on track, since those $5 workers were going to spend and create demand for lots of goods in the new consumer economy I was helping create.

Sendu Packing: How are you going to make a profit if you pay your workers more than the value of what they produce? Why keep people whose labor does not pay their wage?

Henry Ford: Here's where I part ways with you, Packing. If they can't buy, your business won't survive. So, yes, I overpaid my workers—enough to buy my cars. This was why they never turned into a mob storming the Ford Mansion in Detroit.

J. P. Morgan: Let me put in my two cents here—and as a billionaire in 2011 money, I have a lot of two cents—because I differ a bit from my rival Henry. World War I produced an industrial boom for America, but after the war, what the hell were we going to do with all the returning veterans who were at risk of becoming a new surplus population? At home, we built a new consumer capitalism and credit economy, so that ordinary people could go into debt to buy modern conveniences they otherwise couldn't afford: radios, cars, refrigerators, phonographs. We got those veterans to work, producing what Americans learned to buy.

Henry Ford: J.P., that's exactly what I was doing: paying workers more so they could buy.

J. P. Morgan: Yeah, Henry, but my General Motors outdid you. While you kept your Model T for almost 20 years, we changed our models every year and our cars were prettier. This not only created profit, and jobs for all those veterans and other surplus people, but also eased discontent as people didn't feel how underpaid they really were. Driving the latest cars, whether or not they worked better than older models, made people believe they had status, even if they were deeply in debt. It employed people and helped ease the surplus crisis. As people kept buying, we kept hiring.

Max Weber appears on stage.

Ghost of Surplus People Past: Here's Max Weber, a German social theorist of the late 1800s and early 1900s. In some people's eyes, his status surpasses Marx's.

Karl Marx [*scowling, looking at Weber*]: I'm sorry, how many copies have *YOU* sold?

Max Weber [*ignoring Marx*]: Ford, you have brought prosperity, but at great social and psychological cost. Early capitalism had a work ethic that gave people a sense of meaning and purpose, but they ended up producing for the sake of producing with little sense of why they were doing it. They found themselves trapped in an iron cage. Work, produce, and consume just to work, produce, and consume. Buy and possess in order to buy and possess. They are like caged hamsters running on a never-ending exercise wheel to nowhere. They will make money for you, buy your cars and radios, but find little satisfaction in their own life. You temporarily employed the surplus workers, but it was unsustainable, and after the great crash … back to being surplus.

CRASH!!

Sendu Packing: What was that? Was that the PCs stacked in my tower?

Duke of Leisure: It's the stock market crashing and the debt economy imploding. You leeches are paying for the capitalism you built on sand.

Karl Marx: All of your sleazy financial credit schemes got your own stockbrokers jumping out of the windows on the 93rd floor of your Tower of Power. You can't keep Ponzi schemes going forever. You lubricated your new financial consumer-based capitalism with snake-oil debt that crushed US workers and then turned them into the greatest surplus mass America ever saw. But your policies also turned many of your own greedy brokers on Wall Street into surplus people, who faced only two alternatives: surplus or suicide.

Voices in the street [*singing the original lyrics of Woody Guthrie's "This Land Is Your Land"*]: *As I went walking, I saw a sign there / On the sign it said "No Trespassing"/ But on the other side it didn't say nothing / That side was made for you and me!*

J. P. Morgan: Oh God, it's the Great Depression. There is massive unemployment. We don't need their labor, but we still need their consumption.

Sendu Packing: We also need to calm them down; they're about to storm the tower.

Duke of Leisure: What goes around, comes around.

Scene 5: FDR, John Maynard Keynes, and Solving Surplus in the Great Depression and Beyond—Until the Reagan Revolution

Ghost of Surplus People Past: Packing, welcome to the Great Depression. This is the world of mass surplus people that should have put the fear of God in you. A majority-surplus will rise up against you, just as the duke says. But capitalists were more clever in the 1930s and 1940s than you. Some allied with strange bedfellows such as Franklin Roosevelt, who used the theories of the great economist John Maynard Keynes to put the surplus masses back to work. Let us see the tricks Keynes pulled out of his magic hat of job-creation. Will they work for you today? The answer may determine whether you suffer the same fate as the duke, because if you don't find jobs for the surplus people, they may have a guillotine for you too.

Franklin Roosevelt and John Maynard Keynes appear on stage. Keynes is pushing Roosevelt's wheelchair.

Franklin Roosevelt: We've gotta save capitalism from itself.

Karl Marx: You can *temporarily* save capitalism from itself, but in the long run, it is doomed. Someone's profit must be someone's loss. To maximize profits, capitalists would drive down labor costs of the mass of workers and the growing surplus who won't be able to buy anything. Class struggle will ultimately kill capitalism. Keynes may find a way out of the Great Depression, but the very remedy he proposes can breed a slow cancer that will result in a disease for which capitalism has no cure.

John Maynard Keynes: If you don't want the socialism Marx wants, you better listen to me. Duke, you wouldn't claim the economy could run independently of the government, would you?

Duke of Leisure: We aristocrats, a few hundred years ago, ran both the state and the economy. There is no difference. You capitalist leeches talk about laissez-faire, but you are creatures of the state. It financed the railroads and built other infrastructure such as roads and schools, protected your so-called private property, fought wars for you, cleared the land of savages, quelled discontent. You talk about bringing prosperity to the masses, but all you do is displace people. You care about your workers less than I cared about my peasants. I find all this talk about independent entrepreneurs to be hilarious.

John Maynard Keynes: I wouldn't call the duke a role model of productivity, but he has a point. Let's forget about this pretense of laissez-faire. It never had any basis in reality. Let's admit the state underwrites the economy. In the 1920s, you built an economy based on debt. That's not a problem, as long as the debt stimulates growth. The problem is your private corporations can't afford to maintain continual debt. Morgan, you may have lent Europe, especially Britain, $6 billion during World War I, but what would have happened to you if President Wilson had not entered the war? Ford, you can pay your workers $5 a day, but if almost everyone else pays their workers half that, then your employees can buy radios and refrigerators, but hardly anyone can buy Model Ts. You need a federal minimum wage law.

Henry Ford: No! I will not allow anyone, the government or the unions, to dictate to me.

John Maynard Keynes: If you try to keep your wealth, you will lose your wealth. Government programs are needed that will put more money into the hands of the non-rich. In the search for greater efficiency and higher profit, you need fewer and fewer workers. You breed a surplus population. If surplus people are poor people, they can't consume, and your wealth will wallow in silos, just like the duke's. It is already happening to Packing.

George Pullman [*still sitting in his big padded chair*]: How are you going to pay for all these government programs and the minimum wage?

Andrew Carnegie: That would be like paying people for not working!

Duke of Leisure: You capitalists have certainly paid yourselves for not working.

George Pullman: And we can't finance it through taxes. This country is founded on no taxation without representation.

John Maynard Keynes: There is no such thing as a private economy; there is no such thing as private wealth. Capitalist wealth is created or destroyed by state policy. When the government borrows, the nation is only borrowing from itself, unless it turns to other countries. The state must be in charge of distributing wealth to where it will do the most good. A rising tide raises all ships. If the poor get less poor, the rich get richer.

Henry Ford: The state is a parasite. It cannot create wealth; it can only hinder wealth creation. The state lives on taxes, our money. Any money given to the state is money taken away from productive people.

John Maynard Keynes: Ford, who would buy your cars, what use would your cars have, if the state did not build roads to drive them on? Is building roads any less productive than building cars? The automotive industry is a creature of the state.

Henry Ford: Privatize the roads, then they will be operated profitably and efficiently.

John Maynard Keynes: The New York and Boston subways could not be profitably operated by their private owners. The state had to buy them. If you don't soothe the surplus population, capitalism might not survive. You might have a revolution on your hands.

Duke of Leisure: Welcome to the club.

John Maynard Keynes: Efficiency has a different meaning for the government than for the private corporation. The state's purpose is to invest in the future with public funds that corporations can't spend. This is the key to eliminating surplus. If you don't follow me, you may have to deal with communists like Marx. They would end profit altogether. They say one corporation's profit is another person's misery.

Henry Ford: See, the state cannot produce. Keynes, your strategy for putting the surplus rabble to work with government funds is self-defeating. You want to use the government to support parasites.

John Maynard Keynes: As I said before, there is no reason why the government cannot engage in indisputable productive activity. Look at the Tennessee River Valley; the river floods and destroys crop land. Most people down there don't have electricity. The federal government can dam the river, prevent floods, and generate electricity with water power and employ thousands of surplus people formerly out on the streets.

J. P. Morgan: What would that do to my Commonwealth & Southern Corporation, the main source of electrical power in the region?

John Maynard Keynes: Is your real concern that the state cannot produce wealth, or that it will produce it too well and threaten private industry? We must find a way for the government to provide jobs without competing with private corporations.

Adolph Hitler appears on stage.

Adolph Hitler: Another war would help. When you mobilize for total war, unemployment instantaneously shrinks to zero. That's what I did in Germany.

Franklin Roosevelt: It is you, Hitler; we must fight and conquer, as we have done.

Hitler takes cyanide pill and disappears.

Franklin Roosevelt: The American spirit, or was it American industrial strength, defeated Hitler. During my New Deal, I spent $40 billion; that is almost as much as total federal spending from 1789 to 1932, $45 billion. Yet, even then I felt limited; I could not make the government so large that it would threaten private enterprise. In the war, there was no competition between state and private interests. We were all united in a common goal. During World War II, I felt free to spend $240 billion to assure victory. Although the government was perfectly capable of manufacturing armaments, that would be communism, not the American capitalist way. Most of that $240 billion was contracted out to the private corporations, which made their profit soar and instantly employed almost all surplus people. My New Deal was actually too restricted to end the Depression. The war brought a prosperity that the world had never seen before.

John Maynard Keynes: I would have preferred to spend on social services, which enhances the lives of citizens, but I suppose armaments can also serve as a stimulus. You can have butter alone, guns and butter, or just guns.

Henry Ford: But butter isn't good for you. It's full of cholesterol.
Rosie the Riveter appears on stage.

Rosie the Riveter: One thing the war did was show what women can do. We manned, no, *womanned,* the factories, built the planes, tanks, ships, and bombs, while the men were off killing each other.

John D. Rockefeller: Yes, Rosie, we employed you and made you a heroine. The war proved how much money is to be made through weapons and how many jobs we can create—especially without competition from Europe or Japan, which were in ruins. Let's not reduce our armed forces, who number in the millions and are a hugely important way to soak up surplus young people. Instead, let's maintain a full war-scale economy. We should disguise the creation of a permanent garrison state by renaming the Department of War as the Department of Offense—oops, Defense. War is sporadic; defense is perpetual. The United States should declare itself the world police force and discourage Europe and Japan from rearming. All the profits from military spending will come to us. And we will have a powerful twofold strategy for solving the surplus crisis. First, the cheaper resources and markets our wars guarantee abroad help create jobs for American workers. And all those young US warriors in the marines, army, and navy are no longer candidates for surplus people but suddenly become heroes. Nobody will call them unemployed or surplus.

J. P. Morgan: To gain support for a militaristic empire, we're gonna need an enemy. We always opposed communism, even though the Soviet Union, not us, bore most of the burden of defeating Hitler. They had the deaths and we had the profits. Let's make the commies our enemy. America will dominate the capitalist—oops, free—world and enjoy prosperity like no place else, with the surplus population largely eliminated, absorbed into our great military machine.

Ghost of Surplus People Past: When you prepare for war, it becomes more likely. A warfare economy is built on destruction. It leads to neglecting civilian infrastructure, which, in the long run, results in a weaker country. It absorbs surplus people but creates millions of surplus returning veterans after the war. So you have to keep fighting wars forever.

Franklin Roosevelt: We won the war, ended unemployment, sent our surplus young men to the frontline, and had a labor shortage so severe that we had to send Rosie into the factory. But now, in the 1950s, we have millions of returning veterans, who feel very entitled. We can't guarantee that we can find them all jobs. Unemployment may surge again; consumption may falter. The war may prove to have been an interlude in a continuing great depression.

John D. Rockefeller: Like I said, we can maintain prosperity through a perpetual war economy, but we still must deal with the surplus GIs. If the labor market cannot absorb them, something else must be found.

Andrew Carnegie: Why not use universities? Education will keep unemployment down and production up. We can expand the percentage of the population who have attended universities way beyond the 5 percent it was in 1940. We have used elementary and high schools to produce a disciplined labor force. We can offer a university education as a carrot for being a compliant student or soldier. Graduates will feel they made it, achieved the American dream, attained professional middle-class status. If there are not enough jobs that really require university-level skills, inflate credentials, make a college degree a prerequisite for managing a store, being a nurse, even a cop. This keeps surplus people in student roles, and then gives them inflated work that makes them feel free of the surplus stigma, though in fact they are underemployed and seduced into a kind of ruse to pacify this part of the surplus population.

Karl Marx: Of course, here is a problem for you tycoons. Colleges may sop up surplus young people, but they tend to breed independent critical thinkers. The 1960s proved how big a problem this could be for your capitalists.

Andrew Carnegie: Well, we may have to give college graduates higher pay or the illusion of managerial authority. And, of course, we do need some creative employees. Capitalism depends on innovation. Think about how scientists helped win the war. Steel mills need chemists who can improve quality and engineers who can develop new production techniques. As corporations and governments grow into huge bureaucracies, we need middle managers, people schooled in psychology, who can elicit worker cooperation. And yes, we need social planners who can assuage discontent and control the general population.

Let's have a GI Bill through which the federal government will give grants and loans to returning veterans who attend college.

Sir Edwin Chadwick: Giving workers a university education is like serving meat in the workhouse. It increases entitlements and expectation. Some university graduates might think they know more than their bosses and challenge their authority. Some might even come to understand how their society is really organized and realize what a sham democracy is. Yes, we need some critical thinkers, but you are going to produce far more than needed. Many will be unemployed or at least underemployed. People without jobs or with jobs that do not offer the authority that they feel they deserve will be especially angry. This will certainly be a destabilizing situation. Meanwhile, with all those women in the factories, what are you going to do with the veterans who do not attend college or expect jobs when they graduate?

Henry Ford II appears on the stage.

Henry Ford II: Let's include loans for buying homes in the GI Bill. Homeowners are property owners and are likely to identify with the property-owning class, but since they will be in debt, they will not do anything that might risk their jobs or their ability to pay their mortgages. And they will consume all the more to maintain and furnish their homes, spurring the shift toward a consumer society that absorbs surplus workers, though some of the GIs will struggle with debt and war traumas and will end up in the surplus population.

William Levitt, the founder of the suburban movement in America and the creator of Levittowns, appears on stage.

William Levitt: Rosie, do you really want to work in a factory? Wouldn't you rather get married, have babies, and cook scrumptious meals for your family, as you make the suburban paradise—which I can build for you—spotlessly clean? Picture yourself in beautiful clothes and jewelry.

Rosie the Riveter: Hmmph! I like working, but factories suck and I do like my white picket fence ...

Duke of Leisure: I remember a time when children were an economic asset for peasants. They needed lots of children to work in the fields, and women had to be constantly pregnant because so many babies died. The wives also helped in the field, but cooking and trying to keep dust out of the houses, which usually had dirt floors, was a full-time job. Wood had to be chopped to make fire; whatever ingredients they could find for food had to be prepared from scratch. Daughters had to help mothers make clothes. Levitt, you seem to be implying that the main economic role for housewives and children is consumer, as you tell Rosie to cook as if her husband was a lord.

Karl Marx: You 1950s capitalists were trying to deal with a potential surplus people crisis by luring women out of the workforce altogether, finding their shrunken identity behind the white picket fence of the Levittowns.

Betty Friedan, writer of The Feminine Mystique, *appears on stage.*

Betty Friedan: The housewife role was one of the greatest tricks in capitalist history to solve the surplus people problem by giving half the population a noble place totally outside the workforce. But I called that ruse the "feminine mystique." I knew that it wouldn't work, that it would create for housewives "the problem with no name." The problem was the same faced by all surplus people, the lack of a place in the workplace and society that offered both material and spiritual sustenance. Women intuitively realized that they had been made surplus, and they experienced the silent psychological depression that all surplus people feel.

William Levitt: Friedan's notions ultimately created a tragic backlash, led by feminists. The truth is that many women are happiest raising babies in my suburbs. This was clear in my heyday of the 1950s. As women exit the workforce, greatly easing the surplus problem, men will come to see themselves as the protectors and providers of their families and dare not risk their jobs, dare not challenge their boss. Emphasize "togetherness," the sanctity of the family, with distinct separate roles for father and mother, with women's place in the home. Build the image of cities as crowded centers of crime, sin and vice, unfit places for women or to raise children. Stress that the advantages of a private yard outweigh any sense of urban neighborhood solidarity. Shift resources from public transit to highways. Replace downtown department stores, theaters, and restaurants with rings of suburban malls on the outskirts of the metropolitan areas. With no theaters in the neighborhood, people will buy newly invented televisions. Through television, we can set styles for customers to conform to as we inundate them with advertising. Even if women don't work, they feel they are productive, and even low-wage men can borrow to consume more. What a wonderful way to manage the surplus people crisis!

Henry Ford II: To keep Rosie out of the factory, men are paid enough to maintain a seemingly middle-class lifestyle on one income. Levitt, you're a genius, and you understand my vision. We create a consumer society where identity is built around consumption rather than work. This makes life tolerable for people who have no work because no jobs are available. At the same time, we lure women out of the workforce. This immediately shrank the surplus people crisis by 50 percent.

Andrew Carnegie: When I sold my company to Morgan in 1901, it was the world's largest producer of steel. After I retired, the steel industry continued to have problems—union agitators, increased regulation, complaints of pollution from the mills, workers' health problems being blamed on the factory. Innovation had become too expensive. Now in the 1950s, with hardly any competition from abroad, there is little need to build new steel plants, at least in the United States. We needed the consumer society to replace the producer society, to make surplus people, especially women, feel needed as consumers rather than workers.

John D. Rockefeller: What really sustains the American economy is armaments. Military contracts support the aeronautics industries, chemical industries, mining, electronics, communications, even automobiles, steel, and petroleum. President Eisenhower has built a network of interstate highways through the Department of Defense. As important as it is for our employees to buy our products, the government, as it perpetually prepares for war, is our largest customer. It supports us and it soaks up the surplus workers. Carnegie, you talked about the importance of innovation, but then you admitted there has hardly been any real innovation in the steel industry for decades. Innovation is coming out of military research: computers, microwaves, information storage devices, new plastics like Styrofoam, and transistors. This military spending is a way for the state to help industry and employ the workers who would go jobless without the state intervention.

John Maynard Keynes: Rockefeller, you are talking about "military Keynesianism." Although you hate me, you are an unwitting follower of mine. You use the government, in this case the military, to create jobs and solve the crisis of massive surplus people. This is what presidents did all through the Cold War.

John D. Rockefeller: There is another obvious benefit we capitalists receive from military spending. Our soldiers and sailors are prepared to go from "the Halls of Montezuma to the shores of Tripoli" to prevent revolutions and buttress governments friendly to American investments, to secure oil and cheap labor.

Sir Edwin Chadwick: Empires are costly. We British extracted wealth from India, Jamaica, and Africa, which we used to build industries at home. But to defend our colonies, we got involved in wars with the Boers and then two world wars. We spent too much on armaments, which interfered with civilian industries, and in the end, we surrendered economic dominance to you Americans. Now, you Americans seem be repeating our mistakes, only worse. Military Keynesianism is a lousy way to solve the surplus people crisis. Your militarism helps build your economic empire and solve your jobs crisis in the short run, but as Vietnam showed, your constant resort to futile wars undermined your economy and standing in the world over the long term.

Packing looks down in the streets. He sees throngs of people of about college student age. Many wear dirty clothes, long hair, and, among the boys, beards.

Protestors [*in unison*]: Ho! Ho! Ho Chi Minh! NLF is going to win! One, two, three, four, We don't want your fucking war! Make love, not war!

Sir Edwin Chadwick: See what happens when you train students to be critical thinkers and don't worry about maintaining job discipline? They may understand how capitalism and empire works all too well and turn their critical analysis against you.

Sendu Packing: The spirits who visited Scrooge in Dickens's *Christmas Carol* gave him a chance to repent, but I don't see what you guys are offering me. And the crowd in the street wants my head.

Duke of Leisure: Yes, they want your head.

J. P. Morgan: Dickens focused on one individual. His *Christmas Carol* was almost a fairy tale written for children, but the problem is not the selfish acts of one billionaire. It is a system—a system that we built while we were alive, but you perpetuate and profit from, at least in the short run. One individual capitalist changing his ways will not make much difference. If you become nice or generous, your competitors will just use it to their advantage, and in the end, if the system collapses, you will suffer the same fate they do.

Everyone vanishes except for Packing. All that is left is the Duke of Leisure's lifeless head. The mob breaks the locks to the tower and is racing up 30 flights of stairs.

Sendu Packing: Guys, ghosts, figments of my imagination, whatever you are! Don't leave me!

ACT IV
YEAR 2020: TELECONFERENCE, NEXT DAY

Same participants as Act I in 2020. Loud noises, explosions, fire, and smoke from the streets. Rocks being thrown at Tower of Power windows: total chaos on the streets. Projector has noise playing from live feed or from projected protests.

Yourall Fired: Ladies and gentlemen, welcome back to our teleconference. I appreciate your being here despite the violent uprising by the surplus rabble.

Donal Trumpcard: I am armed [*waving a pistol around*]. This is an outrage that must be suppressed immediately. Let me tell these mobsters "you're fired, and now you'll face the ultimate firing: the firing squad."

General Beatem: Permission to speak?

Yourall Fired: Permission granted, Beatem.

General Beatem: Ladies and gentlemen, the situation is dire. Surplus people are breaking out from retention centers across the nation. This is the biggest domestic disorder since the civil war. The president has authorized contingency plans to mobilize the armed services immediately to crush the mobs. Before a final decision, he wants a response from both the Pentagon and our community in the Tower of Power.

Murmurs of appreciation from participants.

General Beatem: The Pentagon is in favor of a decisive military strike against these internal terrorists. We can use the same techniques we been using for years in Pakistan, Afghanistan, and other hot spots around the world: drone warfare, enhanced interrogation, instant killing of instigators.

Warden Custer: I can assure you that once stability is achieved by the military, our prison system and incarceration specialists in the retention centers will know how to deal with the rebels.

Applause from participants.

Yourall Fired: I hear a lot of support for the military option. But what do you think, Buffer and Gateskeeper?

Warren Buffer: We anticipated a revolt, but not on this scale.

Bill Gateskeeper: Yes, our whole surplus policy marginalizes the masses and doesn't offer them even the illusion that they have any place in our society. This must change—and fast.

Worthy Surper: What are you gentlemen suggesting? This is no time for bleeding-heart sentimentality, even from the world's richest billionaires. There's a zillion of those lunatics out there!

Bill Gateskeeper: Yes, and they could make the madmen guillotiners in the French Revolution look moderate. The surplus masses have nothing to lose. All of us here must support a massive shift of our own resources and wealth to fund a social reconstruction on our own country.

Warren Buffer: We need to tax ourselves to raise billions to rebuild America. We need taxes on international trade and investment. It's time to create zillions of green jobs.

Gasps from the participants.

Chamberpot Commerce: This is treasonous. You would bring down the world economy and our own corporations. It would drain our profits and force us to pay taxes and, for God's sake, force us to abide by regulations.

Paul Krupman: Gentlemen, as an international economist, let me assure you that Buffer and Gateskeeper are offering the only viable solution. A capitalist economy without jobs is a contradiction in terms. Capitalism can only run on near-full employment. Despite the dismantling of the infrastructure at home, there is still time to rebuild. It requires massive resources and new taxes on you all, but it will reemploy most of the surplus population. It is the only way to quell the revolution and save the US and the planet.

Donal Trumpcard [*brandishing his pistol and yelling*]: We face an internal terrorist revolt and we have to listen to communists like Krupman? Who let him in?

Paul Krupman [*stands up and addresses the elites and whole audience*]: Trumpcard, I am a capitalist true-believer. My recommendations are the only way to save your capitalist system. You must rebuild infrastructure at home and support massive public investment in jobs. Strictly regulate banks, energy companies, and all corporations. Rebuild schools and universities for critical thinking. Tax the wealthy and cut the military to pay for these necessities. Without rebuilding the domestic economy, the people in the street will turn against you. They already have. This is the only way to stop the revolution, save the US, and the planet.

Karl Marx [*stands up in response to Krupman*]: Krupman, like you say, you really are still a capitalist at heart. Not even your government spending policies can revive an economy without a social and economic infrastructure. The truth is, you need the people in the streets to run the country, not the thieves on Wall Street. You need co-ops and massive job creation by federal, state, and local governments. The capitalists have killed off capitalism. The 99 percent have to take over ownership; only they can create a real democratic alternative.

Donal Trumpcard [*takes out his pistol again and fires in the air, yelling*]: I won't sit and listen to this communist BS anymore!

Yourall Fired: Gentlemen, let us maintain our civility. We have too much at stake to waste our time on internal squabbling. Does anybody else have other options to suggest?

Donal Trumpcard [*putting down his pistol*]: Yes, and it may surprise you. I propose that we establish security zones around the Towers of Power on Wall Street and other crucial financial and corporate centers around the country. These should be protected by the most advanced security electronic walls and surveillance. These must be protected by the military at all costs, so they can continue to operate globally. But we can let the rest of the country be occupied by the mobs. We don't need the rabble or their hovels. Without our help, most of them will starve or emigrate, solving our surplus problem fast.

General Beatem: Permission to speak?

Yourall Fired: Come off it, General. Yes, speak!

General Beatem: Sounds like Trumpcard is proposing a version of the green zone strategy the Pentagon used ten years ago in Iraq. Essentially, establish a series of bases in the country—to protect the key financial, corporate, oil, and military centers. Everything else can be profitably abandoned.

More windows smashed. Sounds of protesters yelling and entering the building, climbing stairs to reach the participants.

Protester Voice 1: When we get these corporate criminals, what are we going to do with them?

Protester Voice 2: Show no mercy. They have been brutalizing us for years. It's time for us to give them a taste of their own medicine.

Protester Voice 3: We don't have time for that. We will quarantine them as we take over the Towers of Power, convene democratic assemblies in teleconferences around the country, and establish the constitution of our new democratic full-employment society.

Protester Voice 2: First, I'm going to lock them up and put them in the Surplus People Retention Centers. Let them see how we have been living. I personally want to tell them "you're fired."

Protester Voice 3: And, in fact, they will be surplus people after our revolution. They have built their own prisons.

Protester Voice 4: That's too easy for them; send them right to the guillotine.

Protester Voice 5: We destroy our own revolution if we copy their brutal tactics. No, we must be merciful. They will have a chance to start over in our new society, but they must accept the fairness of our revolution and the new rules of the game: People over profit! True democracy! Jobs for all! Even the billionaires!

Protester Voice 4: You're right; we must be better than them, but first we must reeducate them for their own benefit. Let's take them to court and hold them accountable for their crimes. We need them to see that the revolution is just and that we need a fairer and better world.

Protester Voice 2: We must hold them until they repent and confess their past errors and see how cruel, abusive, and destructive they were. But we don't want to treat them the way they treated us in the Surplus People Retention Centers.

Protestor Voice 3: That is true. Revolutionaries often become worse than the elites they overthrow. We will not brainwash them or commit violence. But they must work with us to create a far better world for humanity and for the environment than the one they built solely to serve themselves.

All Protesters [*in unison*]: People over profit! True democracy! Jobs for all! Even the billionaires!

Video returns to teleconference and the participants who have been listening to the protesters. The sounds of the protesters have become very close as they race toward the suites of the Towers of Power.

Yourall Fired: We have little time left. I have my own proposal. We have been abandoning the country for years. Now is the time for us to stay true to our principles. Our solution is to leave the United States ourselves.

Chamberpot Commerce: What, leave this great country we built?

Yourall Fired [*stands and speaks to the audience*]: Chamberpot, there is nothing left of value here. Nearly all of our companies, workers, and consumers are now overseas. We all have lavish palaces to live in and can manage our operations from multiple overseas resorts, islands, and countries. Why stay here? My proposal is the inevitable final solution to the American surplus crisis. We leave America to the surplus people. They will go down with the rotting ship that we have already abandoned here. We can leave them the remaining American industries and infrastructure, but they won't know how to manage it. In their so-called democratic worker self-management, they will reduce themselves to starvation, poverty, and misery. If they are able to organize at all, they will create Soviet-style gulags. Or collapse into anarchy and total economic chaos. They think they are going to have democracy, but before we know it they'll be begging us to come back.

Goldman Sacker: I would hate to leave Wall Street. I love the sounds of money here [*tearing up*].

Loud banging on the doors of the conference rooms: protesters have reached the suites. They are trying to break down the doors.

Yourall Fired: We have no time left. Helicopters to take us away are waiting on the roof. We can all access them directly, without confronting the mobs. How many favor my plan?

Shouts of approval from nearly all the participants.

Yourall Fired: Overwhelming support! We are free from the burden of American surplus masses for all time!

CEOs and other Power Elites [*in unison as they move toward the helicopters*]: Goodbye, America: Free, Free, Free at last!

Protesters break into the empty conference room as helicopters fly off.

Protesters [*waving at the helicopters and shouting up to them*]: You're gone for good! You're fired! You're fired! You're fired!

Part III

I Like Firing People: A Version Performed at Boston College

By *Charles Derber and Yale Magrass*

With the assistance of Courtney Alpaugh, Lauren Antonelli-Zullo, Matt Bartholome, Casey Benson, Brittany Bieber, Sophia Chalmer, Alessandra Corriveau, Nikki Corso, Phil Cushing, Kyle Fitzpatrick, Niva Javed, Hillary Marshall, Marguerite Minshall, Emily Morton, Colin Madigan, Alison Miller, Ivana Perez, Erin Ryan, Roberto Schaefli, and Julia St. Jean

ACT I

Scene 1: The Teleconference, Year 2020

Cast:

Yourall Fired, Secretary of the Department of Surplus People
Goldman Sacker, leading banker
Chamberpot Commerce, head of the biggest business association
Warren Buffer, top investor
Maura Lee Bankrupt, CEO of one of America's largest banks
Mutt Banecapital, vulture capitalist and leading politician
Bill Gateskeeper, investor and philanthropist
Larry Summit, senior economic adviser to the president

Paul Krupman, economist and *New York News* columnist
Donal Trumpcard, New York real estate mogul
General Fourstar Beatem, Director of the Military Absorption Unit of Surplus People
Warden Custer, head of the Division of Surplus People in the Department of Prisons
Enrolle Anibody, Vice President of the Universities of America Responsible for Matriculating Surplus People
Watchi Everywon, of the Mayors' Conference for Surveillance of Vagrants and Homeless People
Worthy Surper, Administrative Director of the Surplus People Retention Centers of America
Sendu Packing, CEO of Hacker-Packer Computer Co.

> *Smoky amorphous images of crowds in different cities, with some on Wall Street sleeping in ragged tents. Fires are lit where people are cooking and eating scraps. Some people have set fire to trash cans and vehicles. Sounds of yelling and protest. Masses of protesters wandering around, talking to each other, shaking their fists up at the sky, yelling at the Towers of Power that line Wall Street.*

Distant shouts: We Want Jobs! Jobs Now! We Want Jobs! Jobs Now!

New image appears of a teleconference on a huge screen.

Yourall Fired: Ladies and gentlemen, welcome to our annual dinner to discuss our national management of the surplus population.

Applause and smiles from participants. Videoscreen shows elegant waiters serving the lavish meal to the participants.

Chamberpot Commerce: Mr. Yourall Fired, I am sure I speak for all of us in appreciation of your feast for us. This firing business is hard work—we all know that.

Yourall Fired: Nothing harder, and you're all doing a remarkable job. Congratulations! We have some special problems to consider this year, as the number of parasites and unworthy surplus rabble is increasing. We have 8 million additional unemployed and surplus people this year.

Participants show interest in what Yourall Fired is saying, but not distress. They are relishing their gourmet lunch.

Yourall Fired: Over 2 million new surplus people have been created in the past month. This increase in volume has created overflow in some of our absorption centers of the surplus population. Just look at those mobs down there on Wall Street!

Return to a video image of the streets below, with people marching, looking like a ragged army, moving in an angry and determined manner. Continuing sounds of protests: JOBS NOW! JOBS NOW! JOBS NOW!

The teleconference participants look up with some interest.

Sendu Packing: I wonder why they are singling me out. I suppose my name is a good excuse for these troublemakers. Why did my mother give me this name?

Goldman Sacker: Well, I'm sure they're thinking about me, too. After all, my Tower of Power is next to yours. And my name doesn't help either.

Yourall Fired: Now, let me turn the meeting over to Worthy Surper, director of the Surplus People Retention Centers of America. He can offer details.

Worthy Surper: Ladies and gentlemen, 10 million new unemployed in the past year and the most recent numbers this year showing a sharp spike upward. This, of course, is consistent with our business strategies over the past decade, as we have moved to outsource rapidly to keep up with the global competition and increase our profitability. In fact, our outsourcing is even ahead of schedule!

Cheers and self-congratulatory applause among most of the participants in the teleconference.

Worthy Surper: You deserve to congratulate yourselves.

Larry Summit: Yes, my National Economic Council examined the national data, and they demonstrate just how profitable our national outsourcing and surplus strategy have been.

Worthy Surper: Thank you, Dr. Summit. High profit levels are a clear indication of the wisdom of the approach adopted after the Great Recession ten years ago; it then became clear that outsourcing was our only way to increase profitability.

Goldman Sacker: Yes. And we on Wall Street have applied billions of dollars annually to help finance the shift in production abroad. We have also applied the same principles to our own industry, finding hundreds of thousands of surplus American workers on Wall Street.

Appreciative nods and applause from others on the teleconference.

Worthy Surper: Thank you, Sacker, but our successes seem to have put us in quite a pickle.

Chamberpot Commerce: Are you are referring to the street mobs that we were discussing earlier?

Worthy Surper: Yes, Chamberpot, of course. The mobs are increasing in numbers, not only on Wall Street but in Washington,

D.C., Chicago, Dallas, and other major urban centers. The unworthy elements of the surplus people, the parasites and freeloaders, are questioning the virtues of our national downsizing and outsourcing strategy. Some are even questioning the wisdom of the shift in our entire production system abroad.

Donal Trumpcard's toupee falls into his food; he dusts it off and nonchalantly places back on his head.

Chamberpot Commerce: After all we have done for them in the Surplus People Retention Centers and in our other surplus-absorption institutions! Outrageous!

Donal Trumpcard [*as he continues to adjust his toupee*]: Never underestimate the ingratitude of those who fail in our great competition. They are inherently lazy and lack talent. They can only think about themselves and their "entitlements," forgetting that our entire system depends on winnowing out parasites like themselves.

Nodding of heads in ascent around the conference screen.

Warren Buffer: Wait, wait gentlemen ... do I have to remind you again that we are taking a dangerous and illogical course here? Haven't Gateskeeper and I been warning you of how these policies might upset the population? WE MUST CHANGE OUR STRATEGIES.

Bill Gateskeeper: I agree, Buffer, we are playing with fire. We need our business strategies to be embraced by the public.

Donal Trumpcard: Buffer and Gateskeeper, stop being wussies! Didn't you all see my big-time TV show ten years ago, "The Upended"? I made firing people the hottest thing on prime-time television, besides me, of course [*flicks his hair, toupee falls off again*]. Most people can understand that firing is necessary and rational, even exciting. Let me show how we can get our popularity back. Unlike most of you who tried to be anonymous and let all the attention and hostility be directed against parasites in the government, I made myself a media celebrity.

Voices from some ordinary people on the street, clapping and cheering.

Audience Member: Yeah! Trumpcard, Fire them!

One soft voice in crowd talking to the person next to her.

Audience Member: Who is "them"? We've already been fired.

Yourall Fired: Let's give our buddy Trumpcard a round of applause; he's taught America about the efficiency of firing the unworthy, turning human tragedy into entertainment.

A general round of applause from most of the participants.

Bill Gateskeeper: But just how large are the crowds? They seem far bigger than anything we have seen in recent decades.

Yourall Fired: I think Ms. Watchi Everywon can offer us some sense of the magnitude of the problem, since she has been central to our National Surveillance System.

Watchi Everywon: It's a pleasure to be here. As you know, as part of our surplus policy, we have installed hundreds of thousands of surveillance cameras in every US city and suburb. Huge numbers of vagrants and homeless drift on the streets, and because we value freedom so highly, we have not rounded them all up and imprisoned them as in so many other countries. Long live our American liberty!

Participants [*clapping*]: Here! Here!

Watchi Everywon: But, of course, our surplus population has grown massively, so in addition to our absorption and retention surplus centers, we have an advanced surveillance system. Take a look at these bad boys [*points to camera*]. I'd like to thank the military for helping keep these homeless rabble in line and keeping our streets safe.

Loud applause from the participants.

Watchi Everywon: But I must tell you that the mobs we are seeing over the last month confirm Trumpcard's concern that the ingratitude of the surplus parasites and free-riders can never be underestimated. It appears to be a national, spontaneous uprising of angry wretches, with no clear leadership and silly demands about jobs and justice.

Sendu Packing: I keep hearing my name. Are they coming after my money?

Watchi Everywon: They do seem to talk about Packing a lot. We think these ignorant folk are just using Packing as a symbol of our national jobs-cutting strategy.

Goldman Sacker: Are they coming after me too? These rabble could use my name too for their demonic purposes.

Watchi Everywon: They do seem to be all moving toward New York, and our listening devices indicate that they are planning to meet up in Wall Street, where a few rabble have already arrived. Sacker, your name does come up in the mob jabber. Our surveillance devices are picking up all kinds of talk about "bank gangsters," "revolution," and "people over profit." But most do not seem to be armed except with posters, ladders, and tent gear.

Goldman Sacker: Say what? [*with attitude*]

Watchi Everywon: Well, they are talking about launching an assault on the Wall Street Towers of Power. The ladders suggest they are going to try to move up from the street blockades around the Towers of Power on the street and break and enter on higher levels.

Bill Gateskeeper: This reminds me of when the Occupy Wall Street protests began 10 years ago. Sounds like the same crowds are coming back to haunt us. In my view, they had a positive effect in starting a new conversation about the extreme inequality in America.

Warren Buffer: Yeah, and I was happy to help them by confessing that the government coddles me and my billionaire friends with low taxes.

Donal Trumpcard: I remember those crazy hippies and treehuggers. This is an even more dangerous and demented group than the Occupy Wall Street idiots 10 years ago. These are mobs pure and simple, and I'll bet a lot of them are armed.

General Beatem: Ladies and gentlemen, please don't let this alarm you. My colleagues in the Pentagon have the situation well under control. Law and order will prevail, I can assure you.
Loud sighs of relief and appreciative nods from the participants.

Yourall Fired: Let me go around and get brief reports on the overflow and how our surplus institutions are coping. General Beatem, why don't we start with you.

General Beatem: Yes, sir, Mr. Fired, sir [*salutes*]. As you all know, the US military is the largest surplus-absorption institution in America, thank God, and the one that builds patriotism and belief in our great American system among our recruits. As we fight terrorists—and the new great Chinese threat—we have been able to absorb many of the downsized and outsourced into our armies. In fact, the vast majority of our 5 million soldiers are drawn from the surplus population. We empower these human failures to become patriotic warriors.
Donal Trumpcard jumps up and salutes and cries "Go Patriots!"

Yourall Fired: And what of the overflow crisis?

General Beatem: We have expanded our wars and interventions abroad to soak up more of the growing surplus people at home, but we still can't absorb all the potential recruits from the surplus population. Our high-tech capabilities mean we can fight more wars with fewer soldiers. Our drones and robot-soldiers are much better fighters than humans. So we are now starting to downsize the military, without ending, of course, our long wars.

Yourall Fired: Thank you, General [*both salute each other, along with Donal Trumpcard*]. Let me turn to Warden Custer, who is the best person to talk about absorption capacity within the prison system.

Warden Custer: Thank you, Yourall Fired. We know that the unworthy surplus population includes millions of angry and violent parasites, who use their jobless status as an excuse to commit crimes against worthy American citizens. We have coordinated with many of the great corporations represented in this room to expand rapidly our prison-industrial complex and house many more of the surplus rabble. But as with the Pentagon, we are experiencing absorption problems. We are in the process of coordinating with prison systems in allied countries to transfer prisoners to other countries as well as to local jails and nuthouses—I mean mental hospitals. This may help to alleviate the overflow crisis.

Yourall Fired: We wish you Godspeed in this prisoner transfer-abroad initiative, Warden Custer. But let's hear now from Ms. Enrolle Anibody, who can report on the absorption functions of our schools and institutions of higher education.

Enrolle Anibody: Thank you, Mr. Fired. Our institutions of higher education realized at least a decade ago that absorption of the surplus population was becoming the major function of the academy. As our graduates found themselves without job prospects, we realized the need to keep them enrolled longer. Prolonging education would siphon off discontent and maintain hope in the younger generation, who are facing lifelong jobless-ness. What could be a better alternative than lifelong learning? Corporations also saw this as a profitable venture, helping us build the university-industrial complex alongside the prison-industrial complex so eloquently discussed by Warden Custer.

Donal Trumpcard: Long live the University of Phoenix! I think I'll buy it!

Yourall Fired: Are you also experiencing an overflow crisis, Enrolle Anibody?

Enrolle Anibody: Yes, we can't build fast enough to accommo-date the need, and the government can no longer provide the grants and loans to help keep our university-industrial complex sustainable. But we are reaching our limits as student loans have become too risky; our bankers know that our graduates will likely join the surplus and be unable to pay them back. Nonetheless, we are committed to educating the worthy sur-plus people, who we all know play a crucial role in managing and guarding the unworthy surplus masses. We realize that it is education that legitimates our surplus economy. To cut costs we have closed many of the weaker traditional univer-sities. Now most classes are conducted online via computer. Students watch lectures on television and input answers to multiple-choice tests through the Web. They think they are being educated, even though very few of them remember anything they were taught and the jobs they prepare for don't exist. *Appreciative loud applause from the participants.*

Yourall Fired: Thank you, Enrolle Anibody. Let's now turn to the Surplus People Retention Centers (SPRC), where the worthy surplus play a major role in housing and guarding the unworthy. Worthy Surper, do you want to update us on the overflow problems?

Worthy Surper: Ladies and gentlemen, I have just received a call indicating major disruptions in the New Jersey SPRC, one of the largest in the country. I'm afraid I have to go there immediately, since the situation there is serious, and we are getting information about similar protests and revolts in other Surplus People Retention Centers around the nation. However, I should be able to rejoin this teleconference in two hours and update all of you on the situation in our SPRCs around the country.

Yourall Fired: It's a good time for us to take a break, anyway. Let's all take a nap after this hard work we've been doing. Good luck to you, Worthy Surper, and we'll be eager to hear the latest news, direct from the New Jersey Retention Center.

Scene 2: The New Jersey Surplus People Retention Center, Two Hours Later

Cast: same as Scene 1 teleconference participants plus:
Guardian of Incarceration
Guardian of Therapy
Guardian of Emigration
Guardian of Immigrant-Expulsion and Work Opportunity

Narrator: Worthy Surper is now reporting to the teleconference from the New Jersey Surplus People Retention Center.
The teleconference resumes and lights focus on Worthy Surper at the New Jersey Surplus People Retention Center. The other teleconference participants are shadows in the background, but can still be heard. Loud noises and yelling can be heard in the New Jersey Retention Center, which is filled with smoke.

Worthy Surper: Can you hear me now, Yourall Fired?

Yourall Fired: Yes, we can hear you, Surper. But it sounds like quite a ruckus going on there. Are you safe?

Worthy Surper: The worthy staff guardians here are in the process of a lockdown. We will restore order but we have had a major incident, with several thousand of our surplus residents breaking out and moving in a large group to escape the retention center. Apparently these rabble are all headed towards you, to Wall Street!

General Beatem: Permission to speak!

Worthy Super: Permission granted!

General Beatem: I have been getting similar reports from the Pentagon. Parallel break-outs are occurring around the country. The military, as we speak, has received an order from the president to set up blockades and disperse the unruly parasites.

Worthy Surper: The situation does seem not fully within our control, so we appreciate the president's call for the military to help stabilize the situation. Here in the New Jersey Surplus People Retention Center, the situation is still up in the air, but our guardians are playing an important role in pacifying the remaining rabble.

General Beatem: Permission to speak!

Worthy Surper [*annoyed*]: Permission granted.

General Beatem: Do you need military units in your New Jersey center?

Worthy Surper: No, General, thank you. Our guardians are trained in military-style and prison control protocols.

Donal Trumpcard: This is an outrage! We do so much for the surplus population in our national Surplus People Retention Centers. These parasites need to be subjected to the most severe discipline. I would think that once control is reestablished, forced emigration should be instituted for the ringleaders.

Worthy Surper: Trumpcard, I think we will soon have the situation under control.

Yourall Fired: Can you give our participants an overview of the surplus center in New Jersey and the various disciplinary and rehabilitation programs operated by your center? This will help us understand the motives of these unfortunate and ungrateful parasites and will help inform our decision making about how to respond to the surplus uprising.

Worthy Surper: Let me remind you that the centers were established by Congress and the president four years ago, in 2016. By 2015, the number of vagrants, drifters, and other surplus rabble on the streets and in our communities was growing so rapidly that they were undermining domestic security and stability. Our Surplus People Retention Centers were established to help set a model for how to manage the surplus population as it mushroomed out of control.

Sendu Packing: It's impressive how much you have achieved in only four years.

Worthy Surper: Thank you, Packing. The total surplus population in our centers is 1,412,000. It is a large number but a small fraction of the estimated 150 million surplus people in the US. Most surplus folks, of course, continue to live in communities and drift on the streets or are sucked into the surplus-absorption institutions we have discussed.

Yourall Fired: Remind us of exactly what the centers do and how they work.

Worthy Surper: Yes, of course. Our central mission is to develop a long-term custodial service to warehouse a sector of the surplus population, while researching other national strategies for dealing with the much larger number of surplus people who are not housed in our centers. We seek to winnow the worthy from the unworthy. The unworthy, who are the majority, must basically be disposed of, controlled, expelled. The worthy are rehabilitated and trained for useful service, largely in the management of the Surplus People Retention Centers themselves. The surplus retention center is managed by a class of guardians. Each guardian is responsible for appropriate treatment of the surplus population. Let me first introduce all of you to our Guardian of Incarceration.

Guardian of Incarceration: Incarceration is the final solution for our most unworthy surplus residents. They blame the system rather than themselves for their unemployment and uselessness, and none of our other treatment options can change their basic mindset.

Goldman Sacker: This must be an expensive operation. Why don't you just send these vagrants and criminals into the prison system?

Guardian of Incarceration: Actually, we are able to incarcerate them more cheaply than in the prisons because we are not bound by the laws governing the judicial and prison systems. According to Supreme Court decisions in 2018, surplus people are not full citizens and are not guaranteed the constitutional rights of other citizens.

> *Video image of a cell bloc. The camera zooms in on one small cell about 10 feet by 15 feet. Twelve people are squeezed into this room, with a toilet in one corner. Inmates are sitting or lying on the floor looking pale, thin, and sickly. Some are trying to sleep.*

Narrator: Here is a scene going on right now from an incarceration bloc.

Conference participants move off stage to make room for this upcoming scene.

Inmate [*grabs the cell bars and yells*]: You barbarians! All we want is a good job. And you lock us up for the crime of wanting to work. You separate us from our families and take away all our freedom. We will never surrender our inner dignity, the one thing we have left.

A guard appears with mace spray.

Guard: What we have here is a failure to communicate! [*sprays the mace into the prisoner's eyes*]

Prisoner [*falls down*]: OOoooooooo, owwwwwwwww! I can't see. I can't see!

Guard [*turning to other prisoners*]: Now, I can be a good guy, or I can be one real mean sum-bitch. It's all up to you. [*turns to camera, speaking to teleconference participants*]: Only brute force works with them. I will admit that some will die, but this is an unfortunate side of our national mandate to keep the surplus population in check.

Everyone in the conference moves back to the main stage.

Donal Trumpcard: If they won't recognize the law of the survival of the fittest, then this is their inevitable fate. They had a chance to show their worthiness and rehabilitate themselves. Some deserve the ultimate firing—a firing squad! [*wildly waves around a pistol; toupee falls off again*]

Applause from the teleconference participants.

Warren Buffer: This kind of inhumane treatment must give rise to some of the explosive riots and demonstrations we are seeing today.

Guardian of Incarceration: Our security systems are very developed and use the latest incarceration techniques. But it's true that the current conditions can breed problems among troublemakers, who have found ingenious ways to escape. If necessary, we will use our domestic drones, on loan from the military, to shoot these surplus rabble from the sky. [*Trumpcard waves his pistol and fires a couple of rounds*]

Worthy Surper: Thank you, Guardian of Incarceration. Incarceration will always be the last resource of our control system in the retention centers. Now let me introduce the Guardian of Emigration.

Guardian of Emigration: Ladies and gentlemen, it's a pleasure to update you on our Emigration Initiative. As you know, in 2018, the president announced formally our transition from an immigration to an emigration society. This reflected the trends of almost a decade, which led more and more surplus Americans to look for jobs in China, India, Brazil, or other foreign countries. This was especially true of educated young people, who couldn't get jobs here and desperately needed to pay back student loans. Once they realized their degrees meant a big zero in the US, they may have felt betrayed, but young people see the world as their big stage, and they always feel hopeful.

Sendu Packing: I know the president has explained the new Emigration Initiative to the nation, indicating the way the US is prepared to help those with the boldness and entrepreneurial spirit to find jobs in other societies. He knows that these workers may end up working for US companies operating in other countries, of course, at far lower wages than they would pay in the US itself. It's a win-win as far as the young people are concerned. They finally get a job while also getting to see the world.

Bill Gateskeeper: But, Guardian of Emigration, how do you select and reeducate people for emigration in the retention centers?

Guardian of Emigration: We want to select as many worthy residents as possible—and even many of the unworthy—for emigration. Getting them out of the US in large numbers, as fast as possible, will stabilize the nation and tamp down the conditions giving rise to the mobs out there.

Donal Trumpcard: This seems a fitting punishment for the surplus rabble. If it were up to me, I'd load these folks up in spaceships and send them off to Pluto.

Loud laughter heard from the teleconference participants.

Guardian of Emigration: Actually, we are coordinating with NASA to discover whether there are cost-efficient ways to send significant numbers of surplus people off the earth into space, Trumpcard. Space travel is becoming more commercially viable, and the population and surplus crises are becoming too intractable. If not Pluto, Mars might be a fitting destination.

Narrator: Look, here's the ghost of the great nineteenth-century social theorist, Karl Marx! [*play Twilight Zone music and have lights flash on and off*]

Karl Marx: Even Malthus would have found you all barbarians as you happily discuss this absurdity.

Sendu Packing: What is this strange apparition? A ghost playing Karl Marx, of all spooks?

Laughter from the teleconference participants.

Karl Marx: You may all laugh. But my spirit lives on—and will as long as capitalism continues to survive and brutalize the world's people. Those people out there on the street are the victims I predicted your ruthless system would produce. I am still a specter haunting your global system, which is doomed by its own successes.

Sendu Packing: Marx, if you are really his spirit, you're irrelevant today. Nobody believes in you. You're living still in the nineteenth century. But let's pretend to take your absurd ideas seriously. As one of the world's great entrepreneurs, I've always been willing to entertain the unimaginable—which is how I see your presence as a ghost. But think, then, you foolish ghost Marx. You, yourself, knew that capitalism had to expand everywhere—and now outer space is a possibility. Of course, most of the surplus population in the emigration programs, for now, will be recruited for emigration to other countries on Earth. I am happy to consider hiring the worthy surplus in my plants in China and India, as long as they accept the wages and hours I require there.

Goldman Sacker: I feel the same way. As we downsize on Wall Street, many of our laid-off workers are good candidates for jobs with us in Rio or Shanghai.

Guardian of Emigration: This is precisely the priority for our emigration policies in the retention centers. We carefully screen our residents to find the most worthy, those who could be productive workers for Goldman Sacker or Sendu Packing.

Sendu Packing: They are desperate to use their skills, and can be trained to desire emigration.

Warren Buffer: But what about those who refuse to emigrate?

Guardian of Emigration: This distinguishes the worthy from the unworthy. Those refusing emigration are proving their unworthiness and lack of motivation. A sign of worthiness is recognizing your place, and not challenging authority. We send many of these unworthy folk abroad, though many will not find work in other countries and will not survive.

Karl Marx: This is even worse than what I predicted 150 years ago. I knew capitalism would hurtle workers in advanced countries down into the sewers of the reserve army of the unemployed. I knew many of these "lumpen" proletariat would suffer and might die. But perhaps because I thought your brutal capitalism would collapse much earlier, I did not consider that you would develop such a systematic policy to expel your own population wholesale, to sink or swim in other nations. But now as I look at the protesters in the street, I think maybe my prophecies are finally becoming true. These ultimate refugees will create a world far better than the one you are destroying.

Warren Buffer: I am hardly a Marxist, but I share his outrage. Your callous emigration policy violates the decency and common sense that I learned as a child in Omaha.

Guardian of Emigration: We are acting on the orders of the president and the nation. This is both a national security and an economic issue. The global markets are the best judges of how to organize the global labor force. Stability at home requires purging many of our surplus people. Expelling the unworthy surplus is economically efficient, since it gives these unworthy folks the largest possible market to find a job. If they cannot find a job anywhere, that is just another indication of their defective nature. Emigration is their best chance to get a life.

Donal Trumpcard: Life is a privilege and they haven't earned it!

Worthy Surper: We do, though, offer some jobs in this country as well, particularly the work that used to be done by illegal immigrants before we expelled them all. Let's turn now to our Guardian of Immigration-Expulsion and Work Opportunity.

Guardian of Immigration-Expulsion and Work Opportunity: It's my duty to tell you a little about the rehabilitation program at our retention center. In 2015, the president signed a law deporting all illegal immigrants in the country. Those parasites took jobs Americans wouldn't accept. Our Mexican Wall never did the job of keeping them out. Therefore, the military had to forcibly remove all undocumented aliens with drones and special forces.

Donal Trumpcard: Thank God we finally cleansed the country of these aliens.

Chamberpot Commerce: We had originally supported some undocumented because Americans were too spoiled to do what they blithely called "slave labor." But we soon realized that the surplus crisis would get Americans to do just about anything. See, Marx, we capitalists know how to benefit from crisis.

Karl Marx [*scoffs*]: Nuttensohn!

Donal Trumpcard: Damn it, I don't care if you're a ghost! In America, we speak American!

Worthy Surper: Exactly, Trumpcard, that's why we started our expulsion immigration program. It offered a new avenue for us not only to prove the opportunity remaining for Americans but also to sort the worthy from the unworthy. We generously offer residents the opportunity to do work the aliens had done, such as lettuce-picking at minimum wages. Many refused, saying no American should be asked to work under such inhumane conditions, without any protections guaranteed by law or the Constitution.

Goldman Sacker: But others accepted this work happily?

Guardian of Immigration-Expulsion and Work Opportunity: Yes, many did. Those willing to pick grapes and dig holes for 15 hours a day at virtually no wages and with minimal protections were showing a willingness to use whatever opportunities opened up. These worthy Americans deserved this opportunity. Nonetheless, many unworthy didn't stick with it.

Worthy Surper: Well, those who refused all work were incarcerated or expelled. But those who showed some initiative were given the chance to enter our large system of therapy programs.

Sendu Packing: Surper, can you tell us more about this form of rehabilitation?

Worthy Surper: Yes, Packing, successful management of surplus populations depends on shifts in their psychology and mindsets. Let me introduce you to our Guardian of Therapy, who oversees this vital work here.

Guardian of Therapy: How are we feeling today, ladies and gentlemen? As you can imagine, rehabilitation is an important part of surplus people treatment. Therapy plays a very big role.

Donal Trumpcard: Forget therapy! Drug them into oblivion.

Guardian of Therapy: Actually, a model of therapy known as cognitive behavioral therapy has demonstrated great effectiveness in recent years. Developed originally to treat clinical depression, we have adapted it to shift the way of thinking of our surplus people residents. I should add, most surplus people experience depression after losing their jobs or realizing how difficult it will be for them ever to find jobs. An important part of treating depression is getting patients to realize it is just a psychological state and there is no reason to be depressed.

Chamberpot Commerce: I have to agree with Trumpcard. Therapy sounds like coddling the rabble. It stinks! Lock 'em up, expel 'em, drug 'em.

C. Wright Mills appears on stage; cue Twilight Zone music and flashing lights

Sendu Packing: Speaking of drugs, is that another ghost?

Karl Marx: It's C. Wright Mills, maybe the greatest American sociologist of the mid-twentieth century!

C. Wright Mills: You members of the "power elite" want to manipulate mass society to serve you. You fear that the surplus population will develop the "sociological imagination." The surplus knows they have many personal troubles: You want them to see all their problems as their own doing. But these are not personal troubles; they are public issues that you have created.

Guardian of Therapy: This spook has just the kind of attitude that we see in our most rebellious and worthless surplus rabble. Give Mills electric shock therapy!

C. Wright Mills: Try therapizing me, you brainwasher. I studied your forms of manipulation for years. If they had the sociological imagination they would recognize that their private troubles are the creation of you, the power elite. The sociological imagination would tell them they must solve their problems collectively. It would cause them to bond together to end your system of oppression. But you failed. Look down in the street; you will see the sociological imagination in action as the people work together for their common good.

Guardian of Therapy: Let's ignore this academic-sounding spook. But Trumpcard and Chamberpot, I understand your skepticism. Let me show you an ongoing session to demonstrate our therapeutic approach.

All teleconference members leave stage.

Stage lights show a room in which a Guardian Therapist and Surplus Resident are facing each other in chairs, engaging in a session. Around the room are signs: "Have the Courage to Blame Yourself," "Think Positively about Your Jobless Future," and "There Is No System."

Surplus Resident [*wearing a straightjacket*]: I still feel that it's not my fault. I studied hard and I always worked hard. I want a job, but they're just not there!

Guardian Therapist: So you're still blaming somebody else? This is exactly the problem.

Surplus Resident: I know that it's partly my fault, but *ALL* of us? There must be a problem with the system.

Guardian Therapist: There you go again. Blaming "the system" [*makes hand gestures with two fingers in each hand elevated to suggest quotations*]. There is only the freedom of the markets, and they are ingrained in the laws of nature. They are self-regulating and don't require any direction from anyone. Questioning this proves that you need more therapy. You're delusional! We'll have to lock you up for your own benefit!

Surplus Resident: OK, maybe nobody controls those markets, but please don't lock me up. There is no need for it. I realize you are only concerned about my welfare. But I don't see how you can blame me when I have studied and worked so hard. [*starts to cry*]

Guardian Therapist [*hands resident a tissue*]: There, there. You are making progress. You understand there really is nobody at the top capable of redirecting the markets. The system, if you want to call it that, runs itself, offering maximum freedom and prosperity around the world. It is really part of nature, part of God's beautiful handiwork for human liberty. But it requires that everyone take personal responsibility.

Surplus Resident [*still crying*]: But what else could I have done? What else can I do?

Guardian Therapist: Oh, there are many options for you to consider. There are jobs abroad. And there is intense competition for the remaining jobs here. The market, on its own, selected the very best. You just didn't make the cut.

Surplus Resident: Is there any hope for me?

Guardian Therapist: It all depends on you. I feel you are beginning to assume responsibility for own failures. Just forget this "system" nonsense.

Surplus Resident: Yes, it doesn't make sense to blame others. I'm the failure!

Guardian Therapist [*handing another tissue*]: Very good. I see signs of progress. This is the beginning of your recovery and redemption.

Surplus Resident [*still crying*]: Oh, therapist, thank you so much for your guidance. I will try harder!

> *Lights go back to Guardian Therapist, talking to teleconference participants.*

Guardian Therapist: Ladies and gentlemen, the rehabilitation process [*points toward Surplus Resident while addressing audience*]

> *Loud applause from the teleconference participants as they return to stage.*

Chamberpot Commerce: Now I see the merits of your approach!

Donal Trumpcard: I have to agree. This is the kind of mindshift we need in the whole surplus population. When they blame themselves they are easier to fire. I've been doing this for years! Do you see the way they kiss my ass on my TV show?

> *Michel Foucault appears on stage.*

Sendu Packing: Not another ghost!

Karl Marx: It's French philosopher and social theorist Michel Foucault. He has a lot to say about mental illness, crime, and rehabilitation.

Michel Foucault: Marx says control of the "means of production," economic institutions, makes you a ruling class. I agree with him. It also gives you control over the "means of reality" or the "terms of discourse." This includes control over how people understand and interpret the world, including control over how an act or even a thought gets labeled insane or criminal. You, the ruling class, decide what is normal or healthy. A challenge to your authority becomes a disease or a crime. The people in the street, who you want to call mentally ill or criminals, are the really healthy ones.

Donal Trumpcard: Who let these psychobabble spooks in? Lock the doors and call the ghost-busters!

Michel Foucault: No ghost-buster can bust me. I'll tell you what your therapy is all about. You use the word "society" to get the masses to identify your interests with their interests. They must recognize you are their protectors, who are going to help them fit in. If this fails, you will then turn to more brutal means: prisons, torture chambers. However, now you are in trouble. You have gone too far, and the people in the streets are seeing through your façade.

Chamberpot Commerce: Thank God this is a spook we don't have to worry about. The French intellectuals are bigger crackpots than ours. After hearing this nonsense, I'm glad I eat my "Freedom fries," not French fries.

Yourall Fired: Ladies and gentlemen, we need to interrupt our teleconference call. We are getting more reports of mob uprisings around the country. The size of these revolts is unprecedented.

General Beatem: I wouldn't be too concerned. The military will crush this revolt if the police and retention center guardians don't get this nonsense under control.

Yourall Fired: I'm sure you're right, General. But listen to the shouts and some of the outrageous disruption right here on Wall Street. These hooligans don't even have the manners to wait for us to digest our lunch and finish our meeting.

Yells from outside: JOBS NOW! DEMOCRACY NOW! JOBS NOW!

Yourall Fired: Can you hear the banging on some of our buildings? The rabble out there are breaking through the police barrier and trying to enter the Towers of Power. Why don't we wrap up the meeting today and convene again tomorrow? By then, we will have the latest security reports and these ingrates should be securely locked down. Please return to your pleasure domes and enjoy the rest of the evening.

Lights dim as the yells from the streets get louder. Glass shatters from building windows on the ground floor, and the camera hones in on trash cans pushed over, with fire smoking out of them. Teleconference participants are seen hastily leaving their offices, looking worried.

ACT II: THE MELTDOWN (TEN YEARS EARLIER)

Scene 1: Back to the Great Recession, 2008-2012

Narrator: 10 years earlier, the meltdown, back in the board room. *Ghost enters; cue Twilight Zone music and flashing lights.*

Ghost of Surplus People Past [*motioning toward Packing*]: Packing, come over here. I'd like to have a word with you.
Packing ambivalently moves toward ghost.
Ghost of Surplus People Past: Packing, I am the Ghost of Surplus People Past. Several years ago you fired me when you relocated a Hacker-Packer Computer plant in Singapore. I never did find another job, and I keeled over a few months ago from a heart attack.
Sendu Packing [*his voice shaking*]: Don't hurt me, don't hurt me!
Ghost of Surplus People Past: You and your corporate posse are monsters.
Sendu Packing [*suddenly shaken to the core*]: What do you want from me?
Ghost of Surplus People Past: Packing, I am here to educate you, not hurt you. To understand how you got to this frightening place, we are going to begin your first history lesson. For hundreds of years, my people have suffered at the hands of people like you: the surplus-makers. You have been around since the beginning of capitalism. Your capitalist ancestors always used job-cutting as a central tool. But never at the scale you have created today.
Sendu Packing: OK, maybe I need to hear a little of your history to save my head.
Ghost of Surplus People Past: Mr. Packing, let's go back to a pivotal moment only a decade ago. Welcome to the world of the Great Recession beginning in 2008.
   Lights turn on in the upper story of one of Wall Street's biggest firms, where bankers and corporate CEOS are discussing the financial and economic meltdown in a luxurious suite. They are drinking whiskey, smoking cigars, and eating caviar as they talk. There are faint echoes of protests down on the street way below them, where noisy groups of angry workers, students, and the unemployed are gathering, calling themselves Occupy Wall Street. Twice daily, they hold a General Assembly to discuss vision and strategy.
Narrator: Ladies and gentlemen, I give you the Wall Street elites in a suite and the Occupy Wall Street protestors in the street.
Protesters yell slogans from the streets: We Are the 99 Percent! You Are the 1 Percent! Your Name Is Corporate Greed!
Protester 1 [*speaking in the General Assembly*]: Show me what democracy looks like!
General Assembly [*replies*]: This is what democracy looks like!
Protestor 2: How do we fix the deficit?
General Assembly: End the war and tax the rich!
Protester 3: Mike check.

General Assembly: Mike check!

Protestor 3: People before profit. Regime change begins at home.

General Assembly: People before profit! Regime change begins at home!

Protester 4: Compassion for all, even the 1 percent!

General Assembly [*waving their fingers, in sign of agreement*]: Compassion for All, Even the One Percent!

Yourall Fired: You can see the kind of nonsense we are hearing from the streets. They seem like a cult, don't they? But don't be concerned. They will fade away as it gets colder out there.

Warren Buffer: Let's admit that we are the 1 percent and we've done pretty well. The rest haven't.

Donal Trumpcard: Spare me, Buffer [*with hand to his face*]. Let them try to Occupy Trump Tower. Then I'll teach them a little about how real democracy works.

Chamberpot Commerce: These idiots know nothing about the way the economy works. But that doesn't stop them from forming their mobs. It's disgusting.

Goldman Sacker: Let us not get distracted by this nonsense from the wretches on the streets. Damn right we've been making out well in this "Great Recession." I got bailed out by our boys in Washington. So did most of you. Those lazy bums on the street aren't doing so well. Of course, it's their own fault. The economy is weeding out these unworthy folk as we go global. We don't need *this scum* [*pointing to protestors below*].

Chamberpot Commerce: Our companies are far more profitable if we downsize at home and outsource to all those cheap labor sites in Asia and Latin America. I mean, look at this [*pulls out ridiculously fat wallet and shakes it*].

Maura Lee Bankrupt: You think that's impressive? [*pulls out even bigger purse*] Size *does* matter, boys. Bank of America. Land of the Fee . . . I mean Free. As the only woman here, let me agree strongly with Sacker. Our responsibility is to our global shareholders, not US workers. We may be Bank of America, but that doesn't mean we need American workers. Only American profits. Don't call us cutters. Call us creatives!

Sendu Packing: Yeah, we just don't need Americans anymore. I like my workers MADE IN CHINA [*using stamping hand motion*].

Mutt Banecapital: Let's be honest. Hell, I just like being able to fire people. Period.

Bill Gateskeeper: In shifting American jobs offshore, we are helping the rest of the world develop. It makes our companies rich and it also sets the table to finally bring the rest of the globe out of poverty.

Chamberpot Commerce: Gateskeeper, you're a dreamer and sentimentalist. It really comes down to basic economics. There's no comparative advantage for business in America any more. We are simply doing what good capitalist business people have always done. Go where the profit is.

Enthusiastic applause from the CEOS drinking their whisky, smoking their cigars and eating their caviar.

Voices of Protesters from the street below: WE WANT JOBS! WE WANT JOBS! WE WANT JOBS! DEMOCRACY NOW! DEMOCRACY NOW

Protester 1: We will, *we will* occupy Wall Street!

General Assembly [*repeats*]: We will, *we will* occupy Wall Street!

Protester 3: We are the 99! You are the 1!

General Assembly: We are the 99! You are the 1!

Protester 4: It's simple. STOP CORPORATE GREED! Create jobs for all! Even for the 1 Percent!

General Assembly [*waving fingers in agreement*]: It's simple. Stop corporate greed! Create Jobs for All! Even for the 1 Percent!

Chamberpot Commerce: Listen to these smelly, pathetic mobs. They don't want to work—they'd rather smoke dope and chant together. When was the last time they took a shower? If we gave into these parasites—who just want to be coddled on welfare and Obamacare—the whole global economy would eventually crash. OCCUPY MY ASS!

CEOs start chanting: We are the 1 percent! We are the 1 percent!

Donal Trumpcard: Get soooooome!

Mutt Banecapital [*throws pink slips out the windows*]: Here, have some of these, free of charge.

Buffer and Gateskeeper look somber.

Robber Rubiner: Our outsourcing will discipline workers and the unemployed to educate themselves and work harder, and restrain them from joining unions and making unreasonable demands. And when most work goes abroad, billions of Asian, Latin, and African workers will demand the highly skilled goods that newly motivated American workers can provide.

Sendu Packing: Yes, I've always said that cutting jobs is the only sensible strategy for long-term jobs building. That's why I call myself a jobs-builder.

Mutt Banecapital: You have to cut some jobs to save others. Especially to save ours.

Warren Buffer: Packing and Banecapital, there you go again. The truth is, you're destroying the very economic infrastructure that made America great. The official unemployment rate is hovering around 10 percent, but the real rate is 20 percent.

You call that creative destruction? I call it massacre. And when you massacre, you're going to get protests like those people gathering beneath us on the streets. Listen to them:

Shouts from the street: JOBS NOW! JUSTICE NOW! JOBS NOW! JUSTICE NOW!

Chamberpot Commerce: Buffer, you're a bleeding-heart billionaire. Leave it to us and our friends in Washington to deal with the mobs.

Goldman Sacker: I'm with you, Chamberpot and Packing. All of us here are just involved in creative destruction.

Maura Lee Bankrupt: Here, here Sacker! We American bankers will be the engine of the global economy. That is now our sacred mission because it will pay the highest return to our one true constituency: our shareholders. (And of course, ourselves.) [*nods head toward huge purse again and winks*]
Smiles and nods all around, even as the chanting on the street gets louder. JOBS NOW! JOBS NOW! JOBS NOW!

Warren Buffer: It doesn't add up, Sacker. Everyone knows this is the "Great Jobless Recession." There are now millions of Americans who don't feel needed and struggle to survive, even though they have much to offer. I wouldn't call that efficiency. It stinks!

Bill Gateskeeper: And what about the people warehoused in prisons, put in the military, admitted into higher education because they couldn't find jobs? Our Great Recession has made it clear to everyone that we have a massive surplus people crisis. It's unacceptable.

Ghost of Surplus People Past [*murmuring to himself*]: Yes, unacceptable, unacceptable, unacceptable.

Chamberpot Commerce [*ignoring the ghost*]: Come off it, Buffer and Gateskeeper. You're the richest men in the world. Both Bush and Obama bailed us all out. The public sees us as job-creators, or, as our Republican flunkies—uh, I mean allies—call us, "the jobs-makers." And all these surplus rabble down on the street are evidence that capitalism is doing its job, weeding out the parasites to make room for the more ambitious and talented workers all over the world.

Robber Rubiner: Chamberpot is making a key point, gentlemen. We are responsible for a global system now, not just for the United States. We can't favor American workers over less expensive and harder working people abroad.

Larry Summit: Speaking as an economist, I can assure all you gentlemen that Rubiner is right on the mark. Globalization— and the technological revolution that made it possible—makes millions of American workers redundant. But we can't coddle them or we undermine the entire global capitalist economy.

Ghost of Surplus People Past: Summit, your idiocy is killing me. Again. Those crowds on the street are going to grow, as you fire millions more American workers in the next ten years. Most working Americans are beginning to realize that the people in this room have no need at all for them. They feel like permanent surplus people—and they're going to come after you. As they say in Texas, it's going to get "pretty ugly" for a lot of you.

Bill Gateskeeper: Summit, I don't need your lectures about how capitalism demands a hard-headed approach. I've been ruthless in my business career and I'm all for globalization and technology. We just have to educate the American worker to compete in a global information age. America doesn't have to have a huge pool of surplus people, if we train them in the technologies of the future.

Chamberpot Commerce: Gateskeeper, I guess only the richest men in the world can afford to have your kind of idealism. Most of those parasites down there want something for nothing. They want fat welfare checks and big unemployment checks. But we have a world of workers dying to work for us. Let those parasites [*pointing down to people on street*] emigrate and see how workers in China and Vietnam are busting their butts for us.

Bill Gateskeeper: I care about people, but I'm making a business case to help our capitalist system. If the majority of Americans become surplus people, they will become dangerously angry and uncontrollable.

Sendu Packing: Gateskeeper, the simple truth is that the new globalization means people all over the US are not going to be needed. Even if they are educated, there are hundreds of millions of well-educated Chinese and Indians who will work as skillfully as Americans, but at one-fourth their wages.

Maura Lee Bankrupt: Yeah, and the cream still will always rise to the top. Just look at me. I'm a woman, and where else in the world can a woman make it in high finance? I'm living proof of the marvels of our opportunistic society.

Loud applause and big smiles from all the assembled CEOs.

Goldman Sacker: Drink up and eat more caviar. Most surplus people don't see us as their enemy. They want to be us because we ARE the American Dream.

Donal Trumpcard: Who wouldn't want to be me? They all do!!!

Chamberpot Commerce: Yeah, they understand everyone is responsible for themselves. They realize that us big money people on Wall Street work 20 hours a day and deserve every freakin' dollar we make.

Warren Buffer: I can't buy into this happy crap. A jobless America is just greed and arrogance, and, I must say, a bit of lack of patriotism, as we see it from Nebraska.

Larry Summit: This isn't about patriotism. It's about the laws of global supply and demand. Let me explain.

The room becomes quiet, all heads turned toward Summit.

Larry Summit: Globalization today is different, built around outsourcing rather than insourcing.

Donal Trumpcard: What the hell does that mean? These fuzzy-headed academics make me nuts.

Larry Summit: Just look at the Brits. They took over India, made it a colony, and shut down the Indian local industry. They built up their own British textile plants in England, and "insourced" the Indian jobs into Britain. That is the exact opposite of what US globalization is doing today. It is shutting down industries in the US and relocating them in India and other poorer countries.

Warren Buffer: Well, Summit, that doesn't justify outsourcing our entire industrial infrastructure today. We still ought to be focused on how we can sustain our economy at home.

Larry Summit: Buffer, you just don't get it, man. The global economy is what it's all about today. But brilliant Americans will do just fine. Did I mention that I won the prize for America's most brilliant economist?

Ghost of Surplus People Past [*holds his spooky head in his hands and just moans*]: You are devils, destroying America. Can't you hear those yells of pain out in the street?"

Sendu Packing: Ignore that spook [*dismissing him with his hand*]. Human pain is tragic, but it diverts us from seeing the magic of the global market.

Warren Buffer: Summit, I'm afraid you've got your head stuck in the Ivy. There's a tipping point where the hollowing out of the US infrastructure goes too far and the US will never compete. You're risking the permanent decline, even collapse, of the US middle classes, since there will be no infrastructure to support them here.

Bill Gateskeeper: It's not just you brainiacs, Summit. The information revolution that I began is going to empower everyone eventually. Everyone with a computer can become a global entrepreneur. Everyone can connect with jobs or customers all over the world. American workers are no exception. If our government invests in education and jobs, which you guys except Buffer are abandoning, we can employ nearly all Americans again.

Larry Summit: Yes, Gateskeeper, government and technology can create jobs, but they also destroy jobs. The effects of your information revolution on jobs is different than what happened during the industrial revolution. The industrial revolution created manufacturing jobs and infrastructure in the developed world. But the information revolution is helping dismantle that Western industrial structure and making it possible to rebuild it more efficiently in Asia and elsewhere.

Bill Gateskeeper: But my technology is the foundation of a new postindustrial high-skill high-tech infrastructure in the US. That is where American surplus people can find jobs, if we have the political will to train them.

Chamberpot Commerce: Gateskeeper, you're a genius, but your philanthropic mission is clouding your business savvy. Software engineers from developing nations are happy to take the jobs of our most talented people for very low wages. And we are more than happy to hire them.

Ghost of Surplus People Past: Chamberpot is cruel and greedy, but he is honest enough to tell the truth. Surplus people in the US know that it is not just factory jobs but office and high-tech jobs that are being outsourced. We know that getting an education in America can win you a diploma that is worth about as much as the piece of paper it's printed on. Sure, educated people are currently finding more jobs in the US than school drop-outs. But the handwriting is on the wall. Having a degree in the future won't mean squat.

Larry Summit: The truth is hard to sort out. Yes, the information age technology is a huge threat to millions of jobs in the US. But it also creates new jobs for the most educated and entrepreneurial American workers of the future. America still has the best universities and the best high-tech companies in the world.

Ghost of Surplus People Past: You're all in denial. Ask those people down in the streets. A lot of them have computer degrees or MBAs. A lot of them are college graduates in the humanities and social sciences. They paid $50,000 a year for their degree, and then they can't find jobs with high enough wages to pay back their student loans. In fact, many can't find any jobs at all.

Young people shouting from the streets: WE STUDIED HARD. WHERE ARE OUR JOBS? WHERE IS OUR AMERICAN DREAM?

Donal Trumpcard [*opens window and yells out*]: Didn't I fire half of you on season one?

Larry Summit: Yeah, I recognize some of you from Ivy. You didn't do a day's work in college.

Chamberpot Commerce [*yelling out the window*]: You over-educated kids are spoiled brats. My grandma works harder than you and she's dead! [*turning back to the others*] Let these bleeding-heart liberals learn something about the real world. If they are entrepreneurial, a lot of them will take jobs in Asia and Latin America, places that can use some of their skills. And there are still service jobs in this country that can't be outsourced, like aides in hospitals or nursing homes.

Bill Gateskeeper: Chamberpot, you're writing off a whole generation of US kids!

Chamberpot Commerce: Gateskeeper, stop talking that philanthropy dribble and be a businessman. Our responsibility is not to America or any other country. It is to our global shareholders.

Bill Gateskeeper: I don't think I need your advice, Chamberpot. I'm the richest man in the world. Philanthropy is good business. We need a prosperous, secure, stable society to invest in.

Goldman Sacker: Chamberpot is right. Our banks don't fly any national flag. Of course, we continue to invent the most creative financial instruments in the world and are still number one. We bankroll the world.

Shouts from the streets: You bastard bankers! We trusted you, and you gambled away our national wealth and played Russian roulette with our loans and credit. You destroyed our future!

Donal Trumpcard [*yelling out window*]: Show me your birth certificates!

Goldman Sacker: Of course, when you hear those idiots in the streets, you realize we do depend on the US government to control these malcontents and parasites on the streets.

Maura Lee Bankrupt: Lock 'em up. Lock 'em up.
    Applause from the CEOs around the room. They refill their
    glasses and get more caviar.

Bill Gateskeeper: It is cheaper and more effective to placate them and win their support than beat them.

Robber Rubiner: Gateskeeper, I think Sacker raises an important point. While our responsibility is to our global shareholders, we still need the US government. Not just for law and order. It also provides the favorable regulatory environment for us to continue our financial innovations. And it provides us with bailouts when we need them. We needed the Fed to keep the global economy from crashing over the last few years.

Chamberpot Commerce [*laughing*]: Let's not go too far with this government socialism, Rubiner. Sure, we rely on the government for lots of things; we know we couldn't survive without it.

But we can't let that dirty little secret out of this room. Imagine if the Tea Partiers supporting us heard.

Laughter breaks out from the CEOs all over the room.

Larry Summit: There's another serious problem you gentlemen have not discussed yet. If we want to keep making our huge profits, we need people to buy. That lavish consumption is very difficult for surplus people.

Goldman Sacker: That is why we created credit cards. Easy money, easy debt. The American way. [*peering out the window*] OK, maybe we took it a little too far, perhaps as our current crisis showed.

Shouts from the streets: You loaned us money, told us to go shopping, but took our jobs away. We can't pay our credit card debt. Now we're bankrupt, you bastards!

Donal Trumpcard [*yelling out window*]: And my casinos took your money too!

Robber Rubiner: The mob down there must be policed and silenced, that is for sure. But the problem of surplus people does threaten our consumer capitalism. Seventy percent of our economy depends on domestic demand for goods by our consumers. We are going to have to continue to find ways to get surplus people to consume, as we slowly build up our exports to the point that consumers in other countries will buy our goods. Then, we won't depend on American consumers as we do now.

Chamberpot Commerce: I agree with you there, Rubiner. As we outsource, we will build the purchasing power of people abroad. They will buy from our companies and keep our profits high.

Goldman Sacker: And those profits are going to come from both production and consumption where most of the world is: in China, India, and other parts of Asia and Latin America. As their people become more prosperous, we will need Americans less and less.

Larry Summit: Yes, that is the future, but you can't have a complete collapse of the American economy or you'll get a revolution. So you need the government to spend just enough to keep the surplus people feeling some hope.

Chamberpot Commerce: There's truth to that, Summit. We talk about jobs, jobs, jobs, but we can't tell the truth to the US public. We need to pretend that we have some continuing interest in US jobs or the hypocrisy will look obvious.

Warren Buffer: You gentlemen ought to be ashamed of yourselves. You're admitting the hypocrisy of your PR. You don't give a damn about jobs.

Robber Rubiner: Buffer, Buffer, you're being unfair to Chamberpot. He'll support some government infrastructure investment because he really does need some US workers to keep their jobs. Otherwise, the American economy will collapse, with no consumption and open rebellion by the surplus mass.

Larry Summit: Right again, Rubiner. The action is going to be in Asia, but America has to be propped up for now. Asia isn't ready yet.

Chamberpot Commerce: There you go again, Summit. Yeah, throw a few bones, like Obama has done, to the surplus rabble. We want Americans to be Tea Partiers, not Occupiers. What can be better for us than to have people who can never be rich identify with us and blame all their troubles on government, the very institution that can save them?

Ghost of Surplus People Past: We need the government to get serious about job-creation at home. That means direct creation of massive numbers of jobs, yes, by the government. That's the real function of government in a nation of surplus people.

Chamberpot Commerce: This ghost sounds like a Marxist, a communist. No wonder he's dead!

Appreciative laughter from the CEOs.

Voices from the Streets [*louder than before, as though closer to the Tower*]: WE WANT JOBS NOW! WE WANT JOBS NOW! *CEOs around the room put down their glasses. Some look worried.*

Warren Buffer: Maybe we should be listening to the ghost, even if he sounds a bit Marxist. Might there be a little revolutionary fever spreading among the surplus masses here?

Bill Gateskeeper: Part of the solution may be to encourage our surplus Americans to work abroad. Young people are idealists. They will work in the Peace Corps or the Marine Corps.

Ghost of Surplus People Past: You have created an emigration nation. You're fighting off immigration even when emigration is becoming the real danger—so many of our best people in 10 or 20 years will leave America, a reverse brain drain.

Chamberpot Commerce: It's one world now. We'll keep the best and most ambitious workers here, and emigration will weed out the surplus. Forget Marx, Ghost. We're living by the laws of Mr. Darwin and Mr. Malthus. Survival of the fittest is the rule now.

Warren Buffer: Nonsense, Chamberpot. Of course, we're going to invest and manufacture globally. But there's plenty of work to reconstruct our infrastructure at home. The ghost is right that his people on the street can be put to work rebuilding our energy infrastructure, saving our rotting roads, bridges, and sewers, and renovating our schools. Green jobs may be the most important solution to the problem of a mass surplus workforce in the US.

Chamberpot Commerce: Now you sound like Obama, Buffer. Are you saying we should be bringing Al Gore, with all his scare tactics about global warming, into this room?

Groans from the CEOs.

Voices from the streets: DOWN WITH WALL STREET! DOWN WITH GLOBALIZATION! DOWN WITH JOBLESS CAPITALISM! *Suddenly there is banging on the doors of the Tower. The crowd has closed in. Some are throwing rocks and breaking windows. The lights flicker.*

Goldman Sacker: Gentlemen, excuse me while I call security and the mayor. Remember, Mayor Bloombug recently warned us that the educated unemployed young people were getting restless and some might take to the streets because they can't find jobs. He compared them to the young protesters in Cairo, Egypt. He sympathized with them, but he's on our side and knows when it's time to get the mob under control. It'll only take a minute. Please have another drink and eat up!

ACT III

Year 2020: Teleconference, Next Day [same participants as Act I in 2020]

Loud noises, explosions, fire, and smoke from the streets. Rocks being thrown at Tower of Power windows: total chaos on the streets. Play violent protests on projector.

Yourall Fired: Ladies and gentlemen, welcome back to our tele-conference. I appreciate your being here despite the violent uprising by the surplus rabble.

Donal Trumpcard: I am armed [*waving a pistol around*]. This is an outrage that must be suppressed immediately. Let me tell these mobsters "you're fired, and now you'll face the ultimate firing: the firing squad."

General Beatem: Ladies and gentlemen, the situation is dire. Surplus people are breaking out from retention centers across the nation. This is the biggest domestic disorder since the civil war. The president has authorized contingency plans to mobilize the armed services immediately to crush the mobs. Before a final decision, he wants a response from both the Pentagon and our community in the Towers of Power.

Murmurs of appreciation from the teleconference participants.

Warden Custer: I can assure you that once stability is achieved by the military, our prison system and incarceration specialists in the retention centers will know how to deal with the rebels.

Applause from participants.

Yourall Fired: I hear a lot of support for the military option. But what do you think, Buffer and Gateskeeper?

Warren Buffer: We anticipated a revolt but not on this scale.

Bill Gateskeeper: Yes, our whole surplus policy marginalizes the masses. This must change—and fast.

Worthy Surper: What are you gentlemen suggesting? There's a zillion of those lunatics out there!

Buffer: We need to tax ourselves to raise billions to rebuild America. We need taxes on international trade and investment. It's time to create zillions of green jobs.

Gasps from the participants.

Chamberpot Commerce: This is treasonous! You would bring down the world economy and our own corporations. It would drain our profits and force us to pay taxes and, for God's sake, force us to abide by regulations.

Paul Krupman: Gentlemen, as an international economist, let me assure you that Buffer and Gateskeeper are offering the only viable solution.

Donal Trumpcard [*brandishing his pistol and yelling*]: We face an internal terrorist revolt and we have to listen to communists like Krupman? Who let him in?

Paul Krupman [*stands up and addresses the elites and whole audience*]: Trumpcard, I am a capitalist. A capitalist economy without jobs is a contradiction. It can only run on near full employment. To rebuild the infrastructure at home you will need to support massive public investment in jobs. Strictly regulate banks, energy companies, and all corporations. Rebuild schools and universities for critical thinking. Tax the wealthy and cut the military to pay for these necessities. Without rebuilding the domestic economy, the people in the street will turn against you. They already have. This is the only way to stop the revolution, save the US, and the planet.

Karl Marx [*stands up in response to Krupman*]: Krupman, you really are still a capitalist at heart; not even your government spending policies can revive an economy without a social and economic infrastructure. The truth is, we need the people in the streets to run the country, not the thieves on Wall Street. We need co-ops and massive job creation by federal, state, and local governments. The capitalists have killed off capitalism. The 99 percent have to take over ownership; only they can create a real democratic alternative.

Donal Trumpcard [*fires his pistol in the air, yelling*]: I won't sit and listen to this communist BS anymore!

More windows smashed. Sounds of protesters yelling and actually entering the Towers of Power. Voices heard from protestors climbing up stairs: video shifts to protestors entering building and talking to one another.

Protester 1: When we get these corporate criminals, what are we going to do with them?

Protester 2: Show no mercy. They have been brutalizing us for years. It's time for us to give them a taste of their own medicine.

Protester 3: We destroy our own revolution if we copy their brutal tactics. No, we must be merciful. They will have a chance to start over in our new society, but they must accept the fairness of our revolution and the new rules of the game: People over profit! True democracy! Jobs for all! Even the billionaires!

Protester 4: You're right; we must be better than them, but first we must reeducate them for their own benefit. Let's take them to court and hold them accountable for their crimes. We need them to see that the revolution is just and that we need a fairer and better world.

Protestors [*turn to the Towers in unison and raise their fists as they chant*]: People over profit! True democracy! Jobs for all! Even the billionaires!

Video returns to teleconference and the participants who have been listening to the protesters. The sounds of the protesters have become very close as they race toward the suites of the Towers of Power.

Yourall Fired: We have little time left. I have my own proposal. We have been abandoning the country for years. Now is the time for us to stay true to our principles. Our solution is to leave the United States ourselves.

Chamberpot Commerce: What, leave this great country we built?

Yourall Fired [*stands and speaks to the audience*]: Chamberpot, there is nothing left of value here. We all have lavish palaces to live in and can manage our operations from multiple overseas resorts, islands, and countries. Why stay here? My proposal is the inevitable final solution to the American surplus crisis. We leave America. Let them have their try at democracy; before we know it they'll be begging us to come back.

Goldman Sacker: I would hate to leave Wall Street. I love the sounds of money here [*tears up*].

Loud banging on the doors of the conference rooms: the protesters have reached the suites. They are trying to break down the doors.

Yourall Fired: We have no time left. Helicopters to take us away are waiting on the roof. We can all access them directly, without confronting the mobs. How many favor my plan?

Shouts of approval from nearly all the participants.

Yourall Fired: Overwhelming support! We are free from the burden of American surplus masses for all time!

CEOs and other Power Elites [*leave the stage and walk up the aisles*]: Goodbye, America! Free, free, free at last!

Protesters take center stage and wave goodbye.

Protestors [*in unison*]: You're gone for good! You're fired! You're fired! You're fired!

Index

About the Authors

Charles Derber, a noted social critic, is professor of sociology at Boston College. He is the author of fifteen internationally acclaimed books, including *Corporation Nation, The Wilding of America, People Before Profit, The Pursuit of Attention, Greed to Green,* and *Marx's Ghost.* His books have been translated into seven languages, and he writes for mass media including the *International Herald Tribune,* the *Boston Globe,* WBUR (Boston Public Radio) Opinion Page, *Newsday, Tikkun,* and the *Christian Science Monitor.* He is a longtime social activist working for democracy and social justice.

Yale Magrass is a chancellor professor of sociology at the University of Massachusetts–Dartmouth, where he teaches social theory, political sociology, social movements, and the social impact of science and technology. He is the author of three other books and more than forty articles, including encyclopedia entries and articles in the mass media. He has served on the board of six journals; has been a recipient of several grants; and has participated in numerous international forums.